DANGEROUS
ENCOUNTERS

Meanings of Violence in a Brazilian City

Daniel Touro Linger

DANGEROUS ENCOUNTERS

Meanings of Violence in a Brazilian City

Stanford University Press
Stanford, California

Stanford University Press
Stanford, California
© 1992 by the Board of Trustees of the
Leland Stanford Junior University
Printed in the United States of America

CIP data appear at the end of the book

Original printing 1992
Last figure below indicates year of this printing:
04   03   02   01

For Lynn and Eli

PREFACE

Doing anthropological fieldwork, I, like many others, sometimes experienced a frustrating relativity effect: the closer I moved to a phenomenon, the faster it seemed to recede from my grasp. Every step forward revealed new complexities. This problem seems especially to bedevil the study of culture, something that when seen from a distance can appear monolithic and systematic but when viewed up close, in the ideas and feelings of individuals, seems to fragment into bewildering shards. Believing as I do, however, that an anthropology that loses sight of actual persons is an impoverished anthropology, there is no alternative but to cultivate a double focus, on both society and the person, in an effort to forge a coherent, sensitive statement about the person-in-society, our common, albeit variably experienced, human condition.

It is with this double focus that I try in this book to say something about Brazilians-in-Brazil without effacing the complexities of persons or of their collectivity. Because I am an outsider, however, and because any ethnography necessarily represents individuals and societies in summary fashion, the picture I draw is inevitably skewed and oversimplified. I think nevertheless that it portrays significant issues in Brazilian lives.

The book discusses two conceptually linked forms of face-to-face encounter in urban Brazil: Carnival, a bacchanalian pre-Lenten festival; and *briga*, a potentially lethal confrontation in the street. As social experience, the face-to-face encounter is elemental, mobilizing our strongest emotions and our strongest controls. Brazilians, like people elsewhere, worry about the perils of coming face-to-face with the wrong person, at the wrong time, under the wrong circumstances. Carnivals and brigas, I argue, highlight such perils, which are products of culturally specific constructions of interpersonal relationships and the self. These turbulent events dramatize distinctive, profound social and psychological dilemmas.

The study is based on my fieldwork in São Luís, capital of the state of Maranhão, where I resided with my wife, Lynn Simons, and our son, Eli from March 1984 to March 1986. This was an exciting time to be in Brazil, for at the midpoint of my stay the country underwent a transition from a discredited, feared, and widely hated military dictatorship, in power for over two decades, to a civilian government. If the new government came in under a black cloud—the popular president-elect, Tancredo Neves, died before he could take office, replaced by his vice president of convenience, the conservative *maranhense* José Sarney—the public mood during this period was nevertheless, by and large, one of restrained hopefulness. The *são-luisenses* I knew were universally pleased that the worst days of repression were past and seemed unlikely, in the short run at least, to recur. Nevertheless, they remained keenly aware that something was deeply wrong in Brazilian society: they had certainly not inherited the power ostensibly relinquished by the military officers. They continued to suffer injuries to their self-respect and, in some cases, to their physical persons long after the generals turned the mess over to civilians.

São-luisenses, most of whom are working people who feel vulnerable to the privileged and the powerful, and resent it, celebrated the election of Tancredo Neves with a Carnival of victory in the city's main square, not because they naively expected immediate and revolutionary change, but because they yearned for a sense of dignity so long denied them. If, as I argue, São Luís's dangerous encounters originate in the experience of social oppression Brazilian style, são-luisenses nevertheless do not accept, and have not surrendered to, the conditions that, lamentably, so often inject rancor and violence into their interactions with one another. If anything redeems the dark and troubled scene I describe, and, moreover, holds a promise of someday dispelling (in Chico Buarque's words) the "tenebrous transactions" of Brazilian society, it is this insistence on dignity by men and women who refuse to consent to their own nullification.

This book could never have been written without the cooperation of many são-luisenses who consented to speak of the not-always-pleasant aspects of their lives. To them I wish to express my gratitude openly and clearly. It has become somewhat of a cliché to say that the people we used to call "informants" are significant participants in the writing of our ethnographies; in this case, the truth of the observation is, I trust, evident. I hope my use of the words of Tito, Joana, and the others who spoke into my tape recorder, identified herein only by pseudonyms, does not betray the spirit in which they were given.

While doing interviews and engaging in that weird activity we call participant observation I often felt as though I were, as Brazilians put it, neither fish nor meat. Here I can mention only a few of those in São Luís who made me feel less a stranger by extending their trust and warm acceptance to Lynn, Eli, and me. The Martins family—Dona Augustinha, Seu Zé, Graça Maria, Augusta, and André—filled our Sundays with their laughter and affection. Among the many others who welcomed us were the Silva family, the Ramos family, the Nunes family, the Andrade family, Beatriz Fontana, Mundicarmo and Sérgio Ferretti, Liene and Francisco Moreira, Cláudia and Ronaldo Cardoso, Mariadne and Clóvis Viana, José Carlos Gomes, Padre Paulo Sampaio, and Gayle and Zequinha Lopes. A special note should be made of the children who enlivened our house and delighted us: Cleferson, André, Juçara, Dudu, Ewerton, and others from our neighborhood and beyond. It is with a keener sense of *saudade*, that melancholy longing for the irretrievable, that I recall the visits of Raquel and Isabel, who died in a drowning accident shortly after our departure from São Luís.

To Carlos Augusto de Sousa Ramos I owe a double debt of gratitude. I could not have had a more valuable research assistant, or a more valued friend. Were it not for his help and the sustaining laughter of our late-afternoon conversations, I could not have carried out this research or delved so deeply into the problems it raised.

For their careful work and patience with my exacting demands, I would like to thank my other research assistants, Cleomar de Jesus Silva and Maria das Graças Pereira.

The rector of the Universidade Federal do Maranhão (UFMA), José Maria Cabral Marques, made that university's resources available in support of my research. Members of the UFMA's faculty of the Department of Sociology and Anthropology, especially Mundicarmo and Sérgio Ferretti and José Carlos Sabóia, provided much helpful information and advice. Valdelino Cécio offered me the use of the research facilities of the Centro de Cultura Popular, and the librarians at the Biblioteca do Estado do Maranhão and at the UFMA assisted me in locating useful archival materials.

For their assistance in São Luís I would also like to thank Pedro Braga, Rossini Corrêa, Beatriz Fontana, Helena Heluy, Nascimento Morais, Lindalva Mota, and Mário Rego. David Cleary gave much thoughtful commentary on my research during his stimulating and hilarious visits to our house on the Rua da Cruz. Nearby, on the Rua dos Craveiros, Darrell Posey offered both the benefits of his long experience in Brazil and the welcome diversion of his company.

The University of California, San Diego, supported my research through a variety of grants. This support was crucial during my first fifteen months of fieldwork, when I was unable to secure other funding. The final nine months in the field, essential for completion of the project, were sponsored by a Fulbright-Hays Doctoral Dissertation Research Abroad Grant. A University of California, Santa Cruz, Faculty Research Grant provided funds for the preparation of maps and photos.

I am grateful to F. G. Bailey for introducing me to anthropology and, through sympathetic counsel and the exchange of ideas, helping make me an anthropologist. The perspectives of Roy D'Andrade and Robert Levy have also unmistakably informed this essay. To my friend and colleague Steve Parish I owe my thanks for countless hours of enjoyable and illuminating discussion. Jorge Soares, my first Brazilian friend, inadvertently taught me many basics of Brazilian life and has always been generous with his time and advice. Jerry Salzman, an old American friend who punctuated our field stay with a memorable visit, has been a constant source of encouragement. I am indebted to Janet Keller for her incisive commentary on an early draft of this book. Sandy Shattuck provided insightful last-minute criticism of key portions of the manuscript. At Stanford Press, my editors Bill Carver, Karen Brown Davison, and Trudie Calvert trimmed excesses, urged me to rethink obscurities, and gently shepherded the manuscript through the publishing process. Regrettably, it is impossible to thank by name the many others, in both Brazil and the United States, who assisted me in this project.

Lynn endured with good humor my periods of doubt and exasperation. She has been a valuable consultant and collaborator. Eli, just two years old when we arrived in São Luís, offered me a vicarious opportunity to view the city through a child's eyes. He has been more than patient during the many hours I have spent tethered to a keyboard writing this book. My brother, David Linger, first invited me to Brazil; he has shared with me his own deep and extensive knowledge of that country. My mother, Mildred Rubin, long ago set an example for me, which I have tried to emulate, of respect for others.

D.T.L.

CONTENTS

MAPS AND TABLES

MAPS

TABLES

STORIES

PART 1

INTRODUCTION

There's more samba in meeting than in waiting

There's more samba in evil than in wounds

There's more samba in port than at sea

There's more samba in forgiveness than in farewell

There's more samba in the hand than in the eye

There's more samba on the ground than in the moonlit sky

—From the song "Tem mais samba"
(There's more samba), by Chico Buarque

1

FATEFUL ENCOUNTERS

The Big House and Canudos

Intimacies of slavery, savageries of civilization: irony is a hallmark of Brazilian self-portraits. Probably the two most penetrating, passionate, and influential social critics Brazil has produced are Gilberto Freyre and Euclides da Cunha. Each created in a classic work an indelible symbol of Brazilian society, a mythic—and ironic—national self-representation.

For Freyre in *The Masters and the Slaves* (1956 [1933]), primordial Brazil is the sugar plantation's Big House, where master ravishes slave in an atmosphere suffused with patriarchal lust, caprice, and indulgence. Such liaisons engender not just a hybrid Brazilian population, but a hybrid Brazilian civilization, a blend of Portuguese, Indian, and African elements. Races and cultures fuse in the sensual and emotional hothouse of the amorphous, inclusive Brazilian family. Paradoxically, the depraved "sexual intoxication" (p. 85) permeating the unequal social relations of colonial Brazil eventually transmutes their antagonism and cruelty into Luso-tropical conciliation and tolerance. Freyre concludes that Brazil has achieved "one of the most harmonious unions of culture with nature and of one culture with another that the lands of this hemisphere have ever known" (p. xii).

EPIGRAPH TO PART I: I consulted Perrone's (1989) translations of this and other songs, though our renditions differ in certain respects. My translation of "Tem mais samba" follows his most closely.

3

Cunha's *Rebellion in the Backlands* (1944 [1902]), by contrast, locates Brazil deep in the Bahian hinterland, where the state sends soldiers and cannons to exterminate a messianic community of atavistic backlanders (*sertanejos*).[1] The prophet Antônio Conselheiro, "a buffoon maddened by a vision of the Apocalypse" (p. 133), has established his celestial city of Canudos, a chaotic warren of mud huts built round a monstrous church, as a refuge from the sinful republic that in 1889 replaced the Brazilian empire. The army's annihilation of the rustics, members of a retrograde mixed "subrace," is part of an implacable, atrocious historical process: the "inevitable crushing of the weak races by the strong" (p. xxix). "Civilization"—Cunha's use of the word, unlike Freyre's, is acid—announces itself with artillery and leaves in its wake a silent "trench of the dead, plastered with blood and running with pus" (p. 475). On the civilized coast, delirious throngs greet the swollen severed head of the backlanders' prophet, a trophy of the army's ghastly triumph, with "carnival joy" (p. 476).

Freyre's Brazilian civilization is a fertile amalgam; Cunha's, a criminal juggernaut. The clashing images invite debate over Brazilian character.[2] Are Brazilians conciliatory or intransigent, peaceful or violent? But such questions are irrelevant to a discussion of Brazilianness, which has more to do with shared predicaments than with shared personalities. Masters and slaves, soldiers and sertanejos are compelling Brazilian figures not because they reject or relish violence, but because they are enmeshed in archetypal Brazilian events, precarious face-to-face encounters charged with uncontrolled passions and characterized by the peremptory exercise of power.

Each of these Brazils, the Big House and Canudos, is a spatially isolated locus of fateful encounters between unequal adversaries who can neither decipher nor avoid each other. Brazil in these modern myths is primeval. Anything can happen in the isolated sugar manors carved from the coastal forest and in the sun-blasted ravines of the infinitely receding interior— places where antagonistic strangers come face-to-face in a hallucinatory setting. For Freyre and Cunha, the encounters are volatile and their outcomes ironic: the arbitrariness and cruelty of slavery yield forbearance, generosity, and a melding of positive qualities; the advanced, sophisticated coastal civilization consolidates progress through genocide.

Together, these Brazilian intellectuals give eloquent expression to popular uncertainties about Brazilian identity and disquiet about the Brazilian self. During my two years in São Luís, a city in Brazil's Northeast, people told me countless versions of the mixed-race, mixed-culture myth. Moreover, I ran across variations of this myth in children's textbooks, political

[1]Portuguese words used repeatedly are briefly defined in the Glossary.
[2]See Leite (1983 [1954]) for a review and criticism of studies of Brazilian "national character."

speeches, television dramas, Carnival pageants, popular songs, and Afro-Brazilian religious practices. The myth's very prevalence and the insistence with which it is propagated arouse suspicion. Is the image of a serene, "beautiful, wheat-colored Brazil"[3] a cornerstone of Brazilian identity? Or does it seek to mask an underlying apprehension that Brazilian society is in fact divided and contentious?

This apprehension is the theme of *Rebellion in the Backlands*. Cunha's gloomy assessment of Brazilian civilization as intransigent, relentless, and cruel emerges in troubled fragments of popular discourse. Everyone in São Luís lamented the violence in Brazilian life; many thought this violence had gotten completely out of hand, issuing as much or more from the government and the police as from hoodlums—a position consistent with Cunha's pessimistic view. Violence was a central theme of eyewitness stories, cautionary anecdotes, and political commentary, but it was downplayed or denied as a component of national identity. Not infrequently, the same person who recounted dreadful tales of fighting and mayhem one day told me a Freyrian harmony myth the next.

Cunha's charter for Brazilian identity is unsettling for the same reason that Freyre's is appealing. One hesitates to embrace danger and violence too closely, to assimilate these qualities into the self, even when—or perhaps especially when—that danger and violence seem always imminent. Both Freyre and Cunha address anxieties over discord, arbitrary violence, and loss of control, but from different positions. Cunha trumpets the fears that Freyre tries to mute. Both stories fascinate because they issue from a region of doubt and distress within Brazilian culture.

Like all myths, histories such as *The Masters and the Slaves* or *Rebellion in the Backlands* have several levels of meaning. On the surface, they are narratives of collectivities and origins; implicitly, they are polemical reflections on the collective present. But I would suggest that they also comment on the *private* present. That is, they make symbolic use of the past to address widespread, insistent personal concerns. Such myths do not simply filter down from intellectuals to the man or woman in the street, though they may find there a responsive audience. It is the concerns of the street—those of direct social experience—that provide grist for the mythmaking mills of the intellectuals, who transpose current, immediate uncertainties and predicaments into historical collective dramas. One can read the Big House and Canudos as condensations of central dilemmas of Brazilian daily life—misgivings over the integrity and stability of interpersonal relationships and of the self—into potent symbols drawn from the past.

[3]This phrase (*esse Brasil lindo e trigueiro*) comes from Ary Barroso's sentimental anthem of 1939, "Aquarela do Brasil" (Watercolor of Brazil), probably the most famous popular song ever written by a Brazilian composer.

Popular concerns also provide grist for our anthropological mills, but the stories we tell have a different quality. Constructing a myth of Brazilian identity is not my business as an American anthropologist. Rather, I am trying to enter into a conversation, to contribute a perspective to an ongoing dialogue that ultimately bears on matters important to Brazilians and Americans alike.

Our primary obligation as anthropologists is, I believe, to take seriously other peoples and other realities. I listened as best I could to what people in São Luís told me about Carnivals, street fights, and the incredibly rich microcosms of their private experience. This book sets down what I heard. But because of my training, my culture, and my own biography, what I heard has some idiosyncratic meanings. That is, *são-luisenses'*[4] reflections have entered into my own reflections on violence, human relationships, and the inner world of thoughts and emotions. Similarly, my reflections, presented in the following pages, might conceivably enter into theirs. Like people everywhere, são-luisenses constantly rework the meanings that help shape their experience. When that experience is confusing or distressing, the work of interpretation takes on added urgency. This is why their attention focuses on multivalent, topsy-turvy events such as Carnivals and street fights, and it is why I wrote this book.

Shortly after we moved into our first house in São Luís, I was unpleasantly awakened in the middle of the night by gunshots and the sound of running feet outside our door. When the commotion had faded into the distance, the street began to buzz with speculations. I was relieved to learn that although a policeman had suffered a slight injury, no one had been killed. More disconcerting was the news that such incidents were not unprecedented: evidently our neighborhood, about which we knew next to nothing, was not very safe. The gunfight brought home to me that the sensational, often grisly daily press reports of assaults and stabbings reflected a fact of life in São Luís. (Our little shootout was too trivial even to receive mention in the newspaper.) I had not come to Brazil to study violence, but I began to wonder about the sources of its fascination for são-luisenses, a fascination I reluctantly recognized that I shared. The riddle, which came to be the central problem of my fieldwork, had two parts: What was the meaning of urban violence in Brazil? And how could the Brazilian case shed light on the general question of interpersonal violence? This book, then, is intended as a contribution to the Brazilian debate over Brazilian violence and to a wider discussion, within anthropology and without, of the confusing and distressing propensity of human beings to do harm to one another.

---

[4]This term designates natives of São Luís. São-luisenses also call themselves *ludovicenses* or simply *maranhenses* (natives of Maranhão).

Like Freyre and Cunha, são-luisenses worry over passions run wild, the abuse of the weak by the strong, and the disjunctions between feelings, intentions, and actions that make social encounters so unpredictable. They have a sharp sense of irony, of the absurd, of the deceptiveness of appearances and (consequently) the necessity for keen attention and incisive interpretation. Not surprisingly, this attitude often shows itself as playfulness or wit, but the play can be deep and the humor dark. And for these modern city dwellers, as for the mythical denizens of the Big House and warriors of Canudos, the face-to-face encounter between strangers or enemies bristles with dangers and ambiguities, crystalizing some of life's fundamental quandaries. Such urban confrontations can put strong passions in play, with appalling consequences—as when, on an August morning in 1909, Euclides da Cunha, armed with a revolver and vowing "to kill or be killed," was himself shot dead by his wife's lover on a Rio street (Malta 1990).

This book is about how people living in a Brazilian city think about and negotiate dangerous encounters, vital and disturbing experiences that mobilize anxieties over self-control, self-esteem, self-preservation, and social cohesion—encounters that, when they go wrong, yield the bitter fruits of moral failure, humiliation, death, and chaos.

In the City, Face-to-Face

The Big House and Canudos belong to the past, but the face-to-face encounter—a greeting in the street, a Sunday visit, an argument, a festival, an embrace, a knife fight, a promise to a saint, or a last touch to a coffin—remains a principal vertex of Brazilian life. One of the first lessons I learned living among Brazilians was that physical presence counts for more than it does in my own country, the United States. To get something done in Brazil, one does it in person. Moreover, relationships grow and sustain themselves through the senses and through the intimate social exchanges of banter and laughter. It is not that others cease to exist when absent, but rather that the joy of friendship blooms when people come face-to-face. It shows itself immediately in greetings: in kisses and embraces, pats on the back, gentle touches, smiles. Visitors to our house would sometimes hail our three year-year-old son, "Come over here, Eli, let me smell you." *Saudade*, the bittersweet emotion usually glossed as "longing" or "nostalgia," is a profound, melancholy sense of physical separation, of apartness, of being literally out of touch with a person, a place, a time.

The same sensitivity to physical intimacy conditions Brazilian sociability. Casual conversations with friends often have a lighthearted, conspiratorial tone. On these occasions, the main purpose of talking is not to deliver opinions or make debating points but to delight in one another's presence—to exchange droll stories, to laugh together, to play. It is a mistake to see this verbal play as frivolity: precisely because such occasions are so valued, one must not squander them by losing sight of their social essence.[5]

As with friends, so it is with enemies: physical presence kindles emotion, though of quite a different sort. Sérgio Buarque de Holanda, the much-misinterpreted historian whose work popularized the image of the Brazilian as the *homem cordial*, the "cordial man," once pointedly remarked (1982 [1936]: 144–45) that Brazilian cordiality is exactly that, cor-diality— a matter of the heart, where not only amity, but also enmity, dwells. When enemies come face-to-face, the desire for vengeance flares, and sometimes with it come knives and physical intimacy of another sort. But meetings with strangers, too, can be charged, especially encounters between those who understand themselves to be, at least in part, mutually indecipherable and, possibly, mutually hostile, like soldier and backlander. Once such strangers take notice of each other, there is always the chance that something of consequence, perhaps something of all too much consequence, will transpire between them.

Within Brazil's vastness one still finds rustic backwaters, but two out of three Brazilians now live in cities. In a country that has become predominantly urban, no encounter is more potentially fateful than a meeting between strangers or enemies, especially at night, on a street corner, in the *praça* (public square), at a bar. The negotiation of such encounters is a central preoccupation of the Brazilian city dwellers among whom I lived. These events never fail to fascinate and move those who directly or vicariously participate in them.

This book examines two related types of urban encounters as they are conceived and as they occur in São Luís, a city of a little over half a million people, capital of the northeastern state of Maranhão. The first, Carnival, acknowledged within the country and without as the chief and most eloquent expression of Brazilian popular culture, is the annual festival of fantasy and merrymaking that precedes Lent. Carnival is a mass bacchanalian gathering in the praça, ideally an exercise in sensuality and harmony suggestive of the Big House. The second event, *briga*, no less salient to Brazilians but hardly considered an emblematic cultural manifestation, can occur anytime, anywhere. Briga is a variant of Canudos writ small.[6] A briga is a

---

[5]This does not mean, obviously, that Brazilians lack strong opinions or that they are reluctant to deliver them under appropriate conditions.

[6]Carnival shares with Freyre's Big House a certain mood and style of interaction, as does briga with Cunha's Canudos. The former are characterized by a (limited) tolerance and an eroticism that (in theory) tend to soften social boundaries; the latter feature intransigence, fury, and revenge. I do not mean to draw these analogies closely in other respects.

violent confrontation, usually involving two individuals: the prototype is a street or bar fight.

Both Carnivals and brigas seem at first glance chaotic. In an early scene of Marcel Camus's film *Black Orpheus* (*Orfeu negro*, 1959), Eurydice, a young woman from the countryside, arrives in Rio de Janeiro just as Carnival is getting under way. Through her eyes a brilliant but vaguely threatening spectacle opens before us. The dock is bedlam—clamoring vendors of baubles and onions, leering faces, frightening masks, dancing, shouting, and whistling, everything engulfed in aggressive, pulsating Carnival rhythms. Eurydice finds herself a center of unwelcome attention, ominously encircled; such images of ensnarement and imprisonment recur as the story unfolds. A masker disguised as a skeleton—Death—shadows her throughout Carnival, claiming her at its zenith during a fateful encounter in an eerily deserted, silent trolley terminus. In reality as in the film, death hovers at Carnival's margins, for in the heat of the festival's communal catharsis some people fight and die in brigas that burst suddenly, seemingly without reason or form, into terrifying violence. As Orfeu learns, seeking his vanished lover as the sounds of police sirens fade into the early empty hours of Ash Wednesday, the frenzy of Carnival has, ironically, filled the city morgue with cold, still bodies.

Carnivals and brigas are in many respects unpredictable, but they are not chaotic. Like initiations, sacred ceremonies, and other events that anthropologists usually classify as rituals, Carnivals and brigas are cultural performances, structured by organized, shared understandings.[7] Both events arise from collective engagement in culturally constructed interactions laden with meaning. Although they are neither sacred nor invariant, they do what rituals, in their most general sense, do—bring people together to participate in or celebrate, in an unordinary or otherworldly atmosphere, a performance that distills some shared conception of the nature of the world and the place of human beings within it.

These two cultural performances, however, portray contradictory worlds. In Brazil, as elsewhere, the universe presents itself in multiple and often conflicting cultural guises.

---

[7]Manning uses the term "cultural performance" as "a rubric encompassing ritual, ceremony, pageantry, popular and folk theatre, sporting and entertainment productions, ethnic, regional and arts festivals, and similar genres of collective expression" (1983: viii). For me, cultural performances are those culturally defined events for which there exist shared cognitive "scripts" for participation. This definition, which includes both more or less formal productions such as those listed by Manning and informal structured interactions such as brigas, focuses more closely on the collectively constructed nature of the event.

Carnival

Annual, licentious mass festivals have long attracted the attention of theorists of ritual. Robert Dirks (1988: 857) usefully delineates this domain, which (following Edward Norbeck [1963]) he calls "rituals of conflict," as follows: "festivals, carnivals, saturnalias, political and religious ceremonies, and other yearly celebrations containing episodes of ridicule, threat, assault, rivalry, or other conflicts that, whether solemnly or playfully enacted, at other times are not prescribed, expected, or considered proper." The domain thus defined has the merit of grouping Carnivals together with what Max Gluckman (1954, 1969 [1956]) terms "rituals of rebellion,"[8] highlighting the crucial fact that both, at regular intervals and for a brief and clearly bounded period, suspend the prevailing rules of social order and permit normally proscribed behavior, including, prominently, aggressive displays.

Rituals of rebellion—Christmas-day mess, when British officers waited table on enlisted men, or the agricultural rites in which Zulu "women and girls committed public obscenities and acted as if they were men" (Gluckman 1969 [1956]: 110)—temporarily reverse social roles. But even though they formally negate the established social order, ultimately, says Gluckman, they preserve and strengthen it—if, that is, "the social order is unquestioned and indubitable—where there are rebels, and not revolutionaries" (p. 134). Gluckman expects that rituals of rebellion can flourish only when profound questioning and open rejection of the political status quo are repressed by force or otherwise (perhaps ideologically?) inhibited.

Gluckman's reasoning is not always explicit, but we can make out at least two major reasons why, paradoxically, such formal inversions could end up reconfirming the social order. For one thing, they seem cathartic. Playing at protest may defuse tensions that might otherwise generate social unrest. Second, Gluckman observes that "socially, the lifting of the normal taboos and restraints obviously serves to emphasize them" (p. 114). One could argue that this works socially because it works cognitively—the norm is entailed in its violation. If people experience catharsis during rituals of rebellion, and if normative inversion administers a cognitive jolt that re-engraves the very norms breached, then Gluckman's conclusion that rituals of rebellion are essentially functional—preservative of things-as-they-are—seems plausible.[9]

The analysis, however, is not altogether convincing. If revolution is ruled

---

[8]Turner (1969) calls these "rituals of status reversal."

[9]Although Gluckman (like most British anthropologists of his and the preceding generation) most emphatically considered himself to be a *social* anthropologist, for whom individual motivations lay in the province of other disciplines, I do not see how the logic of rituals of rebellion can work without a psychological basis of the sort I have outlined here.

out at the start, then why should such rituals be necessary? The explanation is functional in form but the function itself is elusive; the argument seems circular. Moreover, in downplaying the prevalence of acts of resistance in everyday behavior, Gluckman's discussion misses some of the significance of full-blown rituals of rebellion. Consider Dirks's discussion of Christmas, what he calls "Black Saturnalia," in nineteenth-century West Indian plantations, as he contrasts the slaves' usual furtive stealing of food with their ritualized exactions during the festival:

> On Christmas morning, house visitors [i.e., slaves] invaded the masters' space, but rather than intruding with the stealth of the ordinary thief they danced right up to the front door in groups, figuratively demanding food otherwise taken on the sly. Reversals, then, did not consist of negations. They were the playing out, collectively and conspicuously, of what otherwise went on covertly. . . . The net effect . . . was to feature aspects of plantation life so broadly as to render them a burlesque. (1987: 187)

He concludes that Christmas did not reconfirm norms, as Gluckman might have contended:

> The Black Saturnalia did not sanctify; it profaned. It disclaimed a lie by enacting reality. If that disclaimer, that rejection, appeared as a joke, if it was set forth in a ludicrous, foolish manner, what we have is an attestation not to the power of the lie but to the power of the truth to find its way out even in the most repressive societies. (p. 190)

Here, the carnivalization of deviance poses a ludic challenge to the official picture. There is a threat in the slaves' bold parody of their daily subversion. The threat was not idle. This unmasking of the truth was anything but cathartic for the plantation workers: the fact that December was the peak month for slave uprisings (1987: 167–68) suggests that the revelries of Christmas actually inflamed revolt.

The implication is that, *pace* Gluckman, rituals of rebellion can indeed challenge the dominant construction of social relationships by broadly sketching a competing vision that serves as a call to arms. In a penetrating discussion of symbolic inversion, Natalie Davis (1978) makes much the same point. She argues that the long preindustrial European tradition in literature, art, and festival depicting women as disorderly and disobedient cut two ways. Men used these portrayals of the "woman on top" to rationalize the subjection of women: if women were by nature imperfect, inconstant, out of control, then men had the right and the obligation to keep women under their thumbs. But the unruly woman, like Brueghel's frightening "huge, armed, unseeing" Mad Meg, "the emblem of fiery destruction, of brutal oppression and disorder" (p. 151), could also be a symbolic resource in political struggles of both women and other subordinates such as peasants and laborers, whose leaders often donned women's clothes during riots in early modern Europe. Hence for Davis the "woman on top" is a "multivalent image" (p. 154) of ambiguous political significance: whether the inversion draws our minds to the norms inverted or to new possibilities for real-world social arrangements or, perhaps, to both, seems moot.

The arguments of Dirks and Davis recommend caution in interpreting rituals of rebellion. We need to pay close attention to what is being reversed; in any case, the event is likely to communicate diverse, and possibly contradictory, messages.

What, then, is being reversed in Brazilian Carnival? Carnival creates a temporary reality normatively at odds both with hierarchy, in a global sense, and with certain everyday constraints on social interaction, a point that has been underscored by many writers, notably the Brazilian anthropologist Roberto DaMatta. Specifically, the ideal carnivalesque world is one that ushers in a regime of equality and permits the free play of suppressed desires. Carnival subjects hierarchy to a Rabelaisian leveling, insisting that all are mortal creatures of flesh and blood, with flesh-and-blood needs and wants (cf. Bakhtin 1968 [1965]). São-luisenses well understand the main features of this carnivalesque utopia and its oppositional relation to important aspects of day-to-day life. Hence Carnival provides a vision of alternative, superior social arrangements: a harmonious, egalitarian world of spontaneity and license.

But this carnivalesque vision, like Davis's woman on top, is multivalent, ambiguous: it does not mean the same thing to all people or in all contexts. For example, in the hands of a cultural innovator such as the Brazilian composer, singer, playwright, and novelist Chico Buarque, Carnival takes on a decidedly millennial cast. Buarque's song "Vai passar," a hit during the euphoric days of early 1985, invokes Carnival as a celebratory symbol of the unpopular military regime's demise. Chico's Carnival is a jubilee, the joyful close of a benighted, unhappy, stifled era. In this exuberant samba of the wretched and downtrodden, inmates of a Brazil that Buarque calls the "General Sanatorium"—a hint here of Meg-like madness?—hail the revival of ties with their ancient communal past as they march toward the promise of a new dawn.

Buarque's samba of the dispossessed, of the "pitch-black Napoleons," the "famished barons," and the "pygmies of the boulevard" singing in unison as the cobblestones tremble beneath their feet, conjures up a revolutionary specter reminiscent of the Black Saturnalia and Mad Meg. But it would be a mistake to see Carnival's chimera as simply a battle cry. São-luisenses, like Gluckman's enlisted men and Zulu women, understand that (to use a phrase associated with Carnival) "anything goes" for just a few short days: Carnival's normative inversions highlight the norms inverted. Moreover, são-luisenses view Carnival specifically as a chance for emotional cathar-sis—for dancing away dangerous passions. In these respects Carnival draws one's attention to a conservative picture of suffering punctuated only by periodic moments of relief. When all is said and done, the festival is symboli-cally indeterminate: it offers something for reactionaries, revolutionaries, and even the politically ambivalent or indifferent.

However tenuously or equivocally, Carnival, like all rituals of con-flict, proposes alternative, superior social arrangements and corresponding psychological rewards. Ultimately, this proposal constitutes not a Geertzian worldview (1973b [1957])—something that anthropologists tend to asso-ciate with beliefs or local common sense—but an evanescent, hypothetical dream of social peace, of solidarity, of emotional release, of carnal satia-tion. In short, whether one discovers in Carnival political inspiration or apolitical reverie, Carnival counterposes a utopian world vision to a socially constructed, culturally imagined, and experientially insistent "real world" infused by competition, hierarchy, frustration, and violence.

But ironically, within Carnival itself this real world resurges in its most concentrated, disturbing form. In the depths of carnivalesque play one may, unhappily, come face-to-face with the cultural nightmare, partially ob-scured by Carnival's magnificent illusion, that human encounters can be precarious, harrowing, morally and physically devastating events. Danger-ous passions do not always take flight in samba; they sometimes drive the unnerving dance são-luisenses know as briga.

Briga

Carnival is, as são-luisenses say, a time to *brincar, não brigar* (play, not fight). The implication is that violence threatens Carnival, and indeed Carnival, to almost everyone's distress, witnesses a good deal of fighting. If in the West Indies Christmas profaned the planters' fantasy of legitimate privi-lege, in Brazil briga profanes society's carnivalesque fantasy of egalitarian tranquillity.

In its treatment of aggression, Carnival employs a common but some-times fragile ironic device—mimicry. Imitation aggression, more or less stylized, is and always has been a fixture of Carnival. Our earliest records of Brazilian Carnival show slaves pelting their masters with colored powders, water, and scents, and vice versa. Carnival urges one to perform aggres-sive acts, but only in play, and to tolerate aggressions from others as if they were play. It burlesques the violence in society, denying that aggression has serious causes and consequences, again offering a comforting illusion of a civilization without discontents, or at least without dangerous discontents.

There is a hint here that Carnival bears some affinity to rituals of reconciliation, sociodramas in which aggression is acted out in miniature and thereby (so it is said) banished. That such rituals can fail has long been recognized (see, e.g., Leach 1977 [1954]: 281 and Bailey 1977: 9–10). Gregory Bateson, referring to the Andaman Islanders' peacemaking ceremony in which members of one side shout at and shake their antagonists, who must show neither fear nor anger throughout the "attack" (Radcliffe-Brown 1964 [1922]: 238), pinpoints neatly the danger in those rituals that, like Carnival, mimic aggression: "The discrimination between map and territory is always liable to break down, and the ritual blows of peace-making are always liable to be mistaken for the 'real' blows of combat. In this event, the peace-making ceremony becomes a battle" (1972d [1955]: 182). The problem is that mimicry requires a tacit agreement by both parties: the person delivering the blows must not be too enthusiastic, and the person receiving them must be forbearing. But the better the mimicry the harder the blows, and the harder the blows the greater the chance that the agreement will break down.

Bateson's notion of cognitive frames gives us another way to look at such rituals. A frame advises us how to interpret what it encloses; at the same time, changed interpretations of what is enclosed can sometimes redefine the frame. "Ritual" is the frame of the peacemaking ceremony; hence blows are not to be regarded as "real" acts of aggression (cf. Bateson's discussion of play [1972d]). But this ritual frame is, in Erving Goffman's (1974) terminology, easily "broken." One man delivers an energetic ritual blow; the other takes this as a real blow; the frame switches from "ritual" to "aggression," permitting retaliation; and the two are suddenly playing a different game—indeed, the very game the ritual was intended to forestall!

Carnival's frame is similarly precarious. Here and there the festival's parody of the distasteful "real" state of affairs slips, with terrible consequences, into exactly that state. As Orfeu discovered at the morgue, what is normatively an ecstatic but peaceful festival inevitably yields a sizable harvest of injuries and deaths. Aside from accidents, the carnage is typically a product of brigas occurring in clubs, in bars, in the praças, and on the streets. Carnival, an event that is, as every inhabitant of São Luís knows, designed to release social and psychological tensions in a safe and wholly pleasurable manner, ends up in some cases actually *precipitating* the violence it abjures. The most unwelcome of guests, briga suddenly appears in the midst of the celebration, its playful mask torn away.

Carnival's millennial dream comes to an end months before the start of a second eagerly anticipated festival, São João, celebrated over several weeks during June. São João is mellower than Carnival, a festival with a rural ambience of bonfires and accordion music associated with the northeastern countryside. It features many small groups of men and women from the poorer neighborhoods or from rural communities performing *bumba-meu-boi*, a dance-drama set to music and song, in the squares of the city, usually in the hours after midnight. The dramas recount pieces of a well-known story in which a slave, urged by his pregnant wife to secure a bull's tongue for her to eat, kills one of the master's cattle and is caught by his henchmen. The man escapes punishment and his transgression is expunged when a curer miraculously resurrects the bull.

São João presents a Brazil bearing little resemblance to the Brazil of Carnival, a forgiving, magical, but immutable pastoral dominion in which indulgence of desire is risky and there is no question of equality. The two visions—Brazil as urban utopia and Brazil as rural patriarchy—clash, but perhaps the separation in time between Carnival and São João minimizes cognitive and emotional dissonance. Carnival and briga, by contrast, come packaged together: there is no escaping the contradiction between Carnival's vision of harmonious community, civilization minus its discontents, and briga's graphic depiction of wanton aggression. The juxtaposition is not fortuitous, either behaviorally or culturally. It marks a social and emotional situation in which são-luisenses feel deeply vulnerable.

São-luisense culture has an explanation for why playing becomes fighting, but the explanation offers little comfort. São-luisenses see Carnival as a chance to *desabafar*, to expel the frustration and anger inevitably accumulated during the previous year. If one does not relieve this internal pressure through harmless acts of venting (*desabafos*), it may break through as aggression, creating a dangerous situation for the person as well as for others. By this reasoning, Carnival, along with other occasions permitting desabafos, provides a necessary space for psychological and social prophylaxis.

A briga during Carnival indicates that something has gone wrong with desabafo itself, the control mechanism of this psychosocial system. Salutary venting has become pathological aggression. A reveler's frustrations lash out at a human victim, negating Carnival's claim that dangerous emotions can be safely discharged. Blood shed during a briga therefore marks not only a place of mayhem or murder but also a place of social and psychological breakdown, bereft of convincing cultural remedy.

The Argument

Throughout this book I tack between experience-near (phenomenological, or emic) and experience-distant (comparative, or etic) perspectives.[10] My aim, ambitious and not fully realized, is to integrate cultural, social, and

[10]The terms are Heinz Kohut's, as discussed by Geertz (1983 [1974]).

psychological considerations into a substantially recursive general interpretive scheme. Such an exercise has the air, as Robert Levy puts it, "of Alice's croquet game, with both mallets and balls, not to mention the wickets, in eccentric motion" (1984: 214). I have tried to flag my most speculative ventures, asking the reader's indulgence for my deeper, yet tentative, excursions into anthropological Wonderland.

Let me now outline the argument.

Chapter 2 concludes this introductory section. It sketches the urban backdrop for the events and stories that follow—the historical mythology, social conditions, physical environment, and everyday life of the citizens of São Luís.

Part II discusses the connection between Carnival and violence. Although Carnival permits desabafo, at best it can provide only a simulacrum of freedom, an illusory counterpoint to the "real world" (Chapters 3 and 4). This is because desabafo itself must be constrained: one can vent "into the air" (the carnivalesque ideal) or one can discharge one's anger at another person—the first step toward a briga. That is, desabafos can easily trigger explosions of violence that destroy Carnival's peaceful pretensions. For its illusion to work, Carnival must play with violence but discourage revelers from crossing the boundary into briga—a delicate operation.

Hence a successful Carnival requires controlled rather than uninhibited release (Chapter 5). It elicits from its celebrants a social and psychological tour de force as they experiment with ways of convincing themselves, at least momentarily, that freedom and solidarity are possible in spite of the disruptiveness of impulse and the consequent precariousness of social relations.

Carnival often teeters on the edge of violence, but that violence is not simply a chaotic abyss. Part III turns to briga, urban Brazil's characteristic scenario of street violence. Based on são-luisenses' stories and commentary, I infer a cultural (i.e., a shared cognitive) model of briga (Chapters 6–9).[11] This cultural model takes the form of a ramifying script—a set of possible interaction sequences—initiated by a provocation. The briga script rests upon still other shared understandings. Its key constituent, also an important component of Carnival, is a folk psychology that describes a tension between dangerous impulses and the religious, moral, and rational structures charged with safely containing them. A briga escalates when these structures fail. A serious briga displays the devastating consequences of interpersonal conflict and, therefore, of personal disequilibrium.

The last chapter of Part III illustrates how culture and personal motives mesh to generate a recognizable, if unusual, actual event (Chapter 10). The event, a briga that culminated in a bizarre slaying, occurred in a crowded

---

[11] A brief review of my methods can be found in Appendix B.

waterfront bar in early 1984. I show how victim and k⌣
by singular aims and concerns, organized their behavio⌣
knowledge of briga to produce an abhorrent, extraordinary, b⌣
coherent lethal interaction.

Part IV, the conclusion, widens the perspective still further, offer⌣
integrated cultural, social, and psychological explanation of Brazilian stre⌣
violence. I first summarize the interrelationships between Carnival, briga,
and desabafo, which together form a problematic cultural cluster. Desabafos can be benign acts of venting, as during Carnival, or malign acts
of provocation, as in briga (Chapter 11). Next, I identify the social and
psychological predicaments that tend to generate brigas and invest them
with meaning (Chapter 12). Brigas begin with malign desabafos; malign
desabafos are triggered by resentment; resentment is fueled by humiliation; humiliation is a product of são-luisense "culturally laden sociality"
(Rosaldo 1984: 140). That is, in São Luís, power is personalized, highly concentrated, and arbitrarily exercised. The unprotected majority, those with
neither name nor voice, are routinely subjected to symbolic nullifications
by their putative superiors. Such indignities produce resentment, which
(according to são-luisense folk psychology) must be vented. By expelling
resentments at someone else—by provoking, or responding explosively to
a provocation—one makes a claim to personhood, to respect. I conjecture
that brigas permit both spectators (vicariously) and participants (directly)
to explore acute formulations of characteristic dilemmas—how to avoid
humiliation and how to manage aggression—in an unconscious attempt to
master disturbing feelings of social impotence and hostility, the sociocultural system's pernicious emotional residues.

If Brazilian civilization reveals itself in face-to-face encounters like Carnivals and brigas, then it is neither the benign conciliator of the Big House
nor the blind destroyer of Canudos. It is a civilization that is uncertain,
unsettled, unfinished. The Brazilians who speak herein are struggling with
contradictory ideas and emotions, living experiences that are often bewildering and sometimes terrifying. They are making themselves, perhaps
making culture, in places where their guidelines conflict or do not exist. The
scene is a restless one: men and women seeking some way to understand and
to resolve the collision between the urges they feel and the requirements for
social peace—in the end, not just a Brazilian problem, but an intractable,
compelling human predicament.

2

THE CITY

An Anecdotal History

In the still hours before dawn, when its squares are deserted, its houses shuttered, and its cobbled lanes silent, São Luís undergoes a subtle transformation. For a moment the city's past, etched in geography and architecture, in monuments and statues, in the names of streets and praças, becomes palpable. One realizes that this beautiful, run-down provincial metropolis of equatorial Brazil has a collectively recalled and imagined history that continues to echo through its daily life and its extraordinary events.[1]

A Spanish sailor was probably the first European to sight what is now Maranhão, months and perhaps even years before the Portuguese Pedro Álvares Cabral "discovered" Brazil by accident on his way to India in April 1500. According to the Treaty of Tordesillas, Maranhão and the place the

[1]General surveys of the history of Maranhão include Meireles (1980 [1960]) and Lima (1981), the main sources for the following summary. For a discussion of the French period in São Luís, see Meireles (1982); d'Abbeville (1975 [1614]) provides a first-person account. Silveira (1979 [1624]) gives an early Portuguese view. Maranhão's reluctance to join an independent Brazil is discussed in Meireles (1972). For a history of the Church in Maranhão, see Pacheco (1968). Tribuzi (1981) provides a brief but informative overview of the state's economic history. Maranhão has experienced several popular rebellions. On the revolt of Bequimão, see Coutinho (1984). Almeida (1978) has written a fictionalized version. On the Balaiada, see Serra (1946) and Santos (1983). On the so-called strike (*greve*) of 1951, see Buzar (1983). On the so-called strike of 1979, see Leal and Farias Filho (1982).

Tupinambás called Upaon-Açu, or Big Island, the present-day island o
Luís, belonged automatically to Portugal. The city, however, which c̲ ̲ ̲ ̲-
pies the northwest corner of São Luís Island, was the only one of Brazil's
state capitals to be founded by non-Lusitanians, a matter of civic pride in
São Luís. On September 8, 1612, the French nobleman Daniel de La Touche,
Senhor de La Ravardière, established a fort on a bluff overlooking the Bay
of São Marcos, in what is now the Praça Dom Pedro II, home of the governor's palace and the city hall. He named the redoubt Saint-Louis in honor
of Louis XIII, the boy king of France. As often happens in São Luís, a city
in which each street has at least two names, there is more than one version
of this story. It has been said, for example, that Daniel de La Touche was
not a gentleman but a pirate, and that the actual settlement of São Luís was
founded not by the French but by the Portuguese, in 1615 or 1616, after the
French had been expelled (Estado do Maranhão 1984: 17). Nevertheless, the
city's anniversary is celebrated on September 8, and a noble-looking bust
of Ravardière stood for years in front of the city hall until it was ripped
down during a riot in early 1986. Or rather, a bust that was supposed to be
of Ravardière; there have been claims that it was actually modeled from a
photo of a Brazilian railway worker (Estado do Maranhão 1984: 17).

The dream of an "Equinoctial France," a French empire in the South
American tropics, did not last long. The decisive battle between French and
Portuguese occurred at Guaxenduba, a site facing the island of São Luís,
on November 19, 1614, when, according to legend, a beautiful woman appeared before the exhausted, ragtag Portuguese troops, scooped up sand
from the ground, transformed it into gunpowder, and gave it to the Portuguese soldiers, urging them on to a miraculous victory. This apparition of
the Virgin, known as Nossa Senhora da Vitória (Our Lady of Victory), is a
patron saint of the city.

A little less than a year after this battle, the Portuguese drove the French
forever from Maranhão, and only once afterward, in 1641, was their hegemony challenged. The Dutch invaders, villains of maranhense history, not
only sacked São Luís but at one point, in early 1643, frustrated by military
defeats, took revenge upon the populace by casting its women, nude, from
the city, turning over 25 men to Indians from Ceará to be killed and eaten,
and sending 50 more to Barbados to be sold as slaves to the English (Instituto Histórico e Geográfico Brasileiro 1922: 289). On February 28, 1644, the
beleaguered remnants of the Dutch occupying force, having reduced São
Luís to an unrecognizable ruin, abandoned the city, fleeing in three ships for
Pernambuco.

The city's subsequent history has been punctuated by revolts. São-luisenses sometimes call São Luís the "Rebel Island," with good reason. The first
major insurrection of colonial times, aside from early attacks on settlers by

the native inhabitants, had as its primary target the Trading Company of Maranhão and Grão-Pará, created in 1682 and granted a monopoly in the commerce between the colony and the metropolis. The company charged exorbitant prices for the insufficient number of slaves and poor-quality merchandise it brought to Maranhão, paid low prices for colonial products, and indulged in blatant corruption. The uprising, which came to a head in February 1684, was led by Manuel Bequimão (or Beckman), a well-to-do, respected, and politically experienced planter, mill owner, and merchant. The revolutionaries eliminated the company's monopoly, established a governing junta, and expelled the Jesuits, who had exercised their own monopoly over the indigenous peoples. But slowly the revolution lost its momentum, and on November 2, 1685, on a beach not far from the old fort, Bequimão apologized for any offenses he might have committed, declared his satisfaction at dying for Maranhão, and was hanged. Shortly thereafter the colonial authorities wisely rescinded the monopoly. Bequimão is Maranhão's first great hero, a symbol of maranhense pride and resistance to outside powers.

Maranhão asserted itself again when Dom Pedro I proclaimed Brazil's independence from Portugal on September 7, 1822, by refusing to adhere to the new Brazilian state. São Luís, the stronghold of loyalist sentiment in Maranhão, held out until July 28 of the following year, when, under the cannons of the English pirate Alexander Thomas Cochrane (who afterward helped himself to a rich booty of slaves, gunpowder, public monies, ships, and goods confiscated from the Portuguese), the city finally yielded and Maranhão officially became a province of the empire of Brazil.

The independence movement had been strongest in the backlands of Maranhão, the *sertão*, and it was there that a stubborn and fierce jacquerie erupted in 1838. This revolt, known as the Balaiada, featured an odd alliance of former independence fighters, backwoodsmen, and escaped slaves. Although the Balaiada never touched the city of São Luís, the rebels occupied Caxias, then the second city of Maranhão, and controlled (or terrorized) great expanses of the interior, until, three years after it had begun, the movement was quelled by the army.

Slave labor was the backbone of the local economy through most of the nineteenth century. The importation of slaves into Maranhão probably began sometime between 1661 and 1671. By 1800, perhaps two-thirds of Maranhão was black or *mestiço*, of mixed descent (Meireles 1980 [1960]: 191). Throughout the period of slavery, escaped slaves managed to set up small rural communities (*mocambos*, or *quilombos*) in isolated regions of the province.[2] Whenever these came to the attention of the authorities, they were ruthlessly destroyed.

---

[2]Cleary (1990: 30–39) has a nice summary discussion of escaped-slave settlements in Maranhão.

By all accounts Maranhão and the city of São Luís were extremely poor in the early years. What wealth there was came from exploitation of the natural environment (e.g., harvest of wood) and the subsistence cultivation of a few basic crops: cotton, manioc, tobacco, and sugar. But in the second half of the eighteenth century, the pace of production picked up, stimulated by a new trading company, and the impetus carried over into the next century. The late colonial years and the period of the empire (1822–89) are sometimes called a "golden age" in Maranhão.[3] It was golden at least for the landowners and merchants who profited from the cultivation and trade of cotton, sugar, and rice, crops produced by slave labor. This trade attracted the interest of foreign nations other than Portugal, especially the English, who established an enclave within the city. São Luís, the state's administrative and commercial center and only major port, prospered. Indeed, much of central São Luís, including the Praia Grande warehouse district and many of the city's most charming residential streets, featuring graceful buildings faced with glazed tiles imported from Europe, dates from this period, although unfortunately a goodly portion of São Luís's impressive architectural heritage has been lost.

The abolition of slavery in Brazil in 1888 apparently dealt a devastating economic blow to Maranhão. Cotton and especially sugar, the pillars of the maranhense economy, were no longer profitable. The slavocrats who abandoned the *fazendas* (large estates) for São Luís put what capital they could salvage into cotton spinning and weaving, but this industry never fulfilled the exaggerated expectations with which it had been launched, although it limped along for some time. Just as the rusted-out machinery of defunct sugar mills dots the countryside, the ruined shells of old cotton factories, overgrown with greenery, sit crumbling in São Luís. Rice and, to a lesser extent, cotton remain significant crops in Maranhão, ranching retains a certain economic importance, and from around the time of World War I the oil-bearing nuts of the *babaçu* palm, a tree that grows wild in the region, became an important extractive resource. ("We have involuted," says Meireles [1980 (1960): 410], "to the primitivism of a gathering economy!") Light industry—soap, ice, food processing, and so on—continues in the urban areas, and São Luís, the state's capital and largest city, is still the chief commercial and administrative center. Until recently, however, São Luís showed no signs of economic dynamism; the local economic picture was one of long-term stagnation, as if Maranhão had never recovered from the demolition of its forced-labor economy.

But during the period of my fieldwork (March 1984 to March 1986), change was in the air. Several enormous industrial projects began operation

[3]For a discussion of the ideology of a vanished golden age in Maranhão, see Almeida (1983).

or were nearing completion. On August 16, 1984, Alumar, a consortium of the U.S. multinational corporation Alcoa and the Dutch company Billiton Metals (a Shell subsidiary), opened a huge aluminum plant, representing the largest private investment (about US $1.5 billion) ever made in Brazil, on the outskirts of São Luís. Bauxite is shipped in to Alumar's own port from Pará, the neighboring state, which is rich in mineral reserves. The proximity of São Luís to these reserves, which include iron, copper, and nickel among other ores, was a fundamental consideration in launching another monumental enterprise, this one heavily subsidized by the Brazilian government—the Great Carajás Project (Projeto Grande Carajás). An 890-kilometer rail line, opened in February 1985, now links mines in the eastern Amazonian region of Pará to a new deepwater port at Ponta da Madeira, on the city's margin. Finally, a startling project was getting under way near Alcântara, a quiet, mostly rural community across the bay from São Luís: the Brazilian government's construction of a rocket and missile base.

Opposition to this new industrialization—in particular, to the Alumar plant—has been spearheaded by a vociferous grass-roots group known as the Committee for Defense of the Island (Comitê de Defesa da Ilha).[4] The committee charges that Alumar is polluting the environment, contributing to social problems, and exploiting the land and its people; moreover, it claims that many of the project's benefits have accrued to powerful local figures and outsiders. An undercurrent in this opposition is a concern that the maranhense way of life will be overwhelmed by outside influences, whether Brazilian or foreign. Many in the community listen to these arguments with a sympathetic ear but look at the plant as a fait accompli that may offer hope of economic betterment. Probably most politicians, most of the press, and the business community hail Alumar as a sign of progress, although it remains unclear whether new industry will follow in its footsteps and whether the wealth generated will trickle down to the poorer inhabitants of this very poor city.

The incursions of national and foreign capital represented by the Carajás and Alumar projects will, no doubt, further erode São Luís's atmosphere of remoteness in space and time. In the course of the twentieth century the city has slowly but increasingly become integrated with the rest of Brazil through improved communications, greater population mobility, and

---

[4]English (1984) outlines the objections to Alumar's presence in São Luís; Meirelles (1983) does the same with respect to the missile base being constructed near Alcântara. In the past as well, foreign companies have sometimes aroused the ire of the population of São Luís. A 1933 murder case highlighted this antagonism: José de Ribamar Mendonça, a recently fired employee of the Ulen Company, an American firm operating public utilities in São Luís, shot and killed the company's local manager, an American named John Harold Kennedy. The man was later acquitted, a decision received with jubilation by the crowd assembled outside the courtroom. See Joffily (1983).

growing economic interdependence. Politically, however, contemporary Maranhão has been characterized by an archaic system of "bossism" (*mandonismo*). It has been dominated by a succession of powerful figures, the most recent of whom, José Sarney, ex-chairman of the former ruling party and longtime defender of the military regime that came to power in 1964, ironically enough became the first president of postmilitary Brazil.[5]

Revolts still occur in São Luís. In 1951, for example, a bitter dispute over the election of Governor Eugênio Barros paralyzed the city for months; in 1979, a small-scale student movement for a fare concession on city buses blew up into a tense, prolonged, and violent confrontation between *o povo*, the people, on one side, and the state government and police, on the other. Indeed, a dizzying double revolt occurred just before I left Brazil. In November 1985 são-luisenses revolted at the ballot box, rejecting the mayoral candidate handpicked by José Sarney, the only maranhense president in the history of Brazil, in favor of Gardênia Gonçalves, the wife of Sarney's chief local rival. But on January 8, 1986, only a week after Gardênia's inauguration, the people revolted in the streets. Enraged over her dismissal of thousands of city employees hired by the Sarney faction just before the election, a crowd laid siege and set fire to the Palace of La Ravardière, São Luís's ancient city hall. Gardênia, announcing, "The only way I'll leave here is dead," remained barricaded upstairs throughout the attack and survived, though much of the building was gutted (Linger 1993).

A Contemporary Profile

Maranhão

Maranhão is the northern- and westernmost and, with an area of 328,663 square kilometers (about 80 percent the size of California), second largest of the nine states composing the immense and varied region known as the Northeast. It is perhaps the poorest state in this, the poorest region in the country.

The Atlantic Ocean washes Maranhão's northern shore; São Luís is the state's only major port. A rail line and highway run southeast to Teresina, the capital of Piauí. One can continue by bus from Teresina to Fortaleza

[5]Sarney bolted the ruling party in 1984 to become the running mate of opposition leader Tancredo Neves. This enabled Neves to win the January 1985 indirect election, but on the eve of his scheduled March 15 inauguration he was rushed to the hospital for an emergency operation. Sarney took the presidential oath the next day; Tancredo underwent increasingly desperate surgeries, each followed by an optimistic prognosis, finally dying 38 days later without ever assuming office; and despairing Brazilians found themselves, after undergoing a wrenching emotional ordeal, with a president whom most viewed as an opportunistic, reactionary figure.

Map 1. Brazil, 1986. In 1988, after the completion of my research, Amapá and Roraima, two of the three remaining territories, were converted to states; the third, the island Fernando de Noronha (not shown), was annexed to Pernambuco. In addition, the northern portion of Goiás became the new state of Tocantins.

and eventually to the urban industrial centers of the South, an exhausting odyssey lasting several days but a migration route well trodden by north-easterners. Major highways connect São Luís to Brasília, the national capital far to the southwest, but land communication in the backlands of Maranhão is undependable, especially during the rains, and sometimes the road to Bra-sília is impassable. Official Amazônia, a federally designated administrative zone, includes the western portion of Maranhão, and Belém, Pará's capital and the chief entrepôt of the lower Amazon, lies less than a day's journey from São Luís by bus through increasingly lush terrain. From Belém, there are connections by boat to major cities along the Amazon and its tributaries and by air to Miami. Daily flights connect São Luís to Belém, the other capitals of the Northeast, Brasília, and Rio / São Paulo, but air travel is a lux-ury of the well-to-do, and few of the many são-luisenses who travel outside the state are able to afford it.

Travel within Maranhão, except to destinations along the main interstate highways, is arduous, time-consuming, and unreliable. River communi-cations are slow and irregular. Roads are poor and subject to flooding. Imperatriz, the second largest city in the state, lies deep in the interior on the Tocantins River. Journeys from São Luís to Maranhão's remote areas can easily consume a day or more, and some locations may be all but inacces-sible during the rainy season. For most são-luisenses, the thinly populated backcountry of Maranhão might as well be on another planet.

The state is shaped rather like a dagger, or a hand ax, widest near the top and tapering to a point far in the south, where it almost touches Bahia. The coastal region is hot, humid, and relatively well watered. There are two seasons: "winter" (*inverno*), a steamy season marked by very heavy rains and frequently by breathless periods of dead air, extending approximately from January to June; and "summer" (*verão*), the last half of the year, which is generally dry and may be breezy.[6]

Most of the state's population (3,996,404 in 1980)[7] lives in its north-ern tier, within about seven or eight hours (by bus or boat) of the capital, the major exception being the population concentration at Imperatriz. In 1980 Maranhão was, by a wide margin, the least urbanized state or terri-tory in Brazil (31.4 percent versus 67.6 percent for the nation).[8] Although

[6]In São Luís, which sits on the coast at 2°33' south of the equator, temperature variation is minimal, the average high during 1982 having been 30.6°C (87.1°F) and the average low, 23.5° (74.3°F). In that same representative year, São Luís received 1,860.4 mm of rainfall from January through June, and 56.3 mm, or less than 3 percent of the year's total of 1,916.7 mm, from July through December (AEB: 34).

Abbreviations for statistical sources (e.g., "AEB" above) are explained in the Bibliogra-phy, p. 269. Unless otherwise indicated, all statistics cited in the text are for 1980. As of this writing, 1990 census figures are unavailable because the census count did not actually begin until late 1991.

[7]AEB: 76.

[8]AEB: 122.

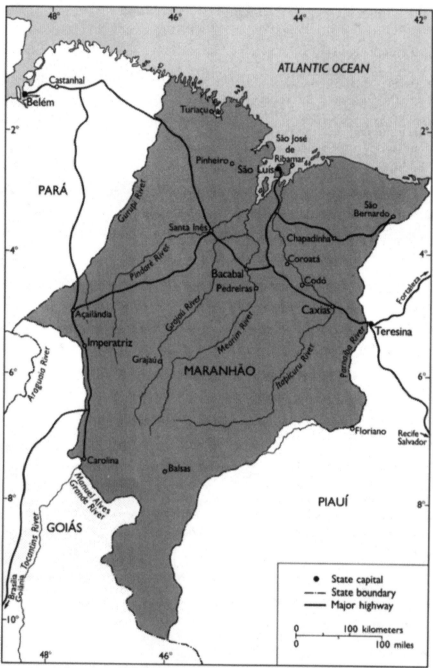

Map 2. Maranhão, 1986. In 1988 the portion of Goiás shown on this map was incorporated into a new state, Tocantins.

in that same year Maranhão experienced a net emigration of almost 50,000,[9] even more people departed from the other states of the Northeast, whose inhabitants have traditionally been driven by economic hardship and periodic drought to less harsh areas, including Maranhão, which has a more benign climate and a low population density. Maranhão's out-migration was more than balanced by natural population growth: during the decade 1970–80, Maranhão showed the highest rate of population increase in the Northeast (an average of 2.93 percent per annum),[10] a rate above the national average and exceeded only in São Paulo and in the sparsely populated and fast-growing frontier regions of the North and Center-West.

Maranhão's people are darker skinned, younger, and more likely to be at least nominal Roman Catholics than Brazilians in general. Whereas in 1980 54 percent of all Brazilians considered themselves "white," in Maranhão the figure was 22 percent.[11] Almost one-third of maranhenses were nine years of age or under; nationally, just over one-quarter of the population fell into this age group.[12] Finally, the percentage of maranhenses who called themselves Catholics (94 percent) was marginally greater than that of all Brazilians who did so (89 percent).[13] As elsewhere in Brazil, virtually all the rest were Protestants; however, these figures hide the fact that many in Maranhão are active participants in Afro-Brazilian religions, remaining at the same time at least nominal, and often devout, Catholics.

The state's population suffers from serious and persistent health and educational deficiencies. Between 1940 and 1970, a maranhense's average life expectancy at birth crept up slightly, from 43 to 49 years—a rise significantly less than the national increase from 42 to 53.[14] During the same period, Brazil's infant mortality rate fell from 164 to 114 per thousand live births, while Maranhão's—again, better than the national average in 1940 but worse in 1970—dropped only from 157 to 133.[15] The state's literacy rate, 43.0 percent in 1980, also fell far short of the national average of 68.0 percent.[16]

The economic situation is, in general, equally bleak. In 1980 about half

[9] AEB: 115.

[10] AEB: 124.

[11] AEB: 126. These distributions are based on respondents' own evaluations of their skin color. Skin color attributions are extremely subjective (Harris and Kottak 1963). For most Brazilians, the category "black" (*preto*) has negative connotations; those whom others might classify as black frequently (but not always) classify themselves in a more ambiguous "brown" category. Brazilian racial ideology takes the black-white-Indian mixture as a key element of national identity.

[12] From AEB: 118 and calculations based on AEB: 85.

[13] AEB: 127.

[14] AEB: 134.

[15] AEB: 134.

[16] Calculated from figures in AEB: 235 and CDM 1-4-7: 174–75. These figures apply to persons five years of age and older. The criteria for literacy are lenient.

(49.8 percent) of maranhense families earned one minimum salary or less,[17] whereas in Brazil as a whole only 23.0 percent of families had a correspondingly low income.[18] This sum was insufficient to provide the basic necessities of life, namely, tolerable housing and adequate quantities of nutritious food. Moreover, each readjustment upward in the minimum salary was quickly eroded by an inflation rate that, during my stay in the field, shot up to well over 200 percent per year.

Together, these comparisons sketch a portrait of a state that falls significantly short of national levels in all important indexes of social welfare.

São Luís

The compact Center of São Luís caps a small peninsula formed by the intersection of the Bacanga and Anil rivers at the northwestern corner of São Luís Island. Bays of the Gulf of Maranhão surround the island on three sides, and a narrow channel known as the Mosquito Strait (Estreito dos Mosquitos), which is crossed by rail and highway bridges, separates it from the mainland. The island is divided into three municipalities (*municípios*): São Luís; Paço do Lumiar, a small inland settlement in the central part of the island; and São José de Ribamar, a fishing community and pilgrimage center on the island's eastern shore, connected to São Luís by a paved highway. The island has a maximum east-west extension of about 45 kilometers (a little longer than the distance from São Luís to São José de Ribamar); along its widest north-south axis, it measures about 30 kilometers.

Although São Luís's Center is compact, a hilly jumble of houses, shops, churches, schools, and government offices lining narrow and congested streets, the rest of the city sprawls over a large chunk of the island: in fact, São Luís, which measures 518 square kilometers, takes up more than half of the island's 905 square kilometers. The outlying neighborhoods of the city vary widely in character. These *bairros* are often internally diverse as well, with rich and poor, city native and newcomer living shoulder to shoulder. Some neighborhoods feature new, luxurious homes set within enormous

---

[17]These figures are from CDM 1-6-7: 30–33. The minimum salary is supposed to provide a minimum standard of living for a worker—not for an entire family. Since much of the economy was indexed to the official minimum salary during my stay, the periodic readjustment in the minimum salary became a tense political issue. Despite huge increases in the minimum salary at the time of readjustment, the raging inflation soon diminished its buying power, and by the end of each readjustment period (if not well before) people were in dire straits. The government sought to hold down increments in the minimum salary to restrain the acceleration in the inflation rate, but the declining standard of living that this policy produced created widespread hardship and dissatisfaction. On September 1, 1980, the minimum salary was 3,189.60 *cruzeiros* (Cr$3,189.60) per month (AEB: 755), or US$57.62 at the prevailing official exchange rate of Cr$55.36 per U.S. dollar.

[18]AEB: 138; this figure is for 1982.

walled gardens; scores of others are dense settlements of small and unpretentious houses along muddy streets; still others, collections of rude earthen
dwellings set in depressions (*buracos*) or long strings of precarious wooden
shacks built out over polluted mangrove swamps (*palafitas*), or even clusters of makeshift cardboard shelters under bridges, lack even minimal conditions of comfort or hygiene. One bairro might have shopping centers,
cinemas, boutiques, and supermarkets; another might be all but indistin-
guishable from a village in the interior, with houses of earth and thatch, and
livestock roaming the surrounding greenery. In some parts of the munici-
pality there are enormous expanses of bush, where as yet no one lives; all
over the island new residential developments, called *conjuntos*, are sprouting
up, and "invasions" (*invasões*) of destitute squatters are claiming vacant land.
Police often evict whole communities of poor settlers, a phenomenon long
familiar to residents of rural Maranhão, where conflict over land is an acute
problem and terror is a long-standing weapon used to oust peasants.[19]

São Luís is growing fast. From 1970 to 1980, its population ballooned
from 265,486 to 449,432[20]—an increase of 69.3 percent over the decade, or
an average of 5.4 percent per year, second among northeastern capitals and
eighth among the 26 capitals of all states and territories of Brazil.[21] In São
Luís one often hears complaints about the numbers of out-of-state new-
comers to the city, but the figures belie this impression. São Luís is an overwhelmingly maranhense city: as of 1980, 93.2 percent of its residents had
been born in the state.[22] Of the 103,208 persons who had migrated into the
city during the preceding ten years, 83.9 percent came from Maranhão.[23]

São Luís's population is slightly older and whiter than that of Maranhão as a whole, and considerably more literate (78.1 percent versus 43.0
percent in 1980).[24] It is also better off economically. Whereas in the state as a
whole almost half (49.8 percent) of households had incomes of or below one
minimum salary, in São Luís the comparable figure was 25.3 percent, still
an appalling proportion but markedly lower.[25] Of course, prices in the city
are high so the difference means less than it might appear. Nuclear families
made up almost half (46.0 percent) of the city's households; most of the rest
were extended families (34.3 percent) and families that included at least one
member who was not a blood or adoptive relation (14.8 percent).[26] Women

[19] Asselin (1982) reviews the problem of *grilagem*, or land grabbing, in the interior of Maranhão. Conceição (1980) gives a maranhense peasant's view of these violent conflicts over land.
[20] AEB: 79.
[21] AEB: 129.
[22] Calculated from CDM 1-4-7: 98–100.
[23] Calculated from CDM 1-4-7: 164–66.
[24] Calculated from CDM 1-3-5: 46 and 57.
[25] Calculated from CDM 1-6-7: 32–33 and 58–59.
[26] Calculated from CDM 1-6-7: 122–23. The remaining 4.9 percent of households consisted
of individuals living alone.

TABLE I

Employment by Sectors of Economic Activity:
São Luís and Maranhão, 1980
(percent)

Sector	São Luís	Maranhão
General services[a]	24.6%	7.1%
Industry	21.1	8.4
Commerce	14.4	5.6
Social activities[b]	13.1	4.0
Public administration	10.1	2.0
Transport/communication	5.2	1.9
Agriculture, livestock, forest products, fishing	3.2	67.6
Other	8.3	3.4
TOTAL	100.0%	100.0%

SOURCE: Calculated from CDM 1-5-7: 226–36 for São Luís and CDM 1-5-7: 35–36 for Maranhão (abbreviations for statistical sources are explained in the Bibliography, p. 269). Figures are for economically active people at least ten years old.

[a]"General services" includes the provision of food and lodging, personal and domestic services, entertainment, repair work, etc.

[b]"Social activities" includes teaching, the medical professions, etc.

headed almost one-quarter of São Luís's households,[27] a significantly greater proportion than in the state as a whole.

Whereas most of the inhabitants of Maranhão make a living in agriculture, livestock raising, gathering of forest crops, or fishing, São Luís's role as capital and largest city is reflected in the disproportionate concentration of its inhabitants in services, commerce, and industry, as the 1980 figures in Table 1 reflect. Within industry, the biggest share was taken by construction; manufacturing remained relatively insignificant, employing a mere 7.2 percent of the working population. The concentration of medical and educational facilities in the capital is reflected by the elevated percentage of persons employed in "social activities" (*atividades sociais*), and more than one-tenth of são-luisenses worked in some branch of public administration: the state and city are major employers.

Finally, consider the population's overall standard of living. Of São Luís's residences in 1980, two-thirds were "durable" (construction with predominantly finished wood or masonry walls), one-third were "rustic" (e.g., earth and wattle), and a fraction were "improvised."[28] These residences were supplied with water, sanitary facilities, and energy as shown in Table 2. Table 3 indicates the percentage of São Luís households with vari-

[27]Calculated from CDM 1-6-7: 61.
[28]Calculated from CDM 1-6-7: 98.

ous durable goods. Table 4 summarizes the distribution of income among these same households.

These three tables, taken together, give a rough idea of the class structure of the city as defined by income and consumption. Telephones, color television sets, and cars are prerogatives of the upper-middle and upper classes: the data indicate that about 15 percent of the population falls into this category. This percentage corresponds to the fraction of São Luís's families

TABLE 2

Utility Installations in São Luís Residences, 1980

Installation	Percentage of residences
Water	
Supply piped in	56.6%
No internal supply	43.2
Not declared	0.2
TOTAL	100.0%
Connected to city system	66.0%
Other source	34.0
TOTAL	100.0%
Sanitation facilities	
Connected to city system	37.3%
Septic tank	11.4
Rudimentary cesspit	29.2
Other (e.g., river)	4.9
No facilities	13.2
Not declared	4.0
TOTAL	100.0%
Electricity	
In some form	78.0%
None	22.0
TOTAL	100.0%
Cooking fuel	
Natural gas in canisters	76.2%
Charcoal	21.2
Firewood	1.1
No cooking facilities	1.3
Other/not declared	0.2
TOTAL	100.0%

SOURCE: Percentages are based on figures for water supply and sewage hookups given in CDM 1-6-7: 110–11. Data for electricity supply are on pp. 118–19; for cooking fuel, on pp. 114–15.

NOTE: There is no network of piped natural gas in São Luís. Cylinders must be purchased from depositories or circulating trucks.

TABLE 3

São Luís Residences with Selected Durable Goods, 1980

Durable good	Percentage of residences
Radio	59.9%
Television (color or black-and-white)	59.7
Refrigerator	53.6
Television (color)	15.6
Automobile	15.4
Telephone	15.4

SOURCE: Calculated from CDM 1-6-7: 118–19.

TABLE 4

Distribution of Income Among São Luís Households, 1980

Family income range, in minimum salaries	Percentage of households
0–1	25.3%
>1–2	26.7
>2–5	28.4
>5–10	10.4
>10–20	5.5
>20	2.5
Not declared	1.3
TOTAL	100.1%

SOURCE: Calculated from CDM 1-6-7: 58–59.

NOTE: The total exceeds 100.0 percent because of rounding. The minimum salary in São Luís on the census date (September 1, 1980) was 3,189.60 cruzeiros (Cr$3,189.60) per month (AEB: 755), or US$57.62 at the prevailing official exchange rate of Cr$55.36 per U.S. dollar.

who earn somewhat in excess of five minimum salaries. At the other end of the scale are those townspeople whose houses have no toilet facilities or electricity, not to speak of running water, gas-fueled stoves, or appliances. This segment of the population, probably around one-quarter or so, for the most part earns less than one minimum salary, lacks material conveniences, and suffers from a high incidence of malnutrition.[29] The remaining one-half

[29]In an article published in the *Jornal do País* of Rio (July 5–11, 1984), Helena Heluy cites a nutritional study headed by Sylvia Parga Martins of the Universidade Federal do Maranhão (UFMA). The researchers found that 61 percent of preschool children from central São Luís showed some degree of protein-caloric malnutrition. Over one-tenth of the children were moderately to severely malnourished. A later UFMA study revealed that less than half of families with incomes under five minimum salaries consumed fish, and only one-fifth ate beef. Milk consumption was minimal. The basic diet of these low-income families consisted of rice, *farinha d'água* (a fibrous, starchy manioc flour), and small quantities of beans.

to two-thirds of families typically earn one to five minimum salaries, live in durable houses supplied with water and electricity (if not necessarily a toilet) hooked up to city systems, cook with natural gas, and own a radio and perhaps a black-and-white television and a refrigerator. These items are considered necessities for anyone with an income surplus, despite their high relative cost in terms of minimum salary. Obviously, not every family with an income of ten minimum salaries will own a color television, and some families with incomes below one minimum salary will have refrigerators, but I believe these figures do give a general sense of how São Luís's population breaks into income and consumption categories.

In 1984–86, the worst off of these groups was living in absolute poverty, deprived to some degree of every essential. The "middle" (but by no means middle-class) group was struggling to survive the ravages of inflation, which accelerated much faster than income. Most são-luisenses felt that they were on a downward spiral and that it was never possible to maintain yesterday's standard of living. They were under constant pressure to make substitutions and to cut corners—to make more use of the charcoal burner than the gas stove, forgo coffee, improvise or skip meals, postpone house repairs or purchases of durable goods, skimp on medical (and eliminate all but emergency dental) care, sew their own clothes instead of buying them, walk long distances rather than take the bus, and so on. The financial margin for these são-luisenses was slight or nonexistent. Every increase in electricity and water rates or bus fares created anxiety and hardship. Hence for the great bulk of the populace of São Luís, the strata to which most of those who contributed to this study belong, this period was, from an economic perspective, unsettled, difficult, and troubling.

Rhythms of City Life

In São Luís, literally all routes lead through the Praça Deodoro, the hub of the city's bus network and a crossroads of city life. What são-luisenses customarily refer to as the Deodoro is really two squares in one. In the smaller Praça Deodoro proper, a traditional site of celebration and protest, petty vendors from Ceará and Bahia hawk cotton clothing by day; at night, maranhenses claim the same spots to sell hot dogs, soft drinks, roasted corn, and cane liquor. Across the busy Rua do Passeio is the grander Praça do Panteon, ringed by large trees and the busts of the "immortals," deceased maranhense writers of renown. To one side, along the Rua da Paz, among the bus stops, taxi stands, and peddlers' trays carefully heaped with candies, cigarettes, and peeled oranges, small kiosks vend the five local newspapers, yesterday's editions from Rio or São Paulo or Belém, and Brazil's myriad and colorful national magazines. Uniformed teenagers from

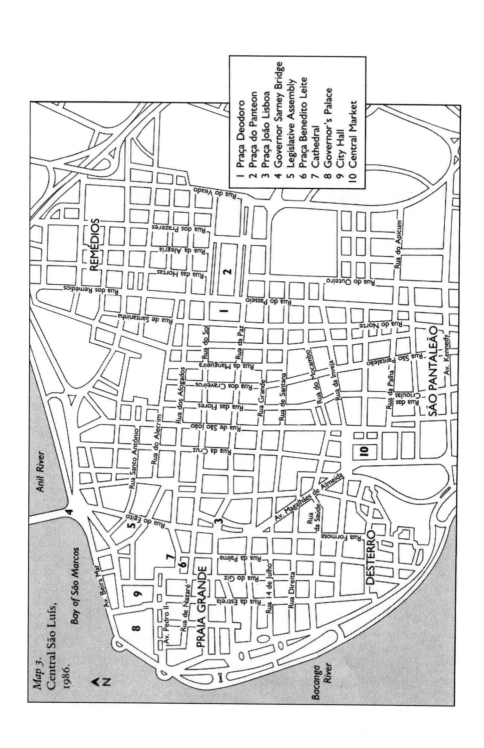

Map 3.
Central São Luís,
1986.

N

Anil River

Bay of São Marcos

Bacanga River

REMÉDIOS

PRAIA GRANDE

DESTERRO

SÃO PANTALEÃO

1 Praça Deodoro
2 Praça do Panteon
3 Praça João Lisboa
4 Governor Sarney Bridge
5 Legislative Assembly
6 Praça Benedito Leite
7 Cathedral
8 Governor's Palace
9 City Hall
10 Central Market

Rua do Veado
Rua dos Prazeres
Rua da Alegria
Rua das Horas
Rua dos Remédios
Rua de Santaninha
Rua de Santana
Rua do Passeio
Rua do Outeiro
Rua do Norte
Rua do Apicum
Rua do Sol
Rua da Paz
Rua da Mangueira
Rua dos Cravelros
Rua das Flores
Rua de São João
Rua Grande
Rua do Mocambo
Rua da Inveja
Rua São Pantaleão
Rua da Palha
Rua das Crioulas
Av. Kennedy
Rua Santo Antônio
Rua do Alecrim
Rua dos Afogados
Rua da Cruz
Av. Magalhães de Almeida
Rua da Saúde
Rua Formosa
Rua do Feito
Av. Beira Mar
Av. Pedro II
Rua de Nazaré
Rua da Palma
Rua do Giz
Rua 4 de Julho
Rua da Estrela
Rua Direita

the nearby schools idle in groups in the shade while the buses, each line bearing its distinctive colors and design, lurch past. And at the rear of the praça, the state's squat public library, one of the bastions of this "Brazilian Athens" (as São Luís sometimes calls itself), presides indifferently over the chance encounters, trysts, festivals, fights, rallies, riots, and Carnivals that go on below its cascading steps.

From the top of these library steps, one can survey the bustle in the square below and see beyond, to the undulating surface of tiled roofs, pierced here and there by a belvedere (*mirante*), church tower, or office building, which eventually falls away toward the bay. The busy thoroughfares on either side of the square, the Rua da Paz and the Rua do Sol, disappear quickly from view among old, gracious houses with enameled facades and iron-barred windows.

If one follows either of these congested but picturesque streets for a quarter of a mile or so, passing near the Fonte do Ribeirão, one of the Center's several ancient public springs, one arrives at another historic nucleus of the city, the Praça João Lisboa, named after the maranhense journalist and historian whose heavy statue dominates the small, shady park at the foot of the square. Pedestrians crisscross the mosaic promenade while groups of older men cluster around the iron benches discussing politics and inflation. With a few unattractive exceptions, notably the post and telegraph office, the praça's buildings date from the eras of colony and empire: they are now banks, pharmacies, travel agencies. On the sidewalks, lined with news and shoeshine stands, disabled men hold up strings of lottery tickets, street vendors exhibit plastic trinkets and toys, beggars play musical instruments, and São Luís's street people call out to passersby. Taxis queue by the clump of stand-up bars at the crown of the praça, the drivers leaning on their cabs or loitering at the zinc counters, sipping small cups of coffee and conversing as they wait for fares. People trickle in and out of the seventeenth-century church opposite, the Igreja do Carmo, whence the square got its original name, the Largo do Carmo.

Business becomes official as one moves off the Praça João Lisboa. Heading toward the Governor Sarney Bridge along the Rua do Egito, one can easily miss the state's Legislative Assembly, cloaked by a blank facade. Going off along the Rua de Nazaré and then veering right across the Praça Benedito Leite, an after-dark gathering spot for transvestites, one comes quickly to the Praça Dom Pedro II, home of the cathedral, the governor's palace, São Luís's city hall, the Bank of Brazil, and the city's two largest in-town hotels. This area is a haven for bureaucrats, lawyers, and politicians. But if one instead descends to the left from the Rua de Nazaré, one enters the Praia Grande, the colonial warehouse district, a working-class neighborhood of old tenements, hardware stores, depots of various kinds, and a small market with basic foodstuffs and tiny, open-air eateries. A certain rough beauty radiates through the Praia Grande's dilapidation, an exhausted elegance that also graces the adjoining neighborhoods of uneven cobblestone and broken tile. Ascending the Rua do Giz, one passes the First District Police Station, whose dull mustard color and heavy air contrast sharply with the flashing lights, loud music, and decrepit but often pleasing old pastel houses of the red-light zone that begins a block or two farther on. Beyond the *zona* is the ancient corner of São Luís known as Desterro (exile, wilderness), site of the old slave market and a curious but beautiful Byzantine-style church built on the ruins of São Luís's first chapel, destroyed by the Dutch invaders. Desterro is home to fishermen, workers in the ice factories and other small industries tucked away here and there on the bairro's narrow streets, and some of the military police officers whose barracks, a former convent, is its dominant structure. These old neighborhoods of central São Luís smell of the sea; of incense, coffee, fish, fruit, laundry soap, and *cachaça*, Brazilian sugarcane rum; of trash and decay; and, during the rainy season, of mold and things that never dry.

Starting out once again from the Praça João Lisboa, but heading away from the bridge, one immediately comes to the Rua Grande, São Luís's main shopping street, a teeming thoroughfare closed to automobile traffic. The Rua Grande is where money and goods change hands: there are opulent department stores; dry-goods shops with roll after roll of brilliant fabrics; peddlers of popcorn and trifles; indigents with begging bowls; and, as the crime pages of the newspapers tell us, pickpockets and shoplifters. Continuing past the Rua Grande and descending along the Avenida Magalhães de Almeida, one passes by the foot of the zona, where blue-uniformed military policemen in boots and pleasure seekers in taxis peel off to climb the Rua da Saúde, the shortest route to the barracks and bordellos. The slope of the Avenida Magalhães de Almeida is a long sidewalk fair, where one finds plastic shoes, hardware, hammocks, dishes, and *literatura de cordel*, popular stories of Brazilian saints and backlands bandits. Soon one reaches the Central Market, situated unhappily in a depression that is permanently flooded during the rains. The market is basic, above all a place to buy food: meat, fish, dried shrimp, manioc (*farinha*), beans, limes, cilantro, rice, coffee, onions, garlic, chilis, sugar, vinegar, tropical fruits. A short distance on, beside the fish market and the Desterro beach with its tangle of masts and bright sails, a Ferris wheel or circus tent often rises on the banks of the Bacanga River. Just opposite is a new outdoor terminus where one can catch a bus for the city's outlying bairros; the bus often circles through the Praça Deodoro before leaving the animated city center.

For someone living in an outlying neighborhood who works in town, the day's tempo is marked by bus trips between Center and bairro. After

São Luís's oldest church, the Byzantine-style Igreja do Desterro, focal point of the bairro Desterro.

The Praça Benedito Leite. On weekends the square, situated in the heart of the city's commercial and government district, is practically deserted during the day, though transvestites (*travestis*) gather here in the evenings.

An upper-middle-class house in central São Luís. The grillwork reflects the climate of insecurity in the city.

An alley in the Center.

Dona Guiomar and her adopted daughter, Dona Conceição, at a child's birthday party, Desterro. Birthdays are significant festive occasions for family and friends.

Dona Neusa in her doorway, Desterro. This woman, by her reckoning over 100 years old, says that as an infant Brazilian officials took her from her natal village, an indigenous settlement in Pará, and gave her to a family in São Luís. She earned her living washing clothes and selling fruit. Two of her three children died as youngsters; the only survivor, a daughter, appears in the above photo, *right*.

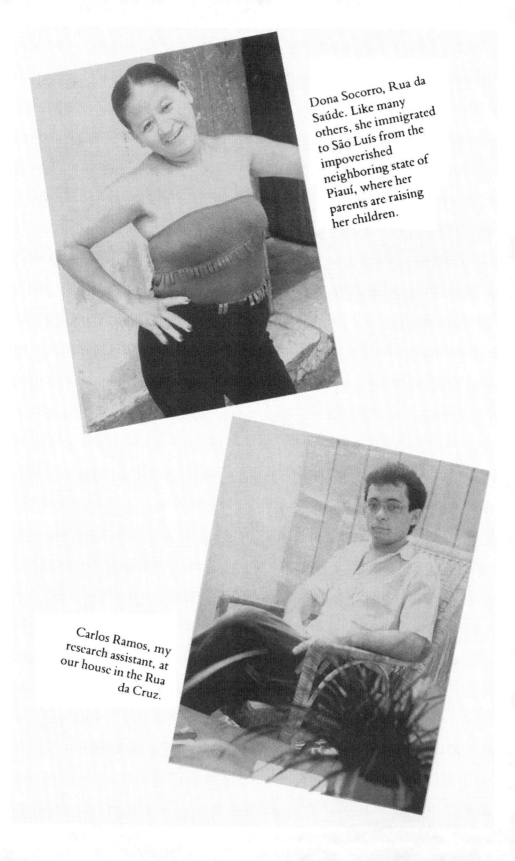

Dona Socorro, Rua da Saúde. Like many others, she immigrated to São Luís from the impoverished neighboring state of Piauí, where her parents are raising her children.

Carlos Ramos, my research assistant, at our house in the Rua da Cruz.

A dancer in an *umbanda* ritual. This modest *terreiro*, one of hundreds scattered throughout São Luís, is located miles from the Center in the humble bairro of Brasília.

Seu Zé (right) and a neighbor relaxing on a Sunday afternoon in a bairro adjacent to the Center.

A vendor in the Central Market. Seafood is plentiful in São Luís, though fresh shrimp is costly for most families.

a small breakfast, typically bread, margarine, and black coffee with sugar, workers catch the bus, which at 7 or 8 A.M. is slow and crowded, taking as long as 45 minutes to arrive in town. After working until noon, many make the equally slow trip home, but this time in the heat of the day. The family gathers for *almoço*, usually the day's only substantial meal. The table is set with rice, farinha, beans, perhaps pasta, and, depending on the family's economic situation, fish, meat, shellfish, or chicken, prepared in a sauce. There may also be fruit or fruit juice or candied fruit as dessert. Vegetables, however, are expensive and (aside from onions and garlic used as seasoning) rarely consumed in most households. Family members will bathe during this midday break, and before returning to work, if there is time, they may nap. Every maranhense house has hooks in the wall or beams suitable for stringing up hammocks; most people sleep in hammocks, for they not only save space but they are cool, comfortable, and inexpensive. Work begins again at 2 P.M., after the bus trip back to town, and continues until nightfall (around 6) or later, when most people go home for good. Dinner is informal: leftovers from lunch, or bread and coffee again, or eggs, or simply rice and farinha. People typically spend the evening hours before the television set, watching (sometimes with fanatical enthusiasm) the succession of *novelas*, or soap operas, for the most part cleverly scripted fantasies of middle- or upper-class life in Rio and São Paulo, that parade across the screen. The evening breeze may tempt some, especially lovers, to sit or stroll outside. Finally, the house is locked and shuttered against the night. São Luís is a sultry place, even in the predawn hours, but são-luisenses prefer to sleep in a house that is sealed up: an open window could invite a *marginal*, a thug, whose natural habitat is the dark, to invade the home.

For a housewife, the daily routine involves going to the market, caring for the children, washing clothes (by hand, in cold water), scrubbing floors, cooking meals, and so on: domestic tasks in a household with no conveniences except perhaps running water and a gas stove. If there are daughters, they may be pressed into service for some of these chores, and children routinely do the shopping for odds and ends at the local *quitanda* (a small neighborhood shop, usually a housefront, selling primarily household staples). Not infrequently, the woman may also seek extra cash by taking in sewing, selling food or drink, or something of the like. Many maranhense families have an *empregada*, or domestic servant.[30] São-luisenses sometimes joke that São Luís is the only place in Brazil where even the poor have servants. This is an ironic exaggeration, but it is true that some families of the lower

---

[30] According to the 1980 census, there were 10,457 such servants, almost all of them women, living full time in São Luís households (CDM 1-6-7: 69). This figure did not include the sizable number of servants who customarily return to their own homes on weekends.

middle class may have young girls, perhaps from the countryside, living with them as servants, and lower-class families occasionally recruit a poor female relation for this role. Domestic work in a typical São Luís household is arduous and time-consuming; men almost never do it.

Although weekdays are punctuated by quick "time-outs"—a *cafezinho* (demitasse of espresso coffee) or shot of cachaça taken at a stand-up bar, a warm and energetic greeting (embraces, perhaps kisses) exchanged between friends surprised to run into each other in the praça, and so on—the weekend brings a dramatic break in the day-to-day routine. The change begins on Saturday afternoon, after most people are done with the week's work and the frenzied Saturday morning shopping rush has ended. Everyone seems to relax, to slow down, to let out a sigh of relief. Cafés and *botequins* (informal neighborhood bars) fill with men sharing tables, beer, and conversation. Girls come out to play hopscotch and boys to play soccer on streets where cars and shoppers had been hurrying a short time before. In the bairros, the houses seem to open up, music spills out, and faces appear at every window, engaged in that grandest of maranhense sports, watching humanity play, flirt, spar, and drift by in the street.

By nightfall, the tempo picks up: people get ready to go out, to a gathering, a party, a bar, a dance hall, the house of a neighbor or relative, a rendezvous in the praça, perhaps a *terreiro* (an Afro-Brazilian ritual center).[31] Eventually Sunday dawns, and if it is sunny São Luís goes to the seashore. Barefoot, in bathing suits—a dramatic switch from the neatness and propriety of everyday dress—são-luisenses jam into the buses, or (if they lack bus fare) stream on foot, to Ponta d'Areia, Olho d'Água, and the island's more distant and uncrowded beaches. Tables are full at the simple beachfront bars, where families or groups of friends drink beer and eat crab or fried fish and farinha. The sun gets low, and the sandy, wet, sometimes drunk beachgoers crowd back onto the buses for the trip home. The bus rocks as some of the young men in the back beat *batucada*, the rhythm of samba, on its metal interior. Sunday night is a time for visiting: relatives drop by, neighbors chat, the children play together and eat and drink special treats made of coconut and corn. "Fantástico," a long-running Sunday-night variety program, comes on, and people drift into their houses and prepare to greet Monday morning.

Finally, superimposed on this weekly rhythm is yet another: the cycle

[31] São Luís has hundreds of terreiros scattered through its bairros. The range of practices is wide, some houses leaning more toward *umbanda*, the more Brazilianized end of the spectrum, and others toward *tambor de mina*, retaining more African elements. (São-luisenses do not, however, always carefully distinguish these terms from one another.) The oldest house of tambor de mina in São Luís is the Casa das Minas, whose African roots are evident. See Pereira (1979) and Ferretti (1985) for discussions of this house and its ritual.

of São Luís's great festivals. Two of these stand far above the others: the June festival (*festas juninas*, usually called São João because his feast day falls during this period) and Carnival. The June festival, which has the air of a country kermis, is celebrated, sometimes tepidly, throughout Brazil, but São Luís's June festival is legendary, in particular the pageant known as bumba-meu-boi,[32] which I described briefly in Chapter 1. Maranhão has dozens of groups of *boi*, literally "bull," so named after the central figure of the performance, a man dancing beneath a magnificently embroidered black velvet "hide" (*couro de boi*) stretched over a frame shaped like the animal. On June nights these groups, clothed in richly decorated, prismatic beaded costumes, circulate among the city's praças, sometimes "playing" (as they say) until dawn, joined by large crowds of são-luisenses who have spent the night in the square drinking and celebrating the visit of each boi.

Almost everyone in São Luís likes bumba-meu-boi and proudly considers it a maranhense trademark. But it does not evoke the same kind or level of participation or catch up the populace in such an intense and concentrated manner as the second grand annual event of São Luís, an event that transforms both the city and the people who live in it. This is Carnival, the great libertine festival that wheels around every year just before Lent.

[32]For introductory discussions of bumba-meu-boi, see Azevedo Neto (1983) and Reis (1984). Prado (1977) analyzes bumba-meu-boi in rural Maranhão.

Groups of bumba-meu-boi with their elaborately decorated bulls pay homage at the Church of St. Peter, marking the culmination of the June festival, June 29, 1984.

PART II

CARNIVAL

Whoever should see me, always quiet and remote
Would guarantee that I don't know how to samba
    I'm just waiting for Carnival
I'm only watching, learning, feeling, listening
I can't speak
    I'm just waiting for Carnival
I watch the porcelain legs of the girl who walks by
And I can't catch hold of her
    I'm just waiting for Carnival
It's been so long that I've wanted your kiss
Moistened with passion fruit
    I'm just waiting for Carnival
And whoever offends me, humiliating me, stepping on me
Thinking that I'll put up with it
    I'm just waiting for Carnival
And whoever sees me taking life's blows
Doubting that I'll fight back
    I'm just waiting for Carnival
I see the day's glow arising
Calling the people to sing
    I'm just waiting for Carnival
I've got so much joy that's been put off and held in
If only I could cry out
    I'm just waiting for Carnival
    I'm just waiting for Carnival
    I'm just waiting for Carnival

—From the song "Quando o Carnaval chegar"
(When Carnival comes), by Chico Buarque

3

THE VIOLENCE
IN CARNIVAL

Events and Scenarios

Carnival and briga may be considered either as observable social interactions, that is, events, or as cognitive scenarios. A scenario (sometimes called a script or event schema) is a conceptual entity that describes an interaction through time. It is because Carnival and briga are intersubjective (i.e., cultural) scenarios that people can bring these events to life. Knowing what Carnival is and what behaviors it permits enables people to "perform" Carnival. Hence Carnival as event is the interactional product of those who share the scenario.

This chapter examines the way that Carnivals and brigas are related as events. The evidence shows that Carnival, an interaction in which aggression is burlesqued, slides all too easily into an overtly violent interaction, briga. This is not to say that brigas do not occur in other settings—they do—or that Carnivals inevitably spawn brigas—though this seems to be the case. But it is to suggest that Carnivals provide felicitous conditions for bloody encounters.

It would be an error to identify these conditions as, at bottom, biological or sociological—say, alcohol-fueled belligerence or excessive crowd density. In chapters to follow I argue that Carnivals spawn brigas because both scenarios draw crucially on the same concepts: the key connection between them is cultural, their common wellsprings of meaning and motivation. The two scenarios rest upon a set of widely held são-luisense notions about mental life—what anthropologists call a folk psychology, or ethno-psychology. The rationale for writing a book that considers Carnival and briga in tandem is that together with são-luisense folk psychology they form a significant (because problematic) cultural cluster. Only by viewing the entire cluster can we appreciate the multilevel dilemma it entails for são-luisenses: that harmonious face-to-face interactions depend fundamentally on the maintenance of psychological equilibrium, which in turn depends on periodic venting (desabafo), a precarious, sometimes unreliable control mechanism.

I begin this chapter with a portrait of São Luís's Carnival and then consider the violence that occurs within it. Brigas mar today's Carnival, and historical reports show that briga has always been the typical form of Carnival violence. Carnival seems to flirt with briga by permitting, even encouraging, stylized provocations. Fights begin when the line between mock provocation and real provocation vanishes.

This line is, of course, subjective; moreover, to provoke someone is to engage in a culturally constructed act. Because actions are not self-evident, the essential ties between Carnival and briga must be sought in minds rather than in behaviors. Accordingly, Chapter 4 considers Carnival and briga as scenarios, examining closely their cultural links. The point of entry into the meaning of Carnival is its slogan "Anything goes!" An exploration of the uses of "Anything goes!" reveals that the scenarios for Carnival and briga not only tap some of the same concepts, such as the notion of provocation and the folk psychology on which it depends, but also jointly profile a pressing cultural dilemma.

Chapter 5 explores this dilemma by contemplating the possible motivations behind the annual playing-to-the-limit of Carnival. São-luisenses want to play Carnival largely because it allows them to expel their frustrations, an act they see as a necessary periodic psychological equilibration. But Carnival requires controlled, not uninhibited, release, because uninhibited release can lead to brigas. The violence in Carnival has a central, unsettling meaning: the blood spilled among the revelers signals the vulnerability of the self-control on which both mental equilibrium and social harmony depend. Playing Carnival well, then, demands a psychological tour de force in which one must modulate the expelling of frustrations so as to forestall violence.

If this analysis is correct, Carnival holds up a mirror to society and to a person's interior world that reflects any signs of failing control. Carnival provides são-luisenses an annual opportunity to dispel anxiety over the specter of violence in self and society by reaffirming their moral and social integrity under challenging circumstances.

These points will be developed in the pages that follow. First, however, it will be useful to provide some background by sketching the outlines of Carnival in São Luís during the mid-1980's.

A Portrait of Carnival

São-luisenses sometimes refer to their Carnival proudly as "the third in Brazil."[1] But pride in their Carnival is coupled with a nagging worry that it is not what it once was, a worry consonant with the Edenic themes that forever crop up in Carnival's great parades. In their yearly postmortems, são-luisenses seem to be asking themselves, "Have we lost our ability to revive our carnivalesque utopia?" More is at stake here than the immediate success of a festival. The veneer of spontaneity and harmony that is Carnival's specialty gives são-luisenses feelings of continuity with their predecessors and solidarity with one another. A crack in the illusion is a serious matter.

In most ways Carnival in São Luís differs little from Carnival elsewhere in Brazil, although the enthusiasm and energy with which são-luisenses play Carnival often impress visitors from other regions of the country. As in all parts of Brazil where Carnival is still vital, immense crowds congregate in the center of the city to drink, dance, sing, shout, and make love. As elsewhere, much attention focuses on the lavish fantasies invented by samba schools. And in São Luís, as everywhere in urban Brazil, Carnival is accompanied by violence.

Because I focus on Carnival's violence, a topic mostly neglected in the literature, my discussion of the festival passes lightly over some of its most significant aspects.[2] Carnival's eroticism, for example, deserves careful and extended consideration. I believe one could develop an analysis of carnivalesque sexuality that would complement my analysis of carnivalesque aggression in revealing ways. But such a project lies beyond the scope of this book. My first Carnival came after I had completed nearly a year of

[1] Everyone cedes first place, by virtue of sheer size and opulence, to Rio. Second place belongs to either Bahia or Olinda, both of which have distinctive and unusually exuberant celebrations.

[2] The bibliography relating to Brazilian Carnival is extensive; I will cite only a few of the most important works here. Richard Parker's remarkable *Bodies, Pleasures, and Passions: Sexual Culture in Contemporary Brazil* (1991), a book I received just as this one was going to press, discusses Carnival's relation to Brazilian erotic concepts and practices (chap. 6: 136–64); it is a valuable counterpoint to my approach. He does not, however, treat at length the *limits* on carnivalesque sexuality, a topic that I believe would be revealing. DaMatta's interpretive writings on Carnival (1973, 1978, 1983, 1984a, 1984b, 1986) are essential. Ortiz (1980a, 1980b), although his approach differs from my own, discusses the regulation of the "disorder" of Carnival, rejecting (as I do) any notion that Carnival lacks strong internal controls.

Samba schools have received more attention than any other single feature of Carnival. Leopoldi (1978) provides a general guide to their organization; Goldwasser (1975) presents a useful case study of Mangueira, one of the Rio schools. Taylor (1982) focuses on certain political aspects of the "aesthetic debate" surrounding samba schools, again in Rio.

fieldwork on urban violence. I wanted to see what light Carnival could shed on the problems I had been examining, so rather than seeking a rounded picture, I looked for Carnival's aggressive components. The reader should be aware of the ways this approach skewed my research: I talked mainly (but not exclusively) to men, who are more likely to engage in violent interactions, and I paid relatively less attention to features of Carnival, however important, bearing only slightly on briga.

Because this is not a holistic study of são-luisense Carnival, a detailed description of the event is unnecessary, but a brief attempt to convey what some call the "smell of Carnival" will provide a context for my subsequent discussion of festive violence. I have used the Carnival of 1985 as representative of the city's recent Carnivals.[3]

Carnival officially spans the three days (the *tríduo*) preceding Ash Wednesday, but in fact the Carnival season begins much earlier. The private clubs of São Luís's *soçaite* (society: the word is taken from English) fete the New Year with the traditional *reveillon*, a ball that initiates a series of *festas* (parties or festivals) with Carnival themes that continues through the tríduo.[4] Samba, the rhythm/dance associated with Carnival, also heralds the New Year at the city's beaches, where massive crowds gather to drink, dance, and throw flowers into the waves as offerings to Iemanjá, Yoruba goddess of the sea. On the weekends that follow, outdoor festas sponsored by the city parallel the celebrations in the clubs. These preparations for Carnival take place in the Praça Deodoro, the nerve center of São Luís and the site of major Carnival events during the tríduo. Like Carnival itself, the pre-Carnival period has two foci, club and street. Both locations feature samba (which takes over the city, temporarily dislodging rock music from cassette players and radios beginning in late December) and plenty of alcohol. The neighborhoods, too, come alive in the weeks before Carnival. Local Carnival bands play in the squares and parade through the streets accompanied by throngs of men, women, and children. Finally, the samba schools hold public rehearsals, providing yet another chance to celebrate in advance Carnival's annual return.

By Fat Saturday[5] the city already has the "smell of Carnival," which is less its odor of sweat and cachaça than a seemingly tangible change in the atmosphere reigning in the city's streets, as a peculiar mix of ease and ex-

---

[3]In contrast, São Luís's Carnival of 1986 was anomalous in certain minor respects. A political faction hostile to the newly elected mayor staged a riverside counter-Carnival in an unsuccessful attempt to compete with the traditional city-sponsored Deodoro festivities.

[4]There is a saying, only half in jest, that in Brazil the New Year does not really start until March—that is, nothing serious can be accomplished until Carnival is over.

[5]"Fat" days are those before Lent, i.e., the days of Carnival and those immediately preceding it. Note that "Mardi Gras," the name usually given the New Orleans Carnival, means "Fat Tuesday."

citement settles over the town. Shops, banks, and public offices have closed, and (except for supermarkets, which will open their doors briefly on Monday) they will remain shut until Wednesday noon. The radio stations play nothing but samba and Carnival marches, interspersing this season's hot releases with Carnival standards dating back half a century or more. Samba floods the streets from open doors and windows. A band passes playing a march, a wave of heat and sound trailing it through the bairro. Those accompanying the band are running, dancing, shouting, drinking cachaça and vodka, and throwing cornstarch and confetti. The pavement begins to take on its distinctive Carnival aspect, spattered with white powder and littered with empty and broken bottles, bits of colored streamers, confetti, tinsel, tin cans, and plastic cups.

By nightfall Carnival is fully under way. The sambas blasting over the loudspeakers at the Praça Deodoro echo throughout the city center. The streets leading to the Deodoro—the Rua do Sol, Rua da Paz, Rua do Passeio—are alive with *foliões* (Carnival revelers). They walk hurriedly, singing, conversing, blowing whistles. The night sky over the Deodoro glows white.

At the Deodoro, the luminous *passarela*—the passageway for tomorrow night's parade of samba schools—is alive with dancers. Arcing over it, and running behind the temporary grandstands mounted alongside, are panels of colored cellophane in abstract designs. Painted on the stands themselves are masked faces, parrots, fruits and flowers, chessboards, peacocks, mandolins, jesters, hearts, streamers, tambourines, and butterflies. A few people wear costumes—a Superman, a sheik, a ballerina, rouged men in dresses, *fofões*,[6] a diapered man sucking cachaça from an enormous pacifier—but the vast majority are dressed down rather than dressed up, as if clothes, like inhibitions, must be shed. Clothing is scanty and brightly colored, in unusual prints. Some foliões add a fanciful touch—a feather, a plastic flower, a headband—but few wear masks.

Thousands of people have jammed the Deodoro. Many are drunk; here and there someone lies unconscious on the sidewalk.

The passarela is the stretch of the Rua do Passeio that runs through the Praça Deodoro.[7] The square opens out behind each row of stands. These

---

[6] The *fofão*, a clown of Portuguese origin, is a traditional figure of Carnival. He (or, less frequently, she) wears a baggy, flowered costume, usually printed in bright and clashing colors, and a hideous papier-mâché mask with an elongated nose. The masquerade is a favorite of boys, but adults also use it. The fofão often carries a wand with a tiny doll perched on it. If you take the doll, you cannot return it unless you also give a small sum of money to the fofão. Young children typically run away and sometimes cry at the sight of one of these grotesque characters.

[7] That is, the passarela is the stretch of the Rua do Passeio that separates the Praça Deodoro proper from the Praça do Panteon.

grounds function for the most part as refueling and relaxation areas crowded with makeshift booths (*barracas*) selling cachaça and fruit juice preparations, beer, cigarettes, and snacks such as corn on the cob, popcorn, candy, and skewered meats. People retreat to the praça mainly to buy food or drink, to talk, to use the temporary bathrooms, to aid a sick friend, or (in the shadows) to kiss and embrace in privacy.

In the praça there are also a fire truck and a first-aid station. Military police, armed with truncheons and often revolvers, monitor the crowd from stationary positions or patrol in groups of six. Occasionally, when an exchange of insults or aggressions goes too far, they usher someone, almost always a young man, into a police van. (On the Friday preceding Carnival, February 15, 1985, a murder occurs at the bus stop in the Deodoro, the second in the praça during this year's pre-Carnival festivities. Three more murders will occur in São Luís before Ash Wednesday.)

Sunday morning and afternoon the city is quiet, but as evening approaches the streets come to life. Tonight is the parade of the major samba schools, for many são-luisenses the highlight of Carnival. A local television station will broadcast the parade live for those not inclined to spend a night in São Luís's inevitable rainy-season downpours. The much more luxurious and sophisticated competition in Rio will be televised in two parts, tonight and tomorrow night, over Brazil's leading network, TV-Globo. At the Deodoro, the stands are packed. Those who did not or could not pay for a seat line the Rua do Passeio for blocks to watch the schools assemble in the darkness before entering the white-lit passarela. It is pouring, and cloudbursts will continue on and off all night. By dawn, when the parade is still going on, the rain will have flooded many streets with rushing water. Most of the Deodoro crowd, however, sticks it out most of the night, chilled and soaked to the bone, because the last two schools to parade—the arch-rivals Turma do Quinto and Flor do Samba—are the grandest schools of São Luís and the only ones with a chance to win.

The parade follows the Rio model, though it is less opulent and less risqué. The motifs are the same: tropical plenitude, sex, Eden, *ufanismo* (superpatriotism), exaltation of o povo (the people), bitter reality versus sweet illusion, homages to local figures. There are nearly nude *mulatas*,[8] clowns, fantasized Indians and Africans, pirates, *baianas*[9] with enormous white skirts and baskets of fruit atop their heads: the stock figures of samba school parades all over Brazil. In the shadows of the Rua do Passeio those who are about to parade drink, banter, fidget, kiss. Some use handker-

[8]The *mulata* (a woman of mixed African and European descent) is the focal female sexual symbol of Carnival. In the samba school's parade, the mulata becomes a stock figure, wearing little more than a *tanga* (the lower portion of a bikini).

[9]The *baiana*, another stock female figure of samba school parades, is typically a fat woman, older than the mulata, clothed in a voluminous dress—a bountiful, maternal figure.

chiefs to inhale *loló*, an illegal home brew containing perfume and ether, made especially for Carnival. Once into the brilliant funnel of the passarela, though, the school bursts into an organized frenzy: percussion, samba, the twirling and gyrations of the dancers, the flashing reflections of foil, glitter, mirrors, and gilt, wave after wave of exotic figures. If the display is sufficiently brilliant, it becomes contagious, and soon the crowd is dancing and singing the *samba-enredo*, the school's theme song for this year's Carnival, repeated over and over for the hour or more that it takes each school to move through the passarela. As the dancers exit from the passarela into the dark street at the other end, the ranks dissolve and people mill about drinking and dancing with each other and with friends who have come to meet and congratulate them, everyone in a state of happy relief.

For the most part the parade proceeds uneventfully, except when Mangueira, one of the schools, delays its entry into the passarela. The crowd becomes impatient and irritable, and there are some scuffles in the stands. The military police arrest and remove a spectator from the passarela—territory that is off-limits to the public during the parade—under a shower of beer cans. At last Mangueira makes its appearance, and things settle down once again.

Turma do Quinto parades next to last, just before dawn, with a samba-enredo in honor of Ferreira Gullar, a maranhense poet of national renown. They sing,

> Today hunger belongs to the people
> Like the sky belongs to the vulture

and energize the drenched crowd, but last year's champion, Flor do Samba, which parades at dawn in a gray torrent of rain, turns out to be the winner with a samba-enredo entitled "Sunday is Ours":[10]

> Forget your obligations
> Today is Sunday
> Explode with rays of happiness, heart
> Life is a circus, the world evil

Monday afternoon arrives: the city is at rest in Carnival. The breeze from the Bay of São Marcos blows tinsel through the streets, which smell of urine. A few people wander here and there. Everything is closed, except

[10] As usual, the loser, in this case Turma do Quinto, later complained bitterly that the decision was rigged and threatened not to compete in the following year's parade. These threats are forgotten when Carnival rolls around again. Owing to the political rivalry that disrupted the Carnival of 1986, however, Flor do Samba did refuse to participate in the traditional Deodoro parade because Flor had ties to the faction opposed to the mayor (see note 3 above).

for some small bars. Three people are drinking on a doorstep. A lone car is stopped by a man in drag, palm held outward police-style, who proceeds to entertain the occupants with a sequence of exaggerated poses before letting them pass. Neighborhood percussion bands of various types, called *blocos*, move through the streets. A *bloco de sujo* (dirty band), a small group of men cross-dressed in old, tattered clothes, smeared with cornstarch and rapping on anything that comes to hand, circulates in a seemingly aimless fashion. A *bloco tradicional*, adults and children disguised identically as jesters, prances slowly and beats out a stately, almost somber rhythm on deep drums. Samba issues from record players, radios, and impromptu bands of children striking tin cans together:

> Mommy, I want to nurse
> Give me the pacifier so baby won't cry[11]

or

> The people's samba
> Is coming down the avenue
> Every cobblestone of this old town
> Will tremble tonight[12]

And children are out in costumes: ballerinas, clowns, fofões, cartoon super-heroes.

In the Deodoro there are more parades tonight, but the attractions are less compelling: the minor samba schools and assorted blocos. In the clubs, people are gearing up for another all-night celebration. At the Casino Maranhense, São Luís's oldest but slightly down-at-the-heels "society" club, the crowd is wall-to-wall. Hot, moist air rolls out of the doorway. Everyone inside is in a sweat. One can just squeeze onto the dance floor, where long lines of inebriated dancers snake through the crowd. During its sets of an hour or more, the band goes nonstop, full tilt. It plays only Carnival music: everyone knows every song, cheering each fanfare and singing along with the music. People are dressed whimsically but, especially the women, elegantly. In many cases they have had clothes made just for Carnival. The club's walls are freshly painted and decorated with geometric motifs. Between sets those who have reserved tables return to them to con-

[11]This perennial Carnival march, "Mamãe eu quero," written by Vicente Paiva and Jara-raca, dates from 1937.
[12]Chico Buarque's samba "Vai passar," from which these lines are taken, was a hit of the 1985 Carnival. It was widely interpreted as heralding the "New Republic," the civilian government scheduled to replace the military regime shortly after Carnival. The 1985 Carnival was sometimes called the "Carnival of the New Republic."

The neighborhood *bloco* "Os Brasinhas" (The Little Devils), assembling in the streets of Desterro before making their Carnival march through the Center, 1985.

Chiquinho, member of the *bloco* "Os Brasinhas," Carnival, 1986. Note the change in costume from one year to the next. Like the festival itself, Carnival masquerades are ephemeral.

Foliões follow the Desterro Band through the streets during a pre-Carnival parade, January 1986. Some are spattered with cornstarch, one of many substances revelers throw at one another.

Children dressed as *fofões*, 1985. This traditional são-luisense Carnival masquerade features grotesque phallic masks and contrasting baggy flowered garb.

tinue drinking, and the others, if there is a break in the rain, thread their way out to the pool area. As soon as the music begins again, everyone jumps up and starts to dance, cheers kicking off the next set.

A man in a bright tropical shirt is making the rounds of the tables with a bag of confetti. He is dumping handfuls on people's heads and down the fronts and backs of their shirts and dresses. Sometimes he rubs the paper dots into their hair. They become irritated and motion for him to stop, but he smiles and persists, saying, "Don't get angry—anything goes, it's Carnival!"

On the dance floor one cannot really dance. People bump into one another. Although it is steamy and hot, everyone is moving and jumping this way and that. Pandemonium reigns. The crowd eventually thins, but the festivities continue till dawn.

Tuesday is the last day of Carnival. The Deodoro is calm until late afternoon, when the barracas set up. The passarela has been turned over to the povo, the people, once again. Some of the samba schools return, but this time the scene is informal: the dancers enter in disarray, often without their fancy costumes or wearing just glittered hats or tinselly skirts, and they mingle with the revelers. Carnival's final curtain is approaching; the crowd's mood turns a bit ragged; here and there a fight breaks out. Around midnight a woman remarks to her friend, "Carnival is over, I'm going home." But samba continues to shake the praça, and many foliões stay to dance and drink until Ash Wednesday dawns.

Festive Violence

Carnival shares its undertone of violence with many other festivals, in Brazil and elsewhere, a quality of saturnalias and similar events long noted in the literature. Consider Emile Durkheim's rather lurid picture of the Australian *corrobbori*, derived from accounts by European observers:

> Commencing at nightfall, all sorts of processions, dances and songs had taken place by torchlight; the general effervescence was constantly increasing. At a given moment, twelve assistants each took a great lighted torch in their hands, and one of them holding his like a bayonet, charged into a group of natives. Blows were warded off with clubs and spears. A general melee followed. The men leaped and pranced about, uttering savage yells all the time; the burning torches continually came crashing down on the heads and bodies of the men, scattering lighted sparks in every direction. (1965 [1912]: 249)

In Durkheim's view, the heightened "collective effervescence" of the cor-robbori easily demolished the "reason and will" of the Australians, whom he regarded as "primitives," exciting them into a frenzy.

Durkheim's sketch probably tells us more about European ethnocen-trism and ethnopsychology than about Australians, but there is no doubt that festivals often feature both ritualized and overt violence. In Sir James George Frazer's words, during saturnalias "the darker passions find a vent which would never be allowed them in the more staid and sober course of everyday life" (1959 [1890]: 559). Goethe's report on Roman Carnival illus-trates Frazer's general point. Noting that mock battles with comfits could escalate to blows, he remarks: "Assuredly many of these frays would end in stabbings, did not the wound-up *corde*, the well-known instrument of Ital-ian police . . . remind people at all moments in the midst of their frolics how dangerous it would be for them to have recourse to dangerous weapons" (1987 [1789]: 25).

What we might call ritualized aggression or agonistic display—the throwing of comfits and the like—is usually directed either at social superi-ors or at social equals. In West Indian Christmas (Dirks 1987), East Indian Holi (Marriott 1966), or the Zulu festivals depicted by Gluckman (1954), the aggressive gesture is directed upward, from putative inferior to putative superior. Despite Gluckman's claim that rituals of rebellion are cathartic, they occasionally overflow the bounds of ritual, as in the West Indies, where the planters, with reason, would build up their defenses as the year drew to a close: between 1649 and 1833 the festive month of December saw four times its share of slave rebellions (Dirks 1987: 167–68).[13]

In contrast, Roman comfit battles, Trinidadian stickfighting (Dorson 1982, Juneja 1988), and the aggressive use of staves during Carnival in Fuen-mayor (Gilmore 1975) are all examples of agonistic displays aimed at social equals. Here, too, the evidence points to a certain danger in ritualized ag-gression: in every case I have cited, play violence sometimes becomes real violence.

Significantly, aggression against peers can become aggression against au-thorities. Trinidad's Carnival of 1881, remembered for the so-called *canbou-lay* riots, is an example.[14] Here, the authorities tried to suppress the canbou-lay bands, groups of black Trinidadians who marched through the streets carrying sticks, drums, and torches, causing the stickfighters to turn their

[13]Taylor (1979: 118) mentions cases of the reverse process: rebellions turning into festivals.
[14]The word "canboulay" comes from the French *cannes brûlées*, cane burning. When a fire occurred in the cane fields of Trinidad, slaves from the neighboring estates would unite to march with drums and flambeaux to the site, where they would grind the burned cane before it became sour (see the account of the *Port-of-Spain Gazette*, March 26, 1881, quoted in Pearse 1956: 181–82). Pearse's paper is an informative summary of nineteenth-century Carnival in Trinidad.

weapons on the British police (Hill 1976: 69), injuring more than a quarter of the detachment (Pearse 1956: 189). The reverse, a displacement of the target of aggression from social superiors (or their agents) to approximate social equals, can also occur. Paul Doughty (1968) indicates that many years ago serious, sometimes fatal, brawling between *indios* (Indians) and *mistis* (mestizos and whites) routinely disrupted the festival of Saint Elizabeth, a major fiesta of Peru's Huaylas district. The authorities therefore decreed that the indios were to celebrate on a different day from the mistis, with the result that the misti festival eventually disappeared and the indios annually divided themselves into two groups who would fight each other. The canboulay riot and the evolution of the festival of Saint Elizabeth suggest that during festivals both aggression directed upward and intraclass aggression may derive from the same source, as I believe they do in Brazilian Carnival as well.

In view of the pervasive reports of festive violence, I find it surprising that social scientists have not looked into the phenomenon more deeply.[15] Of the dozens of papers in three recent edited volumes on the festival (Turner 1982, Manning 1983, Falassi 1987), not one deals substantially with this topic. It is true that ritualized aggression has been a focus of interest since Gluckman's work on rituals of rebellion, but the relationship between *ritualized* aggression and *overt* aggression in festivals has drawn little significant attention from anthropologists. Perhaps this is because students of festival have traditionally concerned themselves with other issues (reversals, social functions, and symbolic exegeses), or maybe because, like Durkheim, we have used a ready-made commonsense folk theory—that collective effervescence turns into aggression—to account for festive violence, so that such violence seems unproblematic. Or, finally, it may be because we credit the use of intoxicants, especially alcohol, with inducing or facilitating the open display of aggression, another commonsense explanation. Whatever the reason, anthropologists and others have on the whole tended to view overt festive violence as a kind of behavioral surplus, worthy of mention but ultimately not particularly interesting.

This attitude reduces such violence to an unintended consequence of "normal" festive behavior. But I think the explanation is not so simple. At least in the Brazilian case, festive violence has meaning, and therefore, I believe, risking festive violence by participating in Carnival also has meaning, which raises the question of motivation. It is not enough to say, for ex-

[15]Dirks's ecological study of "agonistic rites" during the Black Saturnalia (1987) and Gilmore's examination of aggression during Fuenmayor Carnival (1975) stand apart in this respect, though Brazilian Carnival differs in crucial respects from both of these events. Ladurie (1979) presents a fascinating case study of a class-riven sixteenth-century French Carnival that ended in a massacre.

ample, that people fight because they poison their brains with alcohol. The obvious riposte is that the vast majority of people who get drunk during Carnival do not fight; more generally, the cross-cultural evidence on alcohol and aggression demonstrates that there is no necessary connection between the two—indeed, in many cultural settings, alcohol use is associated, both symbolically and behaviorally, with solidarity and pacifism.[16]

The explanation that alcohol causes violence fails to take into account what I consider to be the heart of the matter: according to são-luisense common sense, Carnival is dangerous. São-luisenses share our own folk notions about the effects of alcohol: most would agree that during Carnival people drink to excess and that drinking leads to fighting. They will go further, adducing other aspects of Carnival that tend to precipitate aggressive exchanges, in particular the carnivalesque admonition "Anything goes!" But if they know this, then why do they stage and participate in an event in which many people will fight and some will die? I am suggesting that the proximate causes of violence, whatever they might be, divert our attention from the fact that Carnival's violence has meaning: hence there are human reasons—intentions and motivations—behind both the violence itself and the willingness to risk becoming enmeshed in it. It is this meaning, and these human reasons, that I hope to discover.

There are two possible (though by no means mutually exclusive) answers to the question I have posed. São-luisenses may play Carnival because the pleasure they experience and the perceived benefits they obtain outweigh the perceived dangers of becoming caught up in violent events. Alternatively, they may play Carnival because the perceived risk is itself in some way meaningful. That is, playing Carnival may provide the added fillip of meaningful risk, along with a degree of pleasure and certain straightforward (culturally constituted) benefits. I think there is no blanket answer, for all são-luisenses do not experience Carnival in the same way, but I believe an analysis that fails to take the meaning of Carnival's danger into account cannot adequately describe the motives that drive this festival.

[16]The association of alcohol with violent behavior in some settings is documented: see, for example, Gibbs (1986) on barroom violence. Gibbs cautions, however, that the association is not straightforward: it depends on situational factors. Anthropologists have long noted that the effects of alcohol vary across cultures. Taylor summarizes: "The connection between alcohol and aggression is far from universal, and when they do occur together, the social behavior is patterned rather than random, as we have seen with community drinking occasions in colonial Mexico, where drunken violence is directed against outsiders" (1979: 71). Taylor also notes that whereas in central Mexico drinking among peasants was often associated with homicide, in other areas of the colony such drinking led to little violence and indeed was symbolically (and behaviorally) associated with peacefulness and stability. MacAndrew and Edgerton (1969) forcefully reject the commonsense notion that drinking automatically lowers inhibitions against engaging in forbidden acts. Like Taylor, they defend the position that drinking behavior is strongly culturally patterned. Heath's 1987 review article is the most recent of his periodic surveys of anthropological approaches to alcohol studies.

Let us imagine that during the performance of a play an actor onstage suddenly substituted real bullets for blanks and began shooting randomly. If we thought this actually could happen, theatergoing would take on a radically new meaning. An explanation of why someone went to see the latest mystery drama that referred only to the quality of the script, the direction, and the acting would surely seem incomplete, if not wholly irrelevant. Similarly, Carnival's undertone of violence adds a crucial dimension of meaning to carnivalesque play. In essence, Carnival experiments with behavior that can destroy it as a festival, not to speak of destroying human lives: we are never sure whether its farcical gun is loaded.

But before we can penetrate this recondite problem of motivation, we must first examine closely the nature of carnivalesque violence.

Carnival Murders, 1985

Carnival's violence generally takes the form of briga: a physical fight between two individuals, usually men, involving kicks or blows but at times knives and sometimes, but less often, guns. Murders during Carnival are almost always the result of brigas that explode. Consider the murders associated with Carnival of 1985, as described in these local newspaper reports.[17]

CARNIVAL MURDER NO. 1: Ebinho

DATE: January 28, 1985 (at a pre-Carnival festa)

LOCATION: Praça Deodoro

As Marcelo [the suspect] passed through the Praça Deodoro, he was blocked by the victim [Ebinho, 27], who stood in front of his car, obstructing his passage. Marcelo requested that [the victim] get out of the way and was then struck in the face [esbofeteado] by Ebinho. Fearing that he would be killed [massacrado] by the victim and his friends, Marcelo decided to fire the shots that killed Ebinho. (OI, January 30, 1985)

NOTE: Although witnesses saw the two men arguing, this account, which is Marcelo's, should not be taken at face value. Marcelo was a locally famous hired gun (pistoleiro) with many enemies and was himself later murdered in an unrelated incident. There is no indication, however, that he and Ebinho had ever met before.

---

[17]See the Bibliography, pp. 269–70, for the key to newspaper citations, indicated in the text by a capital-letter code. My use of brackets and other conventions in translated passages is discussed in Appendix B.

CARNIVAL MURDER NO. 2: Adroaldo
DATE: February 15, 1985 (Friday before Carnival)
LOCATION: Praça Deodoro

Amid pre-Carnival euphoria, Adroaldo de Jesus Pacheco Matos, 31, an electrician, was stabbed to death [on Fat Friday] in the Praça Deodoro. Adroaldo said he was going off to buy a cigarette, and he headed toward the Praça Deodoro bus stop. Moments later a rapid and inexplicable tumult broke out and Adroaldo fell dead on the ground, his body perforated with stab wounds.

"It was all very fast, there was hardly any time to see what was happening," declared Galdêncio, who found his brother in a pool of blood. At the moment of the tumult, seeing that one of the criminals was running away, a policeman, who was in the victim's company, fired some shots into the air, trying to intimidate the criminal, who escaped. (*JH*, February 17, 1985)

NOTE: The identity of the killer is unknown; there is no indication that he knew Adroaldo.

CARNIVAL MURDER NO. 3: Elesbão
DATE: February 17, 1985 (Sunday of Carnival)
LOCATION: Vila Bacanga (bairro of São Luís)

In the early hours of yesterday morning, police were informed that at that very moment shots were being fired in the doorway of the Youth Club in Vila Bacanga. When Delegado[18] Luiz Moura and his team arrived there, they found the corpse of Newton Elesbão Costa, 25, married, a housepainter, [along with several other] seriously wounded persons.

Everything began when João Batista Fernandes entered the festa without paying and his friend Raimundo Costa Silva, popularly known as "Fats" [Gordo], was refused entry.

At this an argument [*discussão*] erupted between the doorman of the club, Raimundo Costa Silva, and João Batista Fernandes. When the insults reached a peak, shooting broke out. No one can give a credible explanation for where it

[18] A *delegado* is a high-ranking police officer.

came from. What's certain is that before the police arrived the shooting had ended, with a toll of one fatality, Newton Elesbão Costa, who had fallen at the door of the club. Elesbão had nothing to do with the argument. Raimundo Costa Silva, "Fats," was wounded in the head, arm, and stomach, and José Santana Duarte Ribeiro caught a bullet in the thigh. (*JP*, February 18, 1985)

CARNIVAL MURDER NO. 4: Pelé

DATE: February 18, 1985 (Monday of Carnival)

LOCATION: Barés (bairro of São Luís)

Antônio Edson Nascimento Sousa, 27, known to police by the nickname "Pelé," thief by profession and street vendor by choice, was murdered yesterday in the early hours by the brothers Orlando Cardoso da Silva and Francisco Cardoso da Silva ("Chico the Pilot" [Chico Piloto]), both of whom are also *marginais*.[19] Besides killing their colleague, the brothers robbed him of Cr$40,000 and a pair of shoes that Pelé had bought to play Carnival. At the time he was killed, the victim was costumed as a fofão. (*EM*, February 19, 1985)

NOTE: The two brothers who are accused tell a different story. They say that Pelé had attacked and chased Chico the Pilot with a knife, which Orlando then wrested away and used to kill Pelé. (*OI*, February 27, 1985)

CARNIVAL MURDER NO. 5: Roberto

DATE: February 18, 1985 (Monday of Carnival)

LOCATION: João de Deus (bairro of São Luís)

Victim of a dagger wound in the belly, Roberto Barros Barbosa, 19, unemployed, died at 3 A.M. yesterday in the Intensive Care Unit of President Dutra Hospital. He was wounded at about 10 P.M. Monday night, near the club called Union of Three Brothers, by the marginal known as "Zeca the Nail" [Zeca Prego].

The euphoric trajectory of drunkenness that would result in Roberto's death began toward the end of Monday afternoon. Already somewhat drunk, he went home to ask his lover,

[19]The São Luís press applies the epithet "marginal" (plural: "marginais") loosely and sometimes indiscriminately to young men of the lower class arrested by police or involved in violent incidents.

Raimundinha, for the Cr$400,000 he had given her to keep
for him, so that he could continue his drinking.

The woman refused to hand over the money, and so he
broke up the house [*promoveu um quebra-quebra*], going so far as
to beat up his lover. Afraid of worse to come, Raimundinha
went to her sister-in-law's house to ask for help. Fearing a
violent reaction by her brother, the sister-in-law, Maria de
Jesus Barros, counseled Raimundinha to go to her own relatives' house.

Seconds later, Roberto arrived at his sister's, very drunk,
denying that he had broken up the house. He said that Raimundinha was inventing the story to make him look bad in
front of his relatives. Having finished what he had to say, he
began drinking in the bars nearby.

Around 10 P.M., penniless, he asked a friend of his named
William to buy him a shot of cachaça. William hesitated, observing the drunken state [*o estado etílico*] of his friend, but
ended up giving in to Roberto's request. Drunk and very euphoric, Roberto left the bar. When he was perhaps looking for
another friend from whom to cadge a drink, he ran into the
marginal Zeca the Nail and they began to argue for reasons
unknown.

The argument was rapid and had a violent ending. Zeca the
Nail stabbed his adversary and fled. (*JH*, February 20, 1985)

These descriptions of Carnival murders, although often lacking crucial
details, nevertheless point up certain consistencies. Four of the five murders, and perhaps all five (if we accept the brothers' story of the killing
of Pelé), climaxed arguments that escalated to violence. Four of the five
(again excluding Pelé's murder) occurred at or near locations where a festa
or drinking was under way. At least two (Ebinho and Elesbão) and possibly as many as four (including also Adroaldo and Roberto) of the victims
did not know their assailants. In three cases (those of Marcelo, the brothers
Cardoso da Silva, and Zeca the Nail) the killer was widely assumed to be
a marginal. At least two of the incidents (those involving Adroaldo and
Roberto) and probably more escalated so rapidly that even witnesses had
trouble figuring out exactly what happened and why.

As will gradually become clear, nothing about these Carnival murders
differentiates them from brigas that at other times of the year escalate until
someone gets killed. Observers tell us that such events move like light-

ning and sometimes claim unlikely victims. Moreover, these five murders develop out of certain typically volatile situations. The "entry barred" circumstance of the Elesbão murder is one of these, as is the determinedly provocative (and perhaps self-destructive) pattern of behavior evinced by Roberto. What distinguishes Carnival, therefore, is not that it produces a special kind of murder, but that despite its pacific ideology the festival creates conditions singularly conducive to the briga murder.[20]

Newspaper reports such as those above hold up a mirror to society: são-luisenses take Carnival's violence as an index of the state of health (i.e., degree of solidarity) of their community. São-luisenses repeatedly consult the looking glass because they worry that at some point they fell from grace and that Carnival will deliver the bad news. This raises the question of whether the violence in contemporary Carnival is in fact a by-product of the disintegration of some grand, unified national "family"—that is, whether Carnival was ever peaceful, or whether, on the contrary, briga has always been Carnival's unwelcome partner.

A Historical Perspective

Brazilians see Carnival as an essentially Brazilian phenomenon, as the following Carnival march pointedly demonstrates:[21]

> Who was it that discovered Brazil?
> It was Mr. Cabral, it was Mr. Cabral,
> Two months after Carnival.

Although Carnival's principal roots are European,[22] Brazil's celebration has for many years eclipsed the few remaining carnivals of Europe. In scale and animation, Brazilian Carnival stands alone in the world.[23]

During the nineteenth century, in Brazil as in Portugal, Carnival was known as *entrudo*. Its hallmark was a stylized provocation—a form of ritualized aggression, reminiscent of Rome's comfit battles—also known as

[20] Although it is impossible to cite any figures, everyone agrees that the incidence of briga rises during Carnival, as does the murder rate. There were three killings in São Luís during the tríduo in each of the years 1983, 1984, and 1985. This Carnival rate of one per day is about triple the city's normal rate.

[21] José Chagas (1966) points out that these lyrics make a sly allusion to what are in Brazil comic, fabled attributes of the Portuguese: ineptitude and licentiousness. Cabral's arrival after Carnival proves that Brazil was discovered by accident; otherwise he would never have come two months late and missed the fun.

[22] African idioms, however, strongly influenced Carnival in Brazil. See Verger (1984 [1976]) for a discussion of the origins of Brazilian Carnival.

[23] Trinidad's Carnival is spirited, though Trinidad is of course a much smaller nation than Brazil. For descriptions, see Hill (1972, 1976) and Juneja (1988).

entrudo. In its milder forms, entrudo meant pelting passersby with liquid-filled wax or rubber balls, known variously as *cabacinhas* (little gourds), *laranjinhas* (little oranges), or *limões de cheiro* (lemons of scent), which usually contained perfume but occasionally foul-smelling substances. But sometimes the play was rougher, as when Carnival celebrants doused their fellow citizens with buckets of water, shot them with dye from homemade syringes, or covered them with flour or coal dust.[24] At times repellent or even dangerous materials (sewage, rotten potatoes, even hot pepper sauce or phenol acid—see Coqueiro 1966) were used, and gangs lay in wait for pedestrians, seizing them and throwing them into barrels of water. As one might imagine, the targets of these provocations often resisted, and indeed fighting was the inevitable outcome of certain types of entrudo and one of the principal reasons why frequent, but invariably unsuccessful, attempts were made to suppress it.

Although evidently constructed with an eye to humorous effect—and in this it is not so different from many other *briga* stories—the following fictional incident, related by the contemporary maranhense novelist Josué Montello (1981: 39–41), probably captures the atmosphere of the streets during entrudo. The location is São Luís, near what is today the Praça Deodoro, at the end of the last century. Padre Pimenta has made his way to a church to celebrate a private mass, much against his will, because the Carnival streets are no place for a priest. He is now in the church tower, observing the infernal scene below.

ZEFERINO IS DRENCHED WITH DIRTY WATER AND RETALIATES

Josué Montello, 'Largo do Desterro'

And the padre thought, awed:

"You wouldn't even know there's bubonic plague in the city. Or else these people are dancing and singing to forget their dead. It doesn't make any sense. Everything is crazy."

And the insanity was even greater at the four corners of the praça of the church, all of them occupied by enormous barrels of filthy water, from which a group of foliões served themselves to fill their entrudo syringes and attack whoever ventured out onto the sidewalks.

At this instant the padre heard a loud clamor over toward the Rua dos Remédios. He turned around and didn't want to

---

[24]See Coqueiro (1966) for some fascinating observations on nineteenth- and early twentieth-century Carnival in São Luís.

believe his own eyes. Could it be that it was really Commander [an honorific] Zeferino das Areias who was on his way, at
the head of a bloco, dressed as a pregnant woman, with high-
heeled shoes, immense breasts, rings in his ears, his cloak
falling from his shoulders? Yes, it was he. And wearing on
his fat face the same gold-rimmed spectacles, fanning himself
with a pretty fan, swaying, his left hand on his hip. He hadn't
even trimmed the respectable mustaches behind which, from
Monday to Saturday, in his shop on the corner of the Rua
Grande and the Rua da Cruz, he waited on his customers,
serious, grave, of few words.

And Padre Pimenta thought, awed:

"He's drunk. He's got to be drunk."

The bloco turned now at the Rua do Sol, as if looking for
space to mix in with the multitude in the Largo do Quar-
tel [the present-day Praça do Panteon], with two drummers
flanking the Commander.

And the padre watched, bending down toward the sidewalk, his eye always on the grave Zeferino, who was refining
his shimmying walk, slowing his gaze, still with his hand on
his hip. In a few moments Zeferino would pass by on the
sidewalk in front of the church, right below the bell tower.
Padre Pimenta looked around, as if in search of something.
And hovered over the sidewalk, seeing now Zeferino's head,
his strong shoulders, his swaying hips, thinking:

"Ah, if I just had a can of water handy! The Commander
deserves a good bath of dirty water!"

And he was laughing to himself, the folds of fat shaking
around his stomach, relishing the mischievous punishment,
still draped over the opening in the bell tower, at risk of losing
his balance and plummeting over the edge, when he noticed
that further on, alongside one of the barrels, two stout lads,
each with his bucket full, seemed to be waiting for the Commander, while other foliões, at the other corners, amused
themselves with passersby, covering the pate of an old mulato
with ceruse and shaking powders on a man with glasses,
who responded with kicks, thrusting an umbrella. In front of
the churchyard, almost alongside the central doorway of the
church, were now two overflowing barrels.

On the sidewalk of the church, at this moment, things happened so fast that Padre Pimenta missed the beginning, although he had had his eye on the boys and the Commander, his face bent so far downward to the street that he felt he was going to slip. He clung tightly to the corner of the wall, without averting his curious gaze, and already the Commander was distributing blows, completely wet and dirty as he was, until he managed to put a bear hug on one of the boys, dragging him right up to the barrel. There, without letting the boy loose, he bent him over into the water, which slopped over the side as the uncombed head sank deep into the barrel beneath a thick hairy hand that was clamped angrily onto the boy's neck.

"You're going to die," threatened Zeferino, when he saw that the boy was kicking his legs in the throes of asphyxiation.

But before Padre Pimenta, who was now even more bowed over above the sidewalk, could shout to him to stop, the Commander himself let go of the afflicted head, and from the barrel emerged some staring eyes, some eyebrows in the middle of a forehead, and a mouth blowing out gushes of filthy water, at the same time that Zeferino returned to his high heels and his fan, swaying, fanning himself, heading down the street, between the two deep drums, which were now beating with added force.

Padre Pimenta let out his breath, relieved, sitting down heavily on the long board that served as the sexton's bench, and remained there with legs crossed, gazing at the pandemonium around him. Only then did he understand why Padre Alípio Rodrigues, still in the days of slavery, had ascended that same bell tower on a Tuesday of Carnival and begun ringing the bell, so that he could then cry to the multitude assembling on the church sidewalk:

"The Devil is going to carry all of you off to hell! He's there in the praça, with his eyes of fire! Get out of here! Go home! Fast! Before it's too late!"

Montello's imagined scene is probably not exaggerated. Local newspaper accounts, which in São Luís are fairly reliable reflections of popular sentiment and preoccupations, strongly suggest that entrudo was in the last century a troublesome source of brigas and that these brigas developed much as described above.

The evidence comes from several sources. First, entrudo is one of the activities regulated in the annual Carnival police edicts, which have been published for well over a hundred years and possibly much longer, varying remarkably little over this span of time. These edicts concerned themselves (as do present-day Carnival edicts) with public disturbances, the donning of masks, the use of intoxicants, the wearing of costumes offensive to the authorities, decorum (generally undefined, but certainly applying to behavior that might be considered lewd), and entrudo. From time to time the authorities expressly banned entrudo, the police going so far as to destroy cabacinhas displayed for sale on city streets. But the general rule was that police intervened only in "disagreeable incidents" (*PA*, February 1, 1894), much as present-day police action during Carnival aims not at suppressing provocations—an impossible task—but at breaking up fights.

Second, late-nineteenth-century newspaper columns are full of handwringing over the virulence of entrudo (in bad years) or self-congratulation over its moderation (in good ones), as the following comments illustrate:

> Dear Editor:
> Thank God we had an amusing Carnival: barrels of water and cabacinhas used to be a most beloved pastime, but this year only antiquarian fanatics indulged in this particular diversion. Most attentions turned toward the masked balls, and just as well. (*OG*, February 28, 1852)

> *Carnival*. There were a lot of masked people, some quite spirited. Their appearance has done away with laranjinhas, vermilion, and shoe powder, which have always given rise to maladies and fights [*desordens*]. (*AM*, February 16, 1860)

> This year there is a potential for widespread use of cabacinhas. It is a violent and dangerous situation that peaceful persons, families who are walking in the streets or standing at their windows, should be soaked just because it pleases this or that person with a cabacinha who without reflection often sends death [through illness] to the unlucky person on whom it falls, a consequence of which there are many examples.
> The time has come to banish from among us this and other bad customs that do not go together with our advanced state of civilization. (*DM*, February 6, 1875)

> What is barbarous and incompatible with our pretensions to

be a civilized land is the entrudo, the shower of water, the shoe powders, the dyes, the tapioca, and all the ingredients used to make people dirty and expose them to derision and ridicule. (*PA*, February 17, 1890)

Finally, the problem posed by entrudo is illustrated through cases of violence reported in the press. The earliest example I found in São Luís dates from 1854:

ACCACIO HURLS A CABACINHA AND GOES TO JAIL

press report

Entrudo. Once again this year, cabacinhas were the favorite diversion. Colds, coughs, and fevers are the result.

As is usual, groups of blacks [*negros e moleques*] circulated through the streets with an infernal clamor. A certain Accacio entered a tailor shop along with some others and demanded that the white manager accept the entrudo voluntarily; if not, it would be done by force. The gentleman rejected this insolence, and ordered Accacio to leave, but the aggressor, after insulting the manager repeatedly, threw a cabacinha at his chest, which still bothers him. The alarm was given and Accacio was arrested, but he refused to go to the police barracks without the victim, and every effort was made to oblige him, for his having said that he was *just as good as* [italics in original] the manager!!! We are told that said ruffian [*o tal capoeira*] remains in jail. (*OG*, March 1, 1854)

This incident invites closer examination. Accacio, a black man in a period when slavery still flourished, "invades" a tailor shop and confronts the white manager with the threat of entrudo. Entrudo symbolizes (among other things) an assertion of equality within Carnival: it is rebellious ritual. Accacio gives the manager the option of acknowledging carnivalesque equality, but he refuses, so Accacio makes a unilateral declaration via the cabacinha. The police arrive and arrest him, but again invoking Carnival's egalitarian ideology, he objects that he is just as good as the manager and that therefore the latter should also be detained. The police humor him—a nod to Carnival—but ultimately it is Accacio who ends up in jail.

I cite the case of Accacio because it is an early description of a kind of stylized provocation typical of Carnival that remains in many respects still recognizable—that is, entrudo. It also illustrates DaMatta's observation (1978) that one major impetus of Carnival is to substitute a temporary egalitarianism for hierarchy, though the case also demonstrates that in 1854 (as today) this inversion had its limits. Accacio made the mistake of taking Carnival's license too earnestly: his revolt was too direct, going beyond the jesting or metaphorical protest that Carnival permits, and in the end he suffered the consequences.

The following summary report on the Carnival of 1875 in Salvador, Bahia, a city known for its violent Carnival, illustrates well the dangers of entrudo. The prominence given the report by the São Luís newspaper indicates its salience for local readers.

> During the three days of Carnival, there was furious entrudo that resulted in murders, injuries, beatings, and other acts of vandalism.
>
> Local newspapers reported the following:
>
> Despite prohibition by the police, the pernicious game [*brinquedo*] of entrudo did not disappear from among us this year.
>
> On Sunday there was a lot of water, many limões de cheiro, and other barbarous objects employed in similar amusements.
>
> There were places through which one could not pass with impunity.
>
> Along the entire route of the Bonfim streetcar line, passengers were the victims of savages [*desalmados*] who threw rocks and water in abundance.
>
> One group seized those who were strolling near the shore and gave them a bath in the sea. This practice only ceased when there was a struggle between one of those who had been grabbed and the group, with the result that a person was stabbed in the leg.
>
> Near the Cathedral revolting scenes could be observed. Many citizens received large quantities of water, etc., as they passed near certain houses.
>
> A mass of wet mud was thrown at a respectable priest.
>
> As he was going by the Alvo hill, a black named Constantino was "entruded" by a *parda* [mulata] named Anna Joaquina with a mass of mud in the face; he returned this pleasantry with a blow to the face of the parda. He had subsequently taken only a few steps, however, when he was attacked and beaten by Maurício and others and left for dead in the street, for more than an hour, at which point he returned to consciousness and was medically treated.

Anna Joaquina and Maurício, who is her lover, were arrested. The others got away.

In the city of Valença, Maria Rosa do Sacramento was shot and killed. The cause of this sad occurrence was the abusive game of entrudo.

The offender and his wife were arrested.

Many individuals who were soaked returned the kindness by hurling stones at the houses from which the water had been spilled.

Similar events occurred in Taboão, in Maciel, and in other places during the three days. The obscenities that aggravated these reciprocal attacks disturbed the public order even further.

Streetcars, in particular the open ones, were inundated with basins full of water.

In the streets powders were thrown on passersby; the faces of black men and women were painted and the savagery was carried to the point of making projectiles of dead cats. (*DM,* February 24, 1875)

Additional cases would be redundant. The ones I have given, spanning more than a century, show that Carnival and briga have always gone hand in hand. This is hardly fortuitous. Carnival spawns brigas precisely because it permits, and even encourages, actions that trigger brigas. Entrudo, a stereotyped carnivalesque provocation, is the outstanding example, and it puts us on the trail of a more subtle link between Carnival and briga.

Expelling Evil

São-luisenses worry over the violence accompanying São Luís's Carnival. Warnings and speculations precede the long Carnival weekend. The populace is reassured: the police sweep so-called marginais from the streets, issue the traditional Carnival edict, and mobilize according to a special plan. During Carnival, violent incidents occupy a prominent place in newspaper headlines and in the quiet conversations of the long afternoons. And at Carnival's conclusion comes the media report on injuries and deaths, providing stories and tallies not only from São Luís but from Rio, Recife, Bahia, and the farthest corners of the country. People will judge Carnival partly by its level of violence: other things being equal, a violent Carnival is a bad Carnival and a sign that not only Carnival but the social harmony that is a fundamental value in Brazilian society is deteriorating or vanishing.

Fear of violence is a reason frequently cited for avoiding the street or the club during Carnival. Although the Praça Deodoro and clubs of all kinds, from "society" clubs to the "popular" or "second-class" clubs (*clubes de segunda*), fill with foliões every night of Carnival, no são-luisense, however eager he or she may be to play in the Deodoro or elsewhere, is unaware that doing so entails a certain risk. Those são-luisenses who do not like Carnival or who prefer to stay home watching the Rio Carnival on TV-Globo tend to be most insistent in their warnings, but even those who frequent the Deodoro night after night acknowledge the danger. No one can help but notice that brigas erupt from time to time, that murders occur, that scores of police patrol the praça. And the alertness of the Deodoro crowd is impressive. People respond at once to warning signs of trouble: sudden loud noises, angry shouts, or running brings everyone immediately to attention.

Fights begin by invitation, issued in the form of a provocation.[25] The Deodoro and the clubs are dangerous because there provocations are endemic. Aggressive individuals will provoke others violently, either causing direct physical injury or embroiling strangers in perilous confrontations. Inevitably, some of those provoked will accept (*aceitar*) invitations to fight; brigas will therefore erupt, and even a disinterested spectator might accidentally catch a knife thrust or a bullet. One hears all manner of anecdotes and cautionary tales. During the 1985 Carnival, people often cited the case of Ebinho as an example of the risks involved in playing at the Deodoro. They recalled other Carnival murders from recent years and recounted brigas they had witnessed in clubs or in the streets.

Eduardo is someone who almost never plays Carnival. During his single Carnival visit to a club in the last twenty years, a foray as a guest into one of the city's premier society clubs, he had the bad luck to witness a shooting at an adjoining table. Other persons described fights with knives or broken bottles. Elene warned that during Carnival people "expel their evil"; she cited incidents of acid throwing, resulting in blindings, several years back.[26] She never accompanies her husband on his habitual expeditions to the Deodoro.

Nothing approximates a literal "expelling of evil" so closely as entrudo. The word "entrudo" is disappearing from the vocabularies of são-luisenses under age 30 or so, but the practice remains alive. When the substances used are innocuous, such as water, confetti, or cornstarch, the victim usually stays calm, unless the assault is carried out with particular aggressiveness.

[25] Although I use the English word, the Brazilian-Portuguese cognate *provocação* is much more salient for the people of São Luís than is "provocation" for most Americans, many of whom might be hard-pressed to say exactly what a provocation is or to give examples or identify categories of provocations.

[26] I could not independently confirm these incidents.

But the spewing of noxious substances, such as sewage water, urine, or dyes, is considered not only intrinsically objectionable but socially dangerous because it is likely to touch off *brigas*. These less benign manifestations, when, for example, people fill crude pumps with water from the gutters, still occur. As late as 1982 the local press lamented a significant resurgence of *entrudo*, specifically mentioning the use of mud, sewer water, and eggs (*OI*, February 25, 1982).

Despite its persistence, *entrudo*, by whatever name, is no longer Carnival's dominant form of provocation. Nevertheless, its descendants are legion; what they share is that *conceptually* they involve "expelling one's evil" at another person. São-luisenses complained, for example, of minor, ambiguous physical aggressions: an elbow thrown while dancing, or pushing, jostling, and shoving that can be done (but denied) in the midst of crowds. They likewise deplored the verbal aggressions of drunks. Finally, both men and women emphasized that sexually related provocations were extremely troublesome and dangerous. Women said that if they refused to dance with a man he might "mark" them for insults or physical aggression. Some complained of having been touched or grabbed in an aggressive way. Such affronts also worried the women's partners, because they felt obliged to respond. The men recognized that reacting could lead to an unwanted *briga*, but they felt trapped by the situation and what they saw as their imperative emotional response to it.

This last type of carnivalesque provocation is illustrated in the following story related by Jair during a conversation with Carlos, my research assistant.[27]

BETO GRABS JAIR'S GIRLFRIEND, AND JAIR
THREATENS HIM WITH A .38

    Jair

C: What kinds of provocations happen during Carnival, Jair?

J: A lot, if you go with a woman. If you go with a woman, here in Maranhão there's no respect, the guy goes by and

[27]In passages taken from interviews, I have tried to preserve some of the speech habits and rhythms of informants by retaining Portuguese expletives, sound effects, and other mannerisms. Here, *pa!* and *vap!* are exclamations, at times onomatopoetic. *Porra* is an obscene word, literally "sperm," expressing disapproval, irritation, or anger, often interjected at the beginning of a statement. *Rapaz* (boy), *cara* (guy), *compadre* (a term of fictive kinship), and *bicho* (creature, animal) are various rough equivalents of the English use of "man" in informal speech, as when, toward the end of this passage, Beto says, "No, rapaz, I'm sorry." (I did not use "man" in the translations because I felt it made them read too much like American English slang, with confusing results for American readers.) An ellipsis in interview transcripts indicates a pause; in passages from written materials, it indicates an omission of text.

puts his hand wherever he wants and *pa!* that's where the guy carries you off to perdition, right? For example, you're with your girlfriend, and the guy comes up and feels her up, right in the open, and you're watching. What are you going to do, keep quiet? Are you going to keep watching him do it?

C: Anything goes during Carnival.

J: But I . . . I think that's wrong, that's why sometimes I don't go around with a girlfriend to certain places during Carnival. Because this kind of thing harms you, sometimes it takes you down a bad road, because hey, I, nobody has the blood of a cockroach, but tell me, what would you say if this happened, would you keep quiet?

C: No . . . honestly, no.

J: Exactly, nobody would. Because right away the woman would look at you, what are you going to do? *Porra*, that's why I almost never take a girl to the praça, this praça here, the Deodoro, these are places for brigas. Once I was over there in Maiobão [a distant bairro of São Luís] during Carnival, in a club they have there, just dancing when a short guy comes up, a guy named Beto, I know him, he comes up and *pa!* at the girl. The girl got scared and I said, "What was it?" [and she said,] "No, nothing, nothing, he didn't say anything to me," and then I said, "Porra, what was it?" and then she told me later, "It was a guy who grabbed me in the ass," and *pa!* I got pissed off [*aí eu fiquei puto*]. "How come you didn't tell me?" [and she said,] "But you would've gotten into a briga" [and I said,] "No, I would've just gone and talked with him." Then everything was OK. Afterward I went to dance again, this time I was watching out, keeping a lookout, dancing, and then he came up, he went by with his girlfriend and *vap!* I took off and grabbed his hand, [saying,] "Hey, *rapaz*, what's this?" [and he said,] "How's it going?" [and I said,] "How's it going nothing, *compadre*, you just went by for the second time, are you enjoying it, *cara*?" [and he said,] "Ah, you're making things up" [*tu cismou*], and then I hit him, I was just waiting for him to say that, *pa!* and the guy was on the ground, just once, and the other people stopped it. The next day I went to his house and beat on the door, *pa! pa! pa!* [with] a .38, my father's, excuse me for not even telling

him that I took it. I got there and *pa! pa! pa!* "I want to talk
with Beto." "He isn't here." I went back two more times and
finally I found him. I said, "Hey, citizen, the next time you
do that maybe I won't be around anymore and you either,
[because] I'll be on the run and you'll be dead. Never do that
again and don't play any games with me ever again," and he
said, "No, rapaz, I'm sorry, I was drunk," and so on [and I
said], "Don't even look at my face ever again," and from that
day on he hasn't.

Although this briga had no dire consequences, it is easy to imagine how
it could have. Whether or not Jair's story is the literal truth, he believes that
the provocation, which was of the "hand on the *bunda* [buttocks]" variety
reportedly so prevalent during Carnival, merited both immediate physical
aggression and the subsequent death threat.

Another example of a physical provocation, this time initiated by a
woman, is reported by Joana.

JOANA IS PUSHED AS SHE FOLLOWS THE BAND

Joana

This business of stepping on your foot, usually I don't connect [*ligar*, i.e., pay any attention to it], if you connect you'll
go crazy, I just let it go. But even with me it happened. I was
dancing in the midst of the band [as it was passing one day
before Carnival] and a big woman was coming up behind me,
she stuck her hand in my back [saying], "Get out of the way."
I looked at her and said, "Don't you know how to ask permission?" At that she started insulting me, ridiculing me, "Get
out of the way, you're skinny, get out of the way because I've
got a mind to do this and that to you." I said, "Don't even
try, because you won't get anywhere" [*não vem porque não tem*].
At that she came up to me, sticking her hand in my face. I
grabbed and kicked her, I said, "Did you come here to play or
fight? [*Você veio pra brincar ou pra brigar?*]. If you came to fight,
get lost, because I came to play," and she went away.

Sometimes really a lot of things happen during Carnival,
if you connect, sometimes a person has already left home
with bad intentions, wanting to fight with another person,
and she's obnoxious. Sometimes people really try to get rid
of a lot of things [during Carnival]. [I connected with this

woman] because I thought it was too much. She stuck her hand in my back twice: I don't know if it's because she wanted to show off, because she was with a guy from the police, but this had nothing to do with it, because I knew the guy, a lieutenant from over there at the barracks of the Military Police. He went to talk to her, he said, "Look, I know this girl [Joana], don't bug her [*não mexe com a menina*], because she's not bugging you." She said, "But it's because I don't want anyone in front of me." And then he said, "Then go over to the sidewalk, there you'll have a lot of space but not here. We came here to play and not to fight." [Then the woman went away.] She wasn't drunk. I don't know why she did it, a random provocation [*uma cisma à toa*], I don't know her, I'd never seen her before.

[When a man or a woman does this kind of thing,] it's because they're looking for a briga. Sometimes, in the case of a woman, she's with a guy, maybe she knows he's with the police and she starts to bug somebody, this, that, and the other thing, so that the other person will strike back, maybe to see if he [the policeman] will handle the thing, arrest [the other person], maybe she wants something out of the ordinary. Like last Saturday, too, a man wanted to hit a woman, he went by and was pestering her, "Come on, come on, get out of the way," pushing the woman, he wanted to have things his way and didn't want anyone near him and you can't do this. It's Carnival, you've got to have everybody together, everybody's got to be united.

In this case a provocation led to an exchange of blows between women. Once again, the provoker issued a challenge. Beto fondled Jair's girlfriend not once but twice, flagrantly, as if inviting a response; Joana's antagonist likewise provoked twice, setting up a situation in which "something out of the ordinary" might occur. There are differences, notably in the male partner's position and response (a challenge from another male is a different matter from a call for intervention against a woman), but in both cases we see Carnival being pushed into forbidden territory. The provocation that Jair experienced is the kind that "carries you off to perdition": it is not part of the "anything goes" of Carnival. For Joana this behavior is the antithesis of Carnival, for during Carnival "you've got to have everybody together, everybody's got to be united."

The problem with getting everybody together in a place like the Deodoro is precisely that it is hard to keep them "united." Genival, who unlike Jair and Joana no longer frequents the concentration points of Carnival, summarizes his somewhat pessimistic view:

> I play with the people I know. The time when I wanted to be in the middle of things is now gone. I like [Carnival], but there in the middle of things, no, and not even because of the brigas, the shoving, it's this thing today of being in the middle of that heap of people throwing beer cans full of piss, I mean heavy ones that even hit you in the head and give you a bath of piss. And beer bottles, cachaça bottles, I mean, so a briga isn't even only because of cachaça, because of hot blood, it's also because of the frustrations that people expel [*bota fora*] at that moment, because there's nothing better for expelling things than alcohol, right? It excites you. The guy loses that barrier of his morals, of the law, you know, at the moment the guy, all heated up, says fuck you [*manda porra*] to everybody, I'm going to do whatever I want to.

The urine-filled beer can is clearly an updated version of entrudo, although the man who throws it may never have heard the word. Genival's description here is exaggerated—one would very likely pass Carnival in the Deodoro, as I did, without experiencing a urine bath—but he voices the preoccupation felt by many, probably most, são-luisenses: Carnival means "you've got to have everybody together," but everybody together drunk, "heated up," expelling frustrations, is a recipe for brigas and even murder.
    Like contemporary foliões, today's Carnival is scantily clad.[28] If current-

[28]The bloated samba-school parade aside, contemporary Carnival has a stripped-down quality in comparison with Carnival of even 50 years ago. True, one still encounters fofões and men dressed as pregnant women, but a variety of whimsical characters (the Bear; Colombina and Pierrot; the *cruz-diabo*, a devil decorated with crosses) have vanished. Similarly, although colorful and amusing traditions remain—for example, the Casinha da Roça, a mock rural thatched house that rolls through the streets while those inside cook and distribute foods to onlookers—others are gone: elegant masquerades in the Arthur Azevedo Theater, military bands, confetti battles, processions of decorated vehicles, and a host of stereotypic street dramas. And the popular masked balls, which until recently gave a distinctive (if, for some, scandalous) flavor to São Luís's Carnival, have all but disappeared. The net impression is that much drollery and creative playfulness have fallen away from Carnival but that both the energy and the core of the event persist. At times, however, the festival still shows exceptional vivaciousness and creativity. The highlight of São Luís's 1986 Carnival was a performance by the bloco known as Caroçudo ("Full of Pits," i.e., seeds), headquartered in the lively bairro of Madre Deus, which gave an extraordinarily inventive treatment of a theme that threatened to be deadly boring—the ballyhooed nonevent that was Halley's comet. The performance, which delighted the crowd in the stands and tempted many down into the passarela to join

day Carnival provocations are less organized than the system of barrels on street corners in São Luís and less widespread and obnoxious than appears to have been the case in Salvador, nevertheless they play much the same role within Carnival, in effect testing its limits. During the century between the dousing of Zeferino with sewer water and Beto's pawing of Jair's girlfriend, there has been a move away from the primacy of entrudo toward a more varied, less conventionalized array of Carnival provocations. This deritualization of aggression, which enhances ambiguity, may more readily lead to actual fighting. But the basic configuration is stable: Carnival still tends to generate provocations, which still tend to generate a certain number of brigas, and this predicament is still considered to be one of the great inevitable problems of Carnival.

Yet for most são-luisenses, the danger in Carnival does not vitiate the desire to play. On the contrary, it is difficult to avoid the conclusion that são-luisenses find a certain meaning in pushing their play to a limit. The association between Carnival and briga, then, is not simply a behavioral datum but also a *cultural* linkage. The key to the meaning of the relation between briga and Carnival is the slogan of Carnival, the phrase that both heralds the coming of the festival and seeks to forestall its slide into violence, "It's Carnival: Anything goes!"

---

the bloco, demonstrated clearly that a group can depart from traditional formulas without alienating spectators.

4

ANYTHING GOES!

A Dream of Freedom

Brigas occur during Carnival, but this is not to say that briga is *part* of Carnival. Carnival and briga are related but distinct scenarios. Scenarios do not exist in a cultural vacuum: relations between scenarios, like scenarios themselves, have a cultural structure. Carnival's internal dynamics drive it toward briga; the two meet where mock aggression merges into provocation.

São-luisenses invoke the slogan "Anything goes!" (*Vale tudo!*)[1] at the start of Carnival and, within the festival, at those precarious moments when playing threatens to give way to fighting. "Anything goes!" marks the boundaries of the Carnival scenario; its uses illuminate the cultural truth that Carnival is a zone of tension rather than of pure release.

The first thing to understand about "Anything goes!" is that as a description of Carnival the statement is false. Carnival is regulated in many ways. Public sexual license, for example, is a hallmark of Carnival. Nevertheless, that this license has limits is apparent. Although Carnival encourages unusually suggestive body display and body movement, no one copulates in the glare of the passarela. During Carnival in São Luís, sexual activity (as opposed to seductive behavior or sexual pantomime) is fairly discreet, an af-

[1] Alternatively, people may cry, "Everything is Carnival!" (*Tudo é Carnaval!*). The usage and meaning are essentially the same.

fair of the shadows rather than the bright lights. Carnival relaxes inhibitions and everyday sexual constraints but does not abolish them.

In some clubs, which are less public than the street, sexual play can be more open, but again there are limits. For decades masked balls were a traditional feature of the city's Carnival. These balls took place in so-called popular clubs set up during Carnival in rented houses, generally in the center of town.[2] Although they clearly offered opportunities for sexual liaisons and for a degree of physical sexual play, the popular clubs were not, so far as I could determine, settings for orgies. Nevertheless, they aroused intense controversy within São Luís. The debate revolved around whether the activities in these clubs fell within the boundary of Carnival—not around whether such a boundary exists. In 1966, São Luís's first elected mayor, Epitácio Cafeteira, attempted the righteous gesture of outlawing the masked balls, a crusade that earned him praise from some quarters and ridicule from others. Those who defended the balls considered the festivities a risqué but nonetheless benign, amusing, and traditional component of São Luís's Carnival. Cafeteira's campaign failed, but the masked ball, which had been in decline, died a slow natural death over the following years. Some say this happened because sexual mores in general became less rigid and the popular clubs therefore had no further appeal, an admission that the limits of the permissible could not be expanded indefinitely.

There is no need to belabor this point, which is obvious: Carnival has limits. The acceptable range of sexual behavior is expanded during Carnival, but ultimately bounded: hence alleged excesses can cause controversy and legal intervention. In the last chapter we saw that Carnival permits forms of aggression that would not be tolerated during the rest of the year. Again, excesses are unacceptable, but their treatment depends on the nature of the aggression—whether it expresses political defiance (i.e., rebellion) or interpersonal hostility (i.e., briga).

Carnivalesque criticisms of the political status quo invariably take the form of jests or reveries. Satirical protests and millennial fantasies have their places within a samba-enredo, and the povo can "invade" the center of town, but sober political challenges are out of bounds. I do not, for example, know of a case in the Rebel Island of even an incipient riot during Carnival.[3] The military police who patrol the praça, symbols and incarnations of the state's intolerance of dissent, would surely suppress any

---

[2]The organizers of these balls "imported" young women from the outlying bairros for the entertainment of relatively well-to-do male foliões. The newspapers sometimes argued that this experience caused such women to become prostitutes.

[3]In this respect, São Luís Carnival contrasts strongly with West Indian Christmas (Dirks 1987) and Carnival in sixteenth-century Romans (Ladurie 1979), where violent class conflict was an overt element of the celebration.

such tumult instantly and energetically. The armed and dour soldiers are the ultimate guarantors of Carnival's frontiers, the most tangible evidence that its liberty is constrained, a matter of official sufferance. One would never confound the uniformed police with costumed foliões. The distinction is underscored by the permanent ban on disguises that imitate military or clerical dress: here Carnival forbids even playful mimicry.[4] The police remain unmistakably real police, with real clubs and real guns, a last line of control.

Everyone knows that the state circumscribes Carnival, forbidding protest that threatens to erase the line between playing at revolt and actual revolt.[5] Appealing to "Anything goes!" as a justification for political provocations would be to mistake fantasy for reality (which the Brazilians I knew rarely did) rather than embracing fantasy as a way of enduring the unendurable with dignity and élan. When people do confuse carnivalesque fantasy with reality, as Accacio did, the price is a severe dose of reality—in his case, a trip to jail. Carnival therefore projects an illusion of political freedom and equality against a background of oppressive social reality.

If the state throttles aggression directed toward it, confining carnivalesque rebellion to innuendo and fantasy, it seems a little more tolerant of, and in any case less able to control, interpersonal aggression, that is, briga.[6] Briga is off-limits, and police will intervene in a briga that threatens serious violence, but Carnival nevertheless spills over into this forbidden territory.

Despite the ban on fighting, Carnival stimulates provocative acts such as entrudos. And yet the limit, though sometimes blurred, is there: one

[4]Elaborate restrictions and security measures are taken before and during Carnival. The police organize "blitzes" (the German word is used), the detainment en masse of so-called marginais, or criminals, in pre-Carnival sweeps. The persons thus detained, often arbitrarily, are not released until Ash Wednesday. An annual edict issued just before Carnival seeks to regulate disorderly behavior, indecorous or offensive costumes (including religious habits and military costumes), excessive drinking, entrudo, and the carrying of arms. During Carnival, the police mobilize large numbers of men to deal with violent incidents, especially at night and in the Deodoro. Several of the city's district police stations also go on a round-the-clock schedule. The objective of these precautions is, as the police put it, to allow the folião of São Luís to play Carnival "with tranquillity."

[5]The reductio ad absurdum of state control over Carnival has to be Stalinist Carnival, described by Rosalinde Sartorti (n.d.), introduced by the Communist party in 1935. How, asks Sartorti, could a Carnival be spontaneous when the state arranged to have participants brought to the square in groups, specified what masks and costumes they were to wear, and planned their movements through the park in detail? With the liquidation of the kulaks, Stalin declared the class war at an end. For Stalin, Carnival could therefore be nothing but an expression of equality and brotherhood, or, as Sartorti describes it, a Carnival "reduced to a colorful variety show with no excess whatsoever, moderate, regulated, under control, but pretty to look at"—in short, a Carnival with no room, as Brazilians might put it, to breathe. A thoroughly controlled Carnival is no Carnival.

[6]During Carnival as at other times, fighters generally belong to the working or lumpen classes. I discuss the significance of this in Chapter 12.

cannot attack others with impunity, expecting the attack to be accepted as carnivalesque play. Indeed, whenever someone insists that his or her act of aggression is an "anything" that "goes," an unacceptable provocation has probably occurred.

Everyone knows that the "Anything goes!" of Carnival is delimited. It is not simply false, but rather consciously false—a lie told to oneself, a self-deception. "Anything goes!" is the illusion spun by Carnival about itself, an illusion of grievances resolved, anger spent, and desires satisfied in an atmosphere of social peace, impossible though that is even within the festival. Carnival is not a moment of freedom, but a momentary dream of freedom.[7]

But I think it would be wrong to view "Anything goes!" as an empty slogan. For the dream to work—and it works quite well—Carnival must offer a credible simulacrum of the license that "Anything goes!" promises. An examination of the situations in which the slogan can be invoked reveals exactly how this simulacrum is constructed and where and how it is bounded regarding the dilemma of interpersonal aggression.

Venting

"It's Carnival: Anything goes!" is the cry that ushers in Carnival, that sweeps são-luisenses across the boundary separating the day-to-day world from the world of the festival. It is a call to break free of the daily struggle (*luta*; Scheper-Hughes 1988), to jettison the circumspection, patience, and stoicism so often demanded by everyday life. In contrast, Carnival permits what might be approximately rendered in English as "venting," or, more precisely, the banishing from one's interior world of accumulated frustrations, irritations, resentments, spiritual maladies, anger, and psychological pain in general. Two related terms describe this kind of equilibrating action: *desabafar* (noun: *desabafo*) and *botar para fora* (noun: *bota-fora*). Desabafar is literally to unsmother or unsuffocate, and botar para fora, to cast out. Both have the sense of discharging and bring to mind Elene's warning of foliões who "expel their evil," although clearly she was referring not to innocuous venting but to obnoxious provocations. Indeed, the frontier between desabafo (or bota-fora) and provocation is where Carnival meets briga.

Although "botar para fora" and "desabafar" are sometimes used more or less interchangeably, "botar para fora" has greater force. Tito, a remarkably sensitive and intelligent young man whom I quote extensively in the pages that follow, makes the distinction that a desabafo (typically, the airing

[7]People speak of "falling into the festa" (*cair na festa*) or "falling into the samba" (*cair no samba*) as a way of describing one's surrender to the spirit of the festival or the rhythm of the music. The same idiom is used to describe falling asleep (*cair no sono*).

of a complaint or the verbal or otherwise symbolic expression of irritation or anger) is a limited act that leaves one "with the rest of the neurosis," whereas to botar para fora is to "vomit out" one's anxieties and problems, usually in a highly dramatic manner, so as to separate them in some definitive way from one's interior world. This may be done by getting roaring drunk, shouting, or—and this is where problems arise—provoking or attacking another person. Generally speaking, são-luisenses regard desabafos and bota-foras as providing relief; performed at the proper time and place (for example, during a festival), these actions are neither questionable nor particularly troublesome. On the contrary, the maintenance of psychological well-being requires desabafo, and bota-fora, a more radical act, is also, when done in appropriate circumstances, a salutary measure.

A third related notion is that of playing (*brincar*). Carnival is sometimes described as a gigantic *brincadeira* (an entertainment, game, or joke), and what one does in the streets during Carnival is to brincar—to drink, dance, laugh, and so on. Playing is a way to vent, but it carries a connotation of accompanying laughter:

> The things you do [in your day-to-day life] in one way or another start to irritate [*chatear*] you, maybe because of the monotony. You also usually have some kind of problem to confront, some anxiety to contain, etc. So everything gets heavy. So I'm going to play, I'm going to spend some time doing something that will give me renewed pleasure. There's a thing [in all this] about dreams [i.e., illusions or daydreams], and roaring laughter [*gargalhadas*] specifically. A brincadeira can never be a serious thing. (Tito)

Laughing itself is a metaphorical casting out of the heaviness to which Tito refers. In the guffaw, a carnivalesque act par excellence, the brincadeira, the desabafo, and the bota-fora meet. Says Tito, "You feel your guts set free, you threw [something] out [*você jogou para fora*]." To brincar can also mean to engage in sexual play. Perhaps desabafo and related concepts carry, for males, a connotation of ejaculation, of sexual release, an interpretation suggested by Tito's comments on the psychological effects of sexual play (see pp. 141–43). But both men and women use desabafo to refer to release of the sort experienced during Carnival.

The cry of "Anything goes!" is, among other things, an exhortation to desabafar, to unsmother, to laugh deeply, to cut loose one's afflictions. Some, but not all, of these afflictions are universal. Consider the poem by Fernando R. Vianna, dated 1935, entitled simply "Carnival":

Imbecilic masquerader, in these three days
You seek to convince yourself that you are happy
And, pretending studied joys
A ridiculous role, you leap and laugh!

But despite the alcohol of your orgies
And your clownish attempts to disguise yourself
I see that these mad scurryings
Have their roots in hurt and sadness.

Sharpen your falsetto—and continue
To drink and dance in the middle of the street
In the most unbridled revelry!

Fling away the ancient hurt! Repel the pain!
But . . . Ah! Grab hold of your face—and see that the skin
Is a mask that covers a skull! (*TR*, February 10, 1935)

Here, Vianna sees Carnival as a device for denying, by "flinging away," the "ancient hurt" (the suffering and mortality that are conditions of human existence). Beneath the mask of flesh is a skull: Carnival's animation conceals the irreducible fact of death.[8] Vianna's unmasking is itself pretense, for he, the imbecilic masquerader (whose "joys" are after all "studied"), and the newspaper readers who encounter the poem amid other Carnival notices already know that Carnival is a necessary sham, an exercise in denial not only of mortality but of the whole "hurt and sadness" bound up with living as a human being with other human beings, one's needs and desires never fully satisfied. That it is a sham does not nullify Carnival's psychological utility; to the contrary, Carnival proposes that given the exigencies and intrinsic problems of human existence one had better know how to delude oneself. It prescribes a self-conscious expulsion of burdens as a generalized antidote to fear and suffering.[9]

São–luisenses, unlike Vianna in the poem, rarely specify exactly what it is that is being cast out. (In fact, "desabafar" is an intransitive verb, and "botar

[8]Carnival put in an appearance on the European battlefields of World War II, where consciousness of mortality could hardly have been more acute: Carnival music was relayed by field telephone to the Brazilian troops at the front.

[9]Shortly before Carnival in 1987, a young gay man in Rio told a reporter, "You will see people made up like AIDS victims. . . . Everyone jokes around. *It is better to joke, because AIDS is very sad* [emphasis added]. . . . Before it was like Sodom and Gomorrah. Now AIDS makes people think twice. They are trembling" (*Los Angeles Times*, February 21, 1987). The italicized sentence, shocking as it may seem to a North American, expresses quintessential Carnival logic.

para fora" tends to be used as one.) Venting gets rid of all the garbage, all the distress, rancor, resentment, and rage shut up inside. Carnival is the prototypical festa, a category that also includes parties and other celebrations. By general consensus, festas function as escape valves, permitting one to expel unspecified problems and frustrations collected over a period of time:

> I think that Carnival is an expenditure of energy. It's when you discharge all the rotten stuff that you've been holding in. I think it's the discharge of a wretched, impoverished people who want moments to breathe. Let's say a, a crevice, where I can breathe better, a place where I can go, where I can shout. (Tito)

And Paulista, a recent immigrant from São Paulo, remarks:

> [Carnival means] spilling out [*extravasar*] your accumulated energies, doing what your body demands [*fazer precisão*] in the shadows, getting smashed on cachaça, screwing in the street, four days of euphoria. You've got your pores open, you get more germs, you eat a lot of dust.

The images—expend, breathe, discharge, shout, spill out, "do what your body demands"—converge: Carnival provides the space where the psychological debris or pressure harbored inside for the past year can be vented in a blast of physical, sexual, and mental energy, where the barrier between inner and outer worlds vanishes. In contrast, everyday life is stifling; in it, one can neither "breathe" nor "shout."

The image of suffocation received strong reinforcement during the years of military rule (1964–85), when the regime did its best to silence those who challenged its legitimacy and protested its abuses. This is one reason why Chico Buarque could use Carnival as an expressive symbol of political liberation in the samba "Vai passar," which appeared just before the Carnival of 1985 as the generals' reign was drawing to its close. Buarque himself was a chief target of the censors for many years, but he showed exceptional ingenuity in fashioning seemingly innocent or ambiguous lyrics that had a devastating impact. An example is a song he wrote with another prominent dissident songwriter, Gilberto Gil, entitled "Cálice," literally "chalice," but the title is a homonym for "*Cale-se!*"—"Shut up!" The song as recorded is surely one of the most powerful protests imaginable against censorship, ending abruptly with the command "Cale-se!" Charles Perrone recounts the song's first performance in 1973, a stunning self-indictment by those who would smother dissent:

Censors had not acted when the lyric was published in a São Paulo newspaper. When the composers attempted to sing it in public, however, police came on stage to say the song had been proscribed. When agents removed one microphone, Buarque moved to another. Agents followed him to this and each of the remaining microphones to prevent him from using them. Thus, before a large audience, government agents dramatically enacted the song's central message: "Shut up!" (1989: 34)

Carnivalesque venting therefore has a political—that is, rebellious—dimension as well as an existential one. Especially for those for whom self-censorship is an act of self-protection or survival—those who suffer the most from the demands of and the casual humiliations imposed by social superiors and their agents—Carnival offers a chance not to mask oneself but to cast off, at least temporarily, the everyday mask of silent submission:

The facet of Carnival that I like the best is to be playing, understand? not working. This is Carnival for me. The pleasure of knowing today I don't have a *patrão* [boss], everybody's here, even the patrão is here, the patrão and his wife, they came, *I even give him an elbow and so on while I'm dancing* [emphasis added]. On this day I don't even look at him as a patrão, although he doesn't stop being one. You don't feel like his employee, and even he, I think, at least some patrões, don't feel so much like patrões, on this day, right, which is really the day of liberation. (Genival)

During Carnival, an elbow, a bota-fora straight from some inner world of resentment, can be thrown at the patrão. But one could press this analysis too far: we are not quite convinced, after Genival's hedging, that the patrão will forgive and forget that elbow if it is thrown too directly and maliciously, just as Accacio's ceremonious and pointedly rebellious attack on the white manager of the tailor shop led ultimately to his imprisonment.

Thus once more we catch sight of the limits of the illusion. The tone of Genival's statement denies revolutionary intent. The elbow sounds more like a jesting reminder—a rebellious ritual—than a serious warning: nothing Genival says challenges the view that after Carnival the patrão will once more be patrão and Genival (who works as a scrivener in the police department) will resume his subordinate position. This is not to say, I should emphasize, that Genival sees everyday hierarchical arrangements as desirable or just, any more than one might see mortality as desirable or just. On the contrary, Genival celebrates wholeheartedly the ideology of Carnival as expressed by Joana, "You've got to have everybody together, everybody's got to be united." For those who view and experience subordination within the everyday hierarchy as illegitimate, Carnival offers a defense of feigned egalitarianism, a vision of an alternative order. That is, the defense takes the form of a desabafo (or bota-fora) making concrete a desire recognized as contrary to some reality that is difficult to bear.

Although mortality threatens all, and although everyone experiences frustrations in dealings with others, the weight of hierarchy falls differentially on the inhabitants of São Luís.[10] The distribution of this weight is hard to estimate with any accuracy, for it is a subjective phenomenon, but average são-luisenses complain bitterly over abuses of power on the part of the privileged (and on the part of the government, which is regarded almost universally as a bastion of the privileged). DaMatta (1978) helps interpret this situation by distinguishing between "persons" and "individuals." Persons have a set of determinate social relationships that can be invoked to obtain special treatment. A person can demand exemption from the regulations applied indiscriminately to others, making this claim in the form of the arrogant, fatal question, "Do you know who you're talking to?" (*Você sabe com quem está falando?*). A person, then, is "someone," a human being with a name and connections that identify him or her as a powerful social actor. An individual, by contrast, is a social cipher, a degraded and defenseless human being, powerless in dealings with bosses, with bureaucracies, in short, with patrões of all descriptions. Individuals are victims of purportedly universalistic regulations, which in Brazil function overwhelmingly as weapons of the privileged rather than as guarantees of equal treatment for all.[11] The vast majority of são-luisenses fall into the latter category: for them, as for persons, Carnival presents an opportunity to cast off existential burdens, but they also bear the burdens of powerlessness and social nullification, of deprivation and humiliation. For them, desabafo is doubly important; for them, the dream of equality has its greatest allure.

[10]The literature on hierarchy in its various Brazilian guises is immense; I will cite here just a few representative works. General commentaries include Freyre (1956 [1933], 1964), Galjart (1965), Hutchinson (1966), and Wagley (1971 [1963]: chap. 3). More specific discussions are provided by Brown (1986), on Afro-Brazilian religion; Fernandes (1985), Gross (1971), and Kadt (1967), on Brazilian Catholicism; Leal (1948) and Pang (1973), on *coronelismo*; Leeds (1964) and Weffort (1970), on populism; Lewin (1979), on banditry; Queiroz (1965, 1976 [1965]), on messianism; and Freyre (1956 [1933], 1964), on the family. For an analysis of the relation between hierarchy and Carnival, see DaMatta (1978); he briefly recapitulates some of his points in English in DaMatta (1983).

[11]Laws protect privilege to a considerable extent in every country. DaMatta's claim seems to be that in Brazil they are used more overtly and cynically in this way than they are in those countries of Western Europe and North America with strongly universalistic ideological traditions.

Carnival, then, permits são-luisenses to get rid of frustrations arising from the immutable conditions of human existence (mortality and suffering), from social constraints in general (restrictions on emotional and physical interactions with others, especially those involving the expression of sexuality and aggression), and from the stultifying and often injurious demands of hierarchical superiors in particular. One can expel these frustrations from the interior world for a moment, not to resolve the irresolvable conditions of life, but to obtain temporary relief until the next Carnival. For all its frenzy, Carnival is an accommodation with an intransigent reality, a negotiation with forces that cannot easily be dominated. Desabafo therefore operates as an equilibrating mechanism in what are culturally constituted, cybernetic theories of personality and of society.

Tito sums up more eloquently than I can the experiential importance of Carnival:

> I see in myself, in Brazil, in the people here, this necessity to desabafar, to expel things [botar pra fora] through sound and dance, through . . . expending energies. It's like people say, you simply become depraved, during Carnival you simply become depraved, you throw out everything [você joga tudo pra fora]. "Ah, yesterday I went on a binge, I went on a real binge" [eu tomei um porre mesmo], meaning, I'm OK now, now I'm really OK. You see that woman, that man, there in the middle of things, turning, spinning, shouting, singing. You're seeing the General Sanatorium [he laughs; he is quoting from Chico Buarque's song "Vai passar"], pathology itself, during Carnival, something that's necessary, your ability to express yourself: Let me get rid of this thing, I'm a king, I can do this. I *myself* can't do it, as people say over and over, I myself can't do this, I need *it* [i.e., Carnival] to do this thing. During Carnival the guy gets drunk, during [other festivals] he gets drunk. A whole night of [dancing in the terreiro], three days of Carnival. . . . [He says,] "I feel simply fine, perfect," right? The bota-fora is the result of the thing, it's the relief of the thing. I don't know what would happen if there were some kind of blockage in the middle of all this. I don't know what would happen if we couldn't shout during some brincadeira [he laughs]. I don't know, I don't know if we could stand it all [não sei se a gente poderia agüentar], I think that's it, this is the therapy that allows us to put up with so many things, with *so many things* [his emphasis].

Don't Get Angry, It's Carnival

Earlier I described a man circulating through a club during Carnival with a bag of confetti, handfuls of which he deposited on heads and down dresses and shirts, rubbing the paper circles into people's hair and admonishing them, if they should show signs of irritation, "Don't get angry—anything goes, it's Carnival!" This is a classic scene of Carnival. The substance may be confetti or something less innocuous. Whatever the case, the aggressor's cry to the victim, the proclaimed justification at the moment of attack, particularly if the victim takes offense, is the slogan of Carnival. Clearly this "Anything goes!" is not a call for the victim to expel anything—quite the opposite. Rather, the objective of the cry under these circumstances is to classify the assault: the victim is encouraged to consider the entrudo not as a provocation (an invitation to briga) but as a legitimate equilibrating action, a playful piece of Carnival mischief.

This suggests that desabafos, bota-foras, and brincadeiras can resemble provocations. Indeed, Accacio's cabacinha, Genival's elbow, and Elene's phrase "expel evil" are all suggestive in this respect. To focus more closely on the issue, I propose that we step outside Carnival, to an event (later described by Tito) that occurred around midnight one Saturday in September 1984 at a bus stop near the central market in downtown São Luís. Approximately ten people are waiting, including a young couple. There is little automobile traffic, and few people pass by on foot. I am accompanying Tito as he waits for a bus to take him to his home in an outlying bairro.

> It's really hard to tell or describe something that you see so often, it's because you were born observing this kind of thing. Not briga, not exactly briga, but things that happen all the time. I could see that [there was] a [young] couple, the guy was sitting down [on the sidewalk]. [After I had been waiting there] ten or fifteen minutes, a man who was drunk came walking [up from the central market], maybe high not only on alcohol but also on marijuana. He looked like a stevedore or fisherman, and generally stevedores and fishermen use marijuana to get them through their work and in their free time too. So this man arrived at the bus stop, drunk, drugged, and with serious emotional problems. I noticed a very great resentment [*revolta*] in him, looking for the first person he could find so that he could obtain relief [*para se aliviar*]. [When he got to the bus stop he halted and] he *gave a desabafo that was also a provocation* [emphasis added], saying, "I'm really

stoned" [*xilado*]. This provocation wasn't directed at anybody in particular but at everybody who was there. This gave him a certain aggressive satisfaction. Well, the young guy [sitting on the sidewalk] had *taken the thing as a brincadeira* [emphasis added], or maybe he was happy that somebody, maybe like himself, was drunk or high on marijuana, and he repeated the same word [saying, "Stoned, huh?"]. The man got furious [*revoltado*], maybe not exactly for this reason, so he kicked the guy's leg and made some threats, even threatening to pull a nonexistent revolver.

I will interrupt the story here; it will be completed in a later chapter. Let me begin by commenting briefly on Tito's behavior. When this man appeared, Tito dropped our conversation and gave his full attention to him, urging me quietly at just about the point the story breaks off to move away from the man and the couple, as everyone else at the bus stop was doing. Tito had apparently been assessing the potential danger of this situation from the moment the man appeared. The degree of danger depends, in the first instance, on one's interpretation of the man's statement that he is stoned. This requires an evaluation of the man's emotional state and his objectives. Tito concludes (at least in retrospect, but I think that this was almost surely his judgment at the moment as well) that the man has serious emotional problems: he is seeking a victim upon whom to unload his resentment and thereby obtain relief.

In Tito's view, then, this resentful emotional state demands some sort of venting. The man announces that he is stoned, an action that "[gives] him a certain aggressive satisfaction." This announcement differs from a simple desabafo in that it is a sinister invitation, a provocation. The man is looking for a briga partner, or a victim, whose identity is irrelevant and unknown until the boy foolishly echoes him. To Tito, the boy's great error is in taking the provocative comment as a harmless brincadeira, a playful, perhaps slightly self-deprecating commentary on his drunken state.

This event reveals that provocation is a malign variant of desabafo. In this case the same behavior (the drunk's announcement, "I'm really stoned") could be taken as a brincadeira, an innocuous desabafo, or a provocation, depending on the assumptions made about his motivation. Because the action does not speak for itself, how one responds to it, and therefore the subsequent development of the encounter, depends on how one interprets it.

The ambiguity of venting means that the definition of such an act must be negotiated between the persons involved. Is what So-and-So did a harmless desabafo, a provocation, or (to complicate matters diabolically) a provocation cloaked as a desabafo? This brings us back to Carnival. I can mobilize

"Anything goes!" as a self-interested definition of the situation, a claim that "what I did was a harmless desabafo, not a provocation," meaning, "this is Carnival, not briga; therefore you have no right to impede or take exception to what I am doing." It is as if, through entrudo and other forms of agonistic display, Carnival insists on raising the question, Is this Carnival or briga? over and over (cf. Bateson 1972d [1955]). Entrudos have always fostered brigas because they can elicit multiple interpretations based on an evaluation of the invisible: the interior world of motivation of the individual who is "attacking."

In brief, "Anything goes!" can either invite revelers to cast off the fetters of social control or urge them to rein in their violent impulses. The usages seem contradictory, prescribing emotional release in the first instance and restraint in the second. A closer look reveals that this paradox profiles the limits of Carnival.

Carnival as a Zone of Tension: The Fragile Carnival Frame

"Anything goes!" is a key to the meaning of Carnival's relation both to everyday life and to briga. As the cry of Carnival, that is, as an exhortation to desabafar, the phrase points to the frontier separating the world of "bearing up" (*agüentar*)—the world of day-to-day life, of work, of hierarchy—from the world of venting (desabafar), that of the festa, of play, of mock equality. It announces that a chief condition, or rule, of day-to-day life, the rule that says one must put up with disagreeable, even terrible, things, has been suspended, and it consequently spurs everyone to join in the spirit of the festa. "Anything goes!" is the cry that celebrates and facilitates crossing into a region where desabafo is not only allowed but encouraged.

But in dangerous situations during Carnival, "Anything goes!" illuminates a different sector of cognitive space. Again, the intent is to justify venting—but in relation to a different set of circumstances. Here, "Anything goes!" makes an appeal for tolerance so as to forestall (as inadmissible within Carnival) an aggressive reaction to behavior that would normally be considered provocative. Its aim is to prevent someone from doing what são-luisenses call "connecting" (ligar)—acknowledging a provocation through word or gesture, thereby sealing a hostile compact, in effect a mutual declaration of war.

We can summarize as follows. In the first situation, "Anything goes!" can be read "You are now *permitted* to engage in normally prohibited behaviors." In the second, the message is "You must now *tolerate* normally prohibited behaviors." In the first case, one is roused to activity; in the second, one is cajoled into passivity. By ostensibly defining Carnival as an event in which "anything" is permitted, "Anything goes!" urges são-luisenses to relax their everyday self-control and expel their accumulated frustrations. It thereby marks the frontier between the day-to-day world and the world of Carnival. But such expelling threatens to trigger violence, and hence we encounter "Anything goes!" once more at Carnival's other frontier, which separates Carnival from briga. Here it serves as a reassurance that what is occurring is desabafo, not provocation. In effect, the festival can survive only in a zone of tension that spawns near-provocations but then aborts conflict before it ripens into brigas. By bracketing Carnival between the everyday world and briga, "Anything goes!" succinctly illustrates that in Carnival's rebellious expansiveness lies its peril.

The point can be stated more precisely by considering what Bateson calls "frames." Frames are something like scenarios: they are cognitive interactional settings that influence interpretations of behavior. The word "frame" nicely captures the discontinuous, contextual flavor of Bateson's idea, which he elaborates most clearly in his essay "A Theory of Play and Fantasy" (1972d [1955]), where he elucidates the meaning of the message (implicit or explicit) "This is play." Such a message is "metacommunicative" in that it operates at a higher level of abstraction than playful actions: by framing those actions, it tells one how to interpret them. Three types of messages, says Bateson, may be recognized in or deduced from animal behavior:

> (a) messages of the sort which we here call mood-signs [an involuntary sign of physiological process, e.g., sexual odor];
> (b) messages which simulate mood-signs (in play, threat, histrionics, etc.); and (c) messages which enable the receiver to discriminate between mood-signs and those other signs which resemble them. (p. 189)

Metacommunicative messages like "This is play" fall into the third category, advising the receiver "that certain nips and other meaningful actions are not of the first type" (p. 189). These messages might be called frame (or scenario) markers: they indicate the frame (or scenario) within which a behavior is taking place. In short, they convey information about context.[12] Clearly, the same act can vary widely in meaning depending on which

---

[12]I would expand Bateson's perspective here. Bateson suggests that metamessages distinguish between "mood-signs" and "other signs which resemble them." Perhaps because the culture of Bateson's "informants"—monkeys—is less elaborate than ours, he drew the issue narrowly. For human beings, frame markers distinguish between cultural contexts for behavior, rather than simply between mood signs and feigned mood signs. Certainly both our aggression and our play are highly structured culturally, and it is this structuring—the complex of cultural models that we know and use—to which the frame markers I have discussed refer.

scenario is understood to govern the interaction in which it occurs. João throwing dirty water on José means one thing if both understand that it is part of Carnival, but something quite different if they see it as part of briga.

"Anything goes!" is a frame marker that proposes Carnival as the context of interactions, the relevant scenario. But our evidence allows us to go beyond this simple inference to say something about how this frame marker is used. In particular, we can see that in some cases this marker "erects"— sets up, or puts into place—the Carnival frame, while in other instances it "secures" that frame when it is in danger of being supplanted by another.[13] The distinction between erecting and securing frames is important because an analysis of the ways a particular frame marker is employed can reveal much about the relationships between different frames.

When "Anything goes!" heralds the coming of Carnival, it helps erect a new frame. Society at this time is poised at a frame boundary, about to enter Carnival from the side of the everyday world, and since this entry requires a transformation of certain norms, we can expect a moral inertia, a hesitation as people switch the signs from minus to plus on certain usually proscribed behaviors. To not bear up is a perilous weakness, a lapse in the self-control required to navigate one's way through the hazards of daily life. But now desabafo is to have its moment in the sun. The change of frame signals an inversion of the usual injunction to bear up. Hence "Anything goes!" is part of a symbolic campaign on behalf of a substitution of frames. Its metamessage is "This is play-time (Carnival), not day-to-day life. Therefore desabafo is now permitted."

But when the confetti man utters the same phrase, given the pandemonium in the club and the fact that the festival is days old, no one, unless unconscious, could be unaware that Carnival is in full swing. If the purpose of his admonition is to erect that frame, it seems thoroughly redundant. Is there any other reason, then, for the confetti man's "Anything goes!"?

The answer, of course, is that he is trying not to erect, but rather to defend, the Carnival frame, which is in danger. The frame now threatening to disrupt Carnival is briga. The confetti man's "Anything goes!" is more narrowly focused than the frame-setting cry of Carnival. It is closely analogous to Bateson's monkeys' metacommunication, conveying the metamessage, "This is play (desabafo), not aggression (provocation)." By securing the Carnival frame, and thereby discouraging the interpretation of his entrudo as a provocation, the confetti man can prevent the response that would be appropriate within briga—connection and a slide toward physical aggression.

---

[13]Goffman (1974) speaks of frames being "broken." However, the Carnival frame does not so much "break" as yield to another frame to which it is related.

The marker "Anything goes!" appears at the boundaries of Carnival, thereby indicating those frames cognitively adjacent to it—day-to-day life and briga. The use of this marker suggests that once the Carnival frame has been erected, it can easily dissolve into the briga frame, as desabafo degenerates into provocation. We may infer, I think, that erecting the Carnival frame sets in motion a dynamic that tends later to require its defense.

Carnival is revealed here as an unstable twilight zone, not only because it is a liminal detour between points in social-structural time but also because it is a region poised between a domain requiring submission to everyday social rules and existential facts, on one side, and a perdition of confusion and violence, on the other. Hence by inverting certain aspects of quotidian life—the role usually ascribed to it—Carnival establishes a fragile space that permits, indeed fosters, dangerous play.

The question arises, Why do people put themselves into this volatile emotional and social space?

5

PLAYING TO THE LIMIT

Risking Violence

I have stressed that Carnival and briga come packaged together, and I have presented the package from two perspectives: as a concurrence of social events and as a conjunction of cultural scenarios. As far back as I could trace Carnival in São Luís, briga has been its unwelcome guest. This suggests that it is rooted in certain enduring features of Brazilian society and culture.

It is tempting to argue that brigas occur frequently during Carnival because Carnival sets up objective conditions that may encourage fighting, such as mass drunkenness and crowd concentration, which (our folk knowledge tells us) are bound to generate a certain degree of physical aggression. Most são-luisenses would certainly agree with this reasoning. But I have insisted that to leave the explanation here would be to settle for a mechanical analysis that is unconvincing and, worse, misses the main point. For the important question, in my judgment, is this: If, according to the understandings that são-luisenses share about the consequences of mixing crowds, alcohol, and desabafos, they see Carnival as dangerous, why do they fill the praça year after year under exactly these circumstances? What, in other words, are the motivations, what I have called the "human reasons," behind this event?

The question becomes even more interesting when we realize that Carnival not only creates general conditions thought to be *conducive* to violence but seems *to play* with violence by prompting behavior like entrudo. That is, Carnival violence is not simply the price of the party, an unfortunate by-product of what are, for many, intrinsically pleasurable activities, like dancing and drinking in a kaleidoscopic setting. Rather, a perduring feature of Carnival has been behavior that, according to são-luisense cultural understandings, flirts with briga. The carnivalesque brush with violence therefore seems less a lamentable but unavoidable risk (in the way that crashing is a risk that comes with flying) than a goal in and of itself, a meaningful experiential component of the festival. *This* is the riddle of Brazilian Carnival, a puzzle that cannot be solved through some "objective" analysis of the danger or euphoria produced by drunken revelry.

The most fascinating aspect of Carnival is not, therefore, that Carnival yields a toll of fights and murders, but rather that year after year the people re-create Carnival, with great anticipation and excitement, under circumstances in which fights and murders will occupy a more or less deliberately central place in the celebration. Since são-luisenses know that Carnival is dangerous, the annual reproduction of this event in an urban setting like São Luís—a city which, as its residents are uncomfortably aware, *normally* has high rates of violence and a restive population—demands an explanation that looks to the experiential significance of the festival.

Carnival as a Tour de Force

To understand the human reasons behind Carnival one must adopt a cultural perspective that explores patterns of meaning. My analysis of "Anything goes!" revealed that Carnival is a consciously constructed illusion of license (or freedom) suspended between day-to-day life and briga. For são-luisenses, Carnival permits discharge, but a discharge that must be dammed at the point it threatens to spill over into briga.

The need to release dangerous inner pressures is not some abstract deduction from cultural axioms, the idea that after bearing up all year one must expel, but rather an emotional imperative derived from a specific culturally shaped experience of the world. Because Carnival begins but does not end with venting, however, the question of motivation gets complicated. Carnival is not simply release, but *controlled* release, and a moment comes for most people during Carnival when the emphasis falls more on control than on release. This is not just happenstance; Carnival pushes toward that point by encouraging provocative acts that threaten equilibrium.

The tension between release and control arises because the stuff being released is dangerous: for são-luisenses, frustration, resentment, and anger fuel both Carnivals and brigas.[1] In Chapter 4 I noted that the perceived sources of these various unpleasant and disturbing emotions are both existential and social. Especially onerous, and deserving of a more careful examination, are the abasements inflicted by social superiors. Although urbanization and capitalist rationalization are undoubtedly eating away at traditional patron–client arrangements, social organization in São Luís is still a hierarchical amalgam that mixes elements of patronage and clientage with modern (impersonal economic and political) forms of domination.[2] The very term "patrão" (female: *patroa*) points up the hybrid nature of the system, because it can refer either to one's boss in a capitalist or bureaucratic workplace or to a classic patron of the type sketched by George Foster (1963), with all of the term's connotations of asymmetrical exchange, protection, intimacy, fidelity—and, what Foster underplays, capriciousness or abuse.

Employers seem to combine, in different proportions, the roles of (impersonal) boss and (personal) patron. In domestic work, a sector that employs many women in São Luís, employers probably tend to resemble patrons more than bosses. Household servants generally live with their employers, receiving room and board in addition to a small wage. Their treatment varies enormously. Some employers not only provide good food, wages, and accommodations but also grant servants much free time, address them and behave toward them with respect, trust them with sums of money, and assist other members of their families. But I also knew or heard of cases in which employers worked servants mercilessly, sexually abused them, treated them with derision, or even locked them inside the house to prevent them from stealing.

The point, which I believe is fundamental to an understanding of Brazilian social relations, is that inequality in power is coupled with considerable arbitrariness: the treatment one receives depends on eccentricities and dispositions of the social superior as mediated by the particular personal

[1]Occasionally people speak also of discharging "joy" (see Chico Buarque's song "When Carnival Comes," p. 41). At first glance this seems inconsistent with the idea of venting anger or frustration, but I think it refers in part to the exhilaration one feels in throwing off restraints on self-expression. There is an additional implication that everyday life suffocates the expression of all emotions, including feelings of happiness and especially sexual pleasure.

[2]Hierarchy in its patronal guise is an outstanding feature of Brazilian society. It is in little-industrialized, poor, northeastern areas like Maranhão that relations of patronage and clientage remain strongest. In São Luís, horizontal associations—trade unions, neighborhood groups, and so on—are weak and operate in large measure as vehicles for the ambitions of local political cliques. Informal observation also suggests that patriarchy is a strong characteristic of both the family and the workplace in São Luís. Nevertheless, similar tendencies exist throughout Brazil. In São Luís, as elsewhere in Brazil, individuals condemn and groups challenge this pattern, which is often resented by those who bear its brunt but which has a certain emotional and pragmatic validity (Linger 1993).

relationship, if any, that one manages to forge with that man or woman. Although from the client's perspective such relationships can have positive aspects, especially the patron's provision of goods and services and exercise of influence on the client's behalf, the patrão's arbitrary exercise of power and the often summary and demeaning nature of the personal interactions are keenly felt by many são-luisenses, especially those nearer to the base of the social pyramid, as humiliations. Moreover, because people such as household servants are unprotected, they have no recourse other than to quit their jobs, an often impossible luxury for someone in their economic position. São-luisenses talk bitterly of having to "swallow" indignities dealt out by powerful persons. The ultimate indignity, by implication, is having to accommodate oneself to disrespectful or even disgraceful treatment—the indignity of powerlessness.

Joana's sad, deeply wounding experience as a maid in Rio de Janeiro exemplifies some of the worst aspects of working under the thumb of a harsh, contemptuous patron—in this case, a patroa. An agent in São Luís contracted Joana to care and provide companionship for an elderly woman in Rio. Joana was to receive room and board and a salary, in addition to her bus passage south. However, when Joana arrived at the house of her employer in the posh Tijuca neighborhood of Rio, her new patroa told her that her duties were to bathe and look after several dogs (washing their bedding and disposing of their excrement, among other things), clean the husband's adjoining dental office at 5 A.M. every day, and work as the household servant. She was to perform these duties seven days a week, from before dawn to bedtime. Joana protested that she had been hired to care for an old woman; the patroa replied that since she was already in Rio, she had no choice. The woman forbade Joana to watch television or to converse with anyone in the household. Joana's room was located above the place the dogs were kept, and it stank. She stuck it out for two months and then wanted to leave. Meanwhile, the woman had not paid her a cent, claiming she had no money. Joana finally told her to forget the money; all she wanted was her passage back to São Luís. The woman agreed to pay her way back after the third month of work, saying she would also give her some food for the three- or four-day bus trip. On the day of departure, however, she gave Joana just a little fruit and a sandwich and sent her to pack her belongings. When Joana appeared at the door, ready to leave, the patroa insisted on checking her bags to see if she had stolen anything.

This was the only time Joana ever set foot outside the state of Maranhão. During her three months in the Sul Maravilha, the Marvelous South, Joana, who had neither time nor permission to leave her mistress's house, made no friends; she never even managed a trip to one of Rio's fabled beaches. She saw nothing of the city but what passed by the windows of her taxi on the way from the bus station to Tijuca and, three months later, on her return to the station. Even though she was penniless, it was with a tremendous sense of relief that she boarded the bus to go back north. When she got to São Luís, she discovered that her patroa had sent none of the letters Joana had given her to mail to her family, except for a telegram announcing her arrival in Rio. Joana had not known where to find a post office in Rio, nor had she had the opportunity to leave the house in search of one.

Not all são-luisenses find themselves in the position of the household servant, but everyone, from top to bottom, knows what it is to depend on another for access to the things he or she needs or desires. The other may be a relative, a compadre, a husband, a boss, a lover, a landlord, a friend; regardless of the exact nature of the relationship, the person has the power to satisfy some need either directly, through the provision of some good or service, or indirectly, through personal ties with someone who can make such a provision. Inevitably, this dependency at times results in frustrated hopes and expectations, especially for DaMatta's "individuals," those who, like Joana, lack substantial names or connections, whose dealings with powerful, implacable, arbitrary "persons" so often yield not only defeat but also mortification.

Carnival permits são-luisenses to disgorge the indignities, to expel some of the smothered resentment they feel but cannot express without risk in everyday interactions. To desabafar in this fashion means to relinquish the self-control that a prudent person ordinarily must exercise to keep from showing resentment. But playing Carnival successfully does not mean expelling without limit; one should expel *to* a limit—quite a different notion. Discharge itself requires finesse: one must temper spontaneity. Thus we find within Carnival an ironic tension. If Carnival is to survive, then venting, its raison d'être, can proceed only so far. Specifically, foliões should pour out accumulated frustrations but *modulate the outpouring so as to avoid overt violence*. Violent emotions can legitimately receive only partial behavioral expression, in entrudos or other forms of ritualized aggression.

It is therefore possible, if unorthodox, to view Carnival as a test of self-control. Carnival encourages people to expel violent emotions but forbids them to provoke others. Those whose venting of anger or hostility goes too far present a further challenge to the foliões who are targets of their aggressions: resisting the impulse to respond violently. The folião's performance begins to resemble a tour de force, an act of self-mastery under adverse conditions (Genival: "that heap of people throwing beer cans," drunk, "all heated up"), rather than mere abandonment to impulse. Given são-luisenses' understandings of the world they live in, we can easily see why people want to vent, or play, but what is the motive for a virtuosic exercise of self-mastery within a saturnalia?

São-luisenses did not describe Carnival to me as a chance to exhibit self-mastery or as a tour de force. They did not verbalize what it is that attracts them to play to the edge of briga, perhaps because the reason is hard to grasp or articulate. My analysis of their underlying motives is therefore speculative. Playing to the limit strikes me as an effort to engineer the experience of a significant dilemma, a dilemma cast into sharp relief at the place where control over aggression becomes precarious. I think that in creating this experience são-luisenses, at least many of them, simultaneously express an anxiety and ask a question, seeking a reassuring answer. That is, I am guessing that in playing to the limit são-luisenses are trying to ward off demons—to show themselves that even under the most trying circumstances they can manage the chaos of self and society, thereby assuaging their feelings of vulnerability to the powerful, to the violence in the streets, and to their own resentments engendered by the sociocultural conditions in which they live.[3]

Self-Control as Art and as Sign

Let me begin by broadly outlining the são-luisense folk psychology implicit in the set of understandings that make up the Carnival scenario. (I will take up são-luisense ethnopsychology in more detail in Chapter 8.) According to this ethnopsychology, the interior world has two basic components: a core of potentially dangerous impulses, prominent among which are aggressive feelings fed by socially generated frustrations and resentments; and a mental structure (a suppressive device) that normally is charged with containing the pressure created by these accumulating anxieties and frustrations, permitting safe interactions with others in day-to-day situations. On occasions such as Carnival a momentary breach in the structure permits the accumulated pressure to escape. Such discharge—healthful desabafo when it is done correctly and legitimately—is a way of managing a subjective existential and social predicament that has no basic resolution.

Maintaining dynamic self-control is an art. The interior world is unpredictable, inflammable: remember Jair's comment that with one provocative act "the guy carries you off to perdition." "Perdition" here, I think, refers to briga, where both body and soul (one's self-respect as an effective person and as a competent moral agent) are endangered. Being swept into briga signifies that one has lost one's psychological equilibrium—a profoundly important measure of the person in São Luís. In essence, at the frontier where the festival meets briga, one risks both physical and moral integrity.

---

[3]Both men and women strongly resent being subjected to dismissive and abusive treatment, and see such resentment as threatening to psychological equilibrium. There is no doubt, however, that men feel more impelled to express their hostility in physical violence. The dilemma I discuss here is therefore in some respects more acute for men than for women.

If I am right about this, Carnival's flirtation with the frontier is some-thing like a test that sets impulse free ("Anything goes!") so as to challenge equilibrium. Bringing off a virtuoso performance demonstrates to one-self and to others both that the universe, dangerous as it is, is tractable and that one knows how to deal with it, even under trying and fluctu-ating conditions. The community, too, assembled in the praça in a state of Durkheimian "collective effervescence," manifests to itself its fundamental solidity and wholeness. One more Carnival has gone round, and once more, having played to the limit, I—*we*, because the demonstration is public and communal—have brought off the feat of riding the tiger.

This interpretation would imply, of course, much anxiety over both one's own aggressive impulses and the aggression of others, a disturbing uncertainty as to whether self and society can stay intact. No nation is free of violence, and Brazil, despite its relatively peaceful relations with its neigh-bors, is no exception. Brazilian history features slavery, genocide, bloody and savagely quelled rebellions, and repeated episodes of harsh political re-pression, the most recent one barely ended. Brutality by the state continues to be a terrifying fact of life.[4] Moreover, the level of interpersonal violence is high: over 100 homicides occurred in São Luís in each of the years 1982, 1983, and 1984, the latest years for which I have firm statistics.[5] Such vio-lence is frightening in part, I believe, because of its implications for one's experience of the self. Many são-luisenses perceive that everyday social rela-tions, a recognized source of their own dissatisfactions and resentments, provide the emotional raw material of arguments, brigas, and murders.

[4]Brazil has no capital punishment, yet murder by the police and by death squads—unoffi-cial capital punishment—is common. Cáritas Brasileira, a Church group, has been keeping track of violence perpetrated by all organs of the state throughout Maranhão since mid-March 1983. I tabulated from the Cáritas files 8 cases of police killings in São Luís in 1983 (March 17–December 31), 27 cases in 1984, and 15 cases in 1985. I am grateful to Cáritas, and to Padre Victor Asselin, for permission to consult the records so carefully assembled by Cáritas workers. For an overview of torture and extrajudicial execution in urban Brazil, see Am-nesty International (1990). This unofficial punishment shows the disparity between the pacific public image, wishful illusion perhaps, and violent reality.

[5]Numbers of homicides during recent years in the município of São Luís, according to the figures supplied to me by the Secretaria de Justiça e Segurança Pública (SEJUSP) of the state of Maranhão, are as follows:

Year	No. of homicides	Year	No. of homicides
1980	60	1983	105
1981	72	1984	110
1982	110		

Although according to SEJUSP figures homicides have increased precipitously since the early 1970's (from around 20 per year, if the figure can be believed), high murder rates in São Luís are nothing new. In 1822, for example, 31 persons (21 freemen and 10 slaves) were convicted of murder in a city a tiny fraction of its present size (*OC*, January 22 and 25, 1823). An 1853 article gives a figure of 64 murders in 1850, 40 in the first semester of 1851, and 80 "known to the police" between June 1851 and November 1853 (*OE*, November 24, 1853).

This is why they can understand, if not condone, the violent behavior of others. An unsettling corollary of this cultural scheme is a worry, not necessarily conscious, that one's own ability to navigate dangerous situations is unreliable—an apprehension that, I argue, paradoxically motivates both Carnivals and brigas.

The somewhat insistent claim that Brazilian social relations are especially peaceful—a claim most notably associated with Gilberto Freyre, but one that has the status of a popular myth—I therefore find surprising and unconvincing. This is not to deny that there is more than a grain of truth in the common Brazilian self-image of the homem cordial, the cordial man. This phrase, picked up from Ribeiro Couto and made famous by the historian Sérgio Buarque de Holanda,[6] refers to a certain intimacy in face-to-face relations. Writes Buarque de Holanda:

> Sincerity in personal dealings, hospitality, generosity, virtues so highly praised by foreigners who visit us, represent, in effect, a definite feature of the Brazilian character, to the extent at least that the ancient influence of patterns of human sociability arising in the rural and patriarchal milieu remains active and fertile. (Holanda 1982 [1936]: 106–7)

Buarque takes care to distinguish cordiality from mere politeness or civility —"a species of deliberate mimicry of actions that are spontaneous in the 'cordial man'" (p. 207). Buarque was writing over half a century ago, but generosity, hospitality, and personal warmth remain, in my judgment, notable features of relationships with and among Brazilians. On the whole, the claim of cordiality does have certain behavioral correlates.

It is sometimes forgotten, however, that Buarque uses the word "cordial" to mean "from the heart." Hence he also distinguishes cordiality from kindness or goodness (*bondade*): "Enmity can well be just as cordial as friendship, since both are born in the heart [*coração*] and thus issue from the sphere of the intimate, the familial, the private" (p. 107). As the historian pointed out in an open letter (first published in 1948) to Cassiano Ricardo, a defender of the notion that "goodness" was the chief sentiment of Brazilians, "I have to add that I don't much believe in this so-called fundamental goodness of Brazilians either. I don't expect that we are better, or worse, than other peoples" (p. 145).

The confusion between intimacy and peacefulness that seems to dog the discussion of Brazilian cordiality tends to obscure vast regions of experience familiar to all Brazilians, which are characterized by contentiousness,

---

[6]The distinguished historian's son is Francisco Buarque de Holanda, the songwriter and playwright Chico Buarque.

extreme violence, and sometimes brutality. Euclides da Cunha's phantas-magoria of carnage in the Bahian backlands is perhaps the most vivid lit-erary representation of such violence, but são-luisenses sometimes told me stories that were, in their immediacy, equally hair-raising, some of which I will reproduce in Part III. Thus I remember listening more than once in a state of puzzlement to friends and acquaintances—sometimes the same people who on other occasions had related appalling tales of bloodshed—telling me proudly, "Here in São Luís things are peaceful; we don't have all that fighting that you have over there in your country." All Americans know that the United States is extremely violent by most standards, but São Luís is not a city that could be called peaceful except in relation to one of the world's great murder capitals such as Washington, D.C., or São Paulo (or the crime-ridden Metropolises of the American police dramas that parade across Brazilian TV screens). In short, the allegation of Brazilian pacifism is a comfortable half-truth stretched so thin as to resemble denial: it sig-nals, I think, in part an underlying anxiety over the violence that everybody knows is epidemic.

Denial is one way to cope with anxiety; ritual is another. If são-luisenses are especially anxious about the violence in their society and in themselves, Carnival, with its annual testing of self-control under circumstances that ostensibly liberate the impulses, might serve exactly this purpose of self-reassurance. A "good" Carnival—one that is animated, expansive, and ex-citing but minimally violent—delivers the message that the danger at the heart of both person and collectivity can still be held in check. Is this why cases of and statistics on violence are so minutely examined and analyzed after each Carnival?

Be all this as it may, we can hardly escape the conclusion that, in the cultural scheme thrown into relief by Carnival, harmonious interpersonal relations depend on holding the line that separates aggressive emotions from violent behavior. Carnival liberates dangerous passions in a tenuously controlled outburst of song, dance, and play. In going to the brink, Car-nival challenges people to undertake what it would seem to define as the supremely human task—the willful donning of the mask of hope and soli-darity in defiance of their own desperate plight and quarrelsome nature.

PART III

BRIGA

There's a corpse on the ground over there
Instead of a face, the photo of a goal
Instead of a prayer, someone's curse
And silence serving as "amen"

Soon the bar next door filled up
With scoundrels and workers
A man got up on a table
And made a campaign speech

Peddlers sold rings, neckchains and cheap perfume
Baianas cooked pastries and some good barbecued cat
At 4 a.m. a spirit came down in the flag-bearer
Everyone called it quits, and then—

Slowly each went his own way
Thinking of a woman or his favorite team
I looked at the corpse on the ground
And closed my window to the crime

—From the song "De frente pro crime"
(Facing the crime),
by João Bosco and Aldir Blanc

6

PRELIMINARIES

The Way into Briga

The examination in Part II of Carnival's dynamics, ideology, and conceptual structure revealed its behavioral and cognitive links with briga. The route to briga runs through a passageway where carnivalesque agonistic display becomes provocation. This is (to change the metaphor) the point of vulnerability in Carnival's frame, for Carnival's original impulse, the need and desire to desabafar, to "unsmother" disagreeable and often hostile feelings, must itself be smothered if the festival is to survive.

Part III looks at what happens when desabafo goes bad—when aggression intrudes upon, and then comes to dominate, face-to-face encounters. My focus shifts here to briga itself. Brigas do not lend themselves to field observation because they rarely draw attention until the antagonists are actually fighting. The origins of the fight are typically subtle and hidden from public view: the most interesting part of the interaction is invisible. And in any case, these origins (as well as later developments) are for the most part subjective: provocations are in the eye of the beholder.

During a briga, each antagonist reads and encodes her or his actions according to the set of related ideas that constitutes the briga scenario. Briga-as-event is an interactional product of particular individuals sharing a set of understandings, a "language" of briga. Before I discuss an actual briga, my project in Chapter 10, I must first lay out in detail this constellation of shared understandings that make up the briga scenario.

I take up where Carnival leaves off, with the invitation to fight. Brigas do not begin out of the blue, with a sudden physical attack by one person on another. Two people cannot fight until they have gone through certain ritualized preliminaries, which then "permit"—the word são-luisenses use—one to attack the other.

The first step down the road to briga, according to são-luisenses, is a provocation. The major exception to this rule occurs when the relationship between the two antagonists is one of *rixa*, that is, of enmity or feud. A rixa, however, is almost inevitably the result of a previous briga, or series of brigas, and hence if we trace a rixa back to first cause we encounter a provocation. Some say that brigas occasionally begin as a result of a *besteira*, an act of foolishness or stupidity, or by accident. But one person's besteira or accident is another's provocation: the person on the receiving end of an unintentionally aggressive act may well view it as an offense.

Provocations are moral constructs, in that they are "bad" and merit, or at least understandably elicit, retribution. A provocation is a violation of one's integrity, an infringement on the subjectively experienced rightful boundaries of the person. A. Irving Hallowell argues that in any society, a

> positive evaluation of the self represents the keystone of the
> characteristic motivational structure that we find in man. . . .
> Motivations that are related to the needs of the self as an
> object of primary value in its behavioral environment are not
> in the same category as the needs of animals whose behavior
> is motivated in a psychological field in which any form of
> self-reference is lacking. (1988 [1954]: 102)

The nature of the self and its needs are in large part culturally variable, but everywhere these needs include self-defense and self-respect, corollaries of a "positive evaluation of the self." In São Luís, where capricious demands are daily fare, self-respect depends crucially on one's ability and will to defend oneself. Because personal efficacy is often at risk, an outstanding feature of the são-luisense self is the heightened attention given to protecting its frontiers. A provocation strikes at the very core of são-luisense self-respect: it attacks the self. People describe the effect of being provoked as a feeling of being "invaded," "challenged," "violated." The Ojibwa self, says Hallowell, is endangered by sorcery; the são-luisense self is vulnerable to different culturally specific incursions—to various forms of invasive humiliation (*humilhação*), symbolic nullifications that trespass the borders of the self to assault one's fundamental dignity.

Such violations are, of course, subjective phenomena, and são-luisense cultural guidelines do not always provide unambiguous interpretations of real-world actions. (The boy's response to the drunk at the bus stop is a striking example.) Moreover, sometimes a provocative act is calculatedly equivocal. Was it or was it not a provocation? If I ignore it, has he won? If I respond, will he deny it? If he denies it, is this a lie enabling him to get away with it?[1] So to say that a briga begins with a provocation is to give a slightly misleading air of concreteness to a deed whose meaning may be far from self-evident.

Nevertheless, provocations always appear in briga stories, and my primary focus here is briga-as-construct rather than briga-as-event. That these stories might not correspond to any real event—that we are living in the world of Rashomon[2]—is, for present purposes, beside the point: I am concerned instead with the logic of the sequences they recount. And whatever the reality, these narratives seem organized around a common conceptual model (a scenario) of briga.

One element of this model is the dilemma faced by the person who is provoked: whether or not to "connect" with the provocation. To connect means to acknowledge the provocation in some fashion, thereby confirming the briga frame and risking a violent confrontation. Not connecting (*não ligar*) means ignoring the affront, thereby (in all probability) avoiding a briga but accepting the intrusion of an unanswered provocation.

A briga unfolds in the region between its subjective beginnings (the provocation and connection) and a hypothetical end point (a killing). Death shadows a briga almost from the beginning. The drama grows out of the uncertainty about how the escalating aggressive exchange will end: as the briga progresses, the exits available to the antagonists rapidly shut down; the stakes, moral and physical, rise; and everyone comes face-to-face with the growing possibility that a bloody spectacle will be staged in the street.

Although brigas do sometimes result in murder, usually confrontations fizzle out early on, before they receive any public attention, much less come to blows. Because of their public invisibility and inconsequence, these might look like nonevents—until one realizes that precisely because such incidents may escalate disastrously, because they mark the beginning of the

---

[1] An intentionally ambiguous provocation is a subtle variety of *sacanagem* (see Chapter 7): its very prevarication is an aggression, an invasion of the self, for it forces the person who is provoked to play the provoker's game. Perhaps Stoller (1978: 33) is hinting at something like this when he says, with respect to Songrai ritual insults, "ambiguity [can] precipitate offensiveness just as easily as nonoffensiveness."

[2] Akira Kurosawa's well-known film, which highlights the ambiguity of human events by presenting narratives of a rape and murder from multiple, conflicting perspectives, was inspired by Ryunosuke Akutagawa's two short stories "Rashomon" and "In a Grove" (1959 [1922]).

road to briga, they tend to be negotiated with great care. Far from being nonevents, they are often emotional and tensely calculated exchanges. It is by passing through the provocation and connection, then, that the situation gets redefined (i.e., reframed) from "drinking in a bar," "walking through the praça," "Carnival," or whatever, to "briga."

Anonymous Confrontations

Anonymous confrontations highlight the dynamics of aborted brigas. This is because the fundamental barrier to a briga involving strangers is the delicate problem of making initial contact and agreeing to fight—the dance of provocation and connection. In other words, the provocation and the dilemma it creates are mandatory elements of anonymous confrontations, which is not the case with personal confrontations between those who have a preexisting relationship of enmity.

Encounters with strangers are central experiences of what the great theorists of the city (see especially Simmel 1950 [1902–3], Wirth 1938) have considered the "urban way of life,"[3] a mode that is impersonal and, to a greater or lesser extent, alienating. Anonymity is the blessing and curse of the city. Intimate face-to-face relationships are of prime importance to the city dweller, just as they are to the man or woman of the village, but the city, unlike the village, routinely brings people into contact who have never met before. Such a meeting may be pleasant or unpleasant, prosaic or exciting; it may be a transient incident or it may give rise to an ongoing relationship. Anonymous encounters are wild-card events that provide much of the spice and the danger of city life.

A hostile encounter with a stranger is for most urban residents, in Brazil as elsewhere, one of the most nightmarish surprises that the modern city has to offer. Aside from illuminating the preliminary stages of briga, anonymous confrontations are intrinsically compelling urban events. They are examples of what Marshall Berman (1982: 148) calls "primal modern scenes," urban experiences that "carry a mythic resonance and depth that propel them beyond their place and time and transform them into archetypes of modern life." In focusing on anonymous confrontations, we are therefore examining briga at its most elemental and, in the modern world, most distinctively urban.

[3]This purportedly universal "urban way of life," an atomized, impersonal existence, is a caricature that at best applies in a limited way to some modern European and American cities. Cities in other historical periods or in other sociocultural settings do not reliably exhibit the atomistic features highlighted by members of the Chicago School (Wirth, Park, Redfield) and their European predecessors (Simmel and Spengler). São Luís is in many respects a "personal" city: most people have a considerable network of enduring, strong relationships with kin and others. Nevertheless, living in São Luís does have an anonymous, impersonal side.

To Connect or To Not Connect?

Of all my informants, Tito, a 22-year-old native são-luisense, was best able to capture in words the nature of anonymous confrontations, fugitive events of Goffmanian subtlety.[4] His account of an anonymous confrontation at a bus stop in central São Luís, which I briefly presented in Chapter 4, revolves around the issue of connecting, that is, acknowledging a provocation.[5] Tito's comments clearly display how perceptions, assumptions, emotions, and reasoning come together in a coherent understanding of how brigas begin and what is at stake when two strangers embark on a potentially violent confrontation. At the time, around midnight on a Saturday, I was accompanying Tito as he waited for a bus to his home in an outlying bairro.

A DRUNK MAKES A DESABAFO AT THE BUS STOP

Tito

It's really hard to tell or describe something that you see so often, it's because you were born observing this kind of thing. Not briga, not exactly briga, but things that happen all the time. I could see that [there was] a [young] couple, the guy was sitting down [on the sidewalk]. [After I had been waiting there] ten or fifteen minutes, a man who was drunk came walking [up from the central market], maybe high not only on alcohol but also on marijuana. He looked like a stevedore or fisherman, and generally stevedores and fishermen use marijuana to get them through their work and in their

---

[4]In this chapter I rely heavily on Tito, a young man with a remarkable ability to clarify the twists and turns of these elusive situations poised on the edge of briga. Although Tito is an exceptionally careful observer of human behavior, others make similar interpretations and show similar preoccupations and emotional responses. Tito is in some ways more reflective and complex, but his alertness is culturally appropriate, marked by acuity, not deviance. I think that his introspective lucidity was honed in the course of our interviews and conversations, which occupied scores of hours during the year and a half or so that I knew him. I believe he manages to articulate what others often feel and think but are not able to state in so many words. By spotlighting an individual in this way, we gain a sense of the overall texture and pattern of his thought—how the concepts fit together for him. Collecting scraps of thought (as reflected in speech and other behavior) from different people gives a broad base to one's conclusions but leaves one open to the suspicion of having stitched together an invented pattern from remnants. I admit to having done both in this study—focusing on a single articulate person (Tito) and collecting scraps of various sizes from many others. This could, I imagine, draw fire from two directions, but my intention was to cross-check my inferences. I believe the evidence converges to suggest that Tito's interpretation of briga is, in its main outlines, a widely shared cultural model.

[5]Tito's account is consistent with my independently recorded field notes of the event.

free time too. So this man arrived at the bus stop, drunk, drugged, and with serious emotional problems. I noticed a very great resentment [*revolta*] in him, looking for the first person he could find so that he could obtain relief [*para se aliviar*]. [When he got to the bus stop he halted and] he gave a desabafo that was also a provocation, saying, "I'm really stoned" [*Eu estou muito xilado*]. This provocation wasn't directed at anybody in particular but at everybody who was there. This gave him a certain aggressive satisfaction. Well, the young guy [sitting on the sidewalk] had taken the thing as a brincadeira, or maybe he was happy that somebody, maybe like himself, was drunk or high on marijuana, and he repeated the same word [saying, "Stoned, huh?"]. The man got furious [*revoltado*], maybe not exactly for this reason, so he kicked the guy's leg and made some threats, even threatening to pull a nonexistent revolver.

And after some arguing [*discussões*], almost without participation by the boy, a guard from a [nearby] building came over and, perhaps because he in some way coerced the drunk, the drunk ended up moving away right after this, and absolutely nothing else happened . . . at least during the part I saw.

[When the thing started, I urged us to move away] because I didn't really know if it would be a large-scale briga. It could have been a serious briga, with stones, knives, and anything else. Maybe not on the part of the boy but on the part of the man, who was drunk. Based on so many crimes that you see in day-to-day life, I think the best thing is . . . is to get as far away as possible [he laughs], but afterward I saw that it wasn't going to develop, that it was a controlled briga.

I think it wasn't exactly that the drunk [wanted to fight,] but that his problems [did], the problems that he was having. They were exacting [*cobrando*] a type of, of, of relief, an expelling [*expulsar*] of some kind of problem that was there just then. But even so, you could see that he really didn't want to fight, or at least, he wanted the other one to start so that he would be able to fight. Because you saw that after an aggression he stood just talking [to the boy] and he calmed down a little, that's all. And afterward he provoked the boy again, when the boy didn't really give him the attention he had hoped for. [The boy] blocked the man. He blocked him at the exact moment when he didn't give his opponent the attention he had hoped for. [If the boy had made an aggressive verbal response,] maybe it would have resulted in an aggressive physical reaction, I think so.

[In the beginning, the boy connected, and this was a mistake.] I tell you in all sincerity that the wisest, the most intelligent action is really to not connect. But I [also] tell you with all sincerity [he laughs] that I don't know, the way things are going there's a certain, uh . . . neurotic atmosphere. I really don't know. I really don't know if . . . if I could take a kick from a drunk and not . . . give him five, right? [He laughs.]

Without any doubt whatsoever [the boy did not want to fight].

[Nobody said anything] for the same reasons we didn't. It's the kind of thing, a lot of people have already died like that, almost every day people try to calm down a briga and end up dying. People who are near a briga [often] are struck with a rock, a knife, a shot, these things happen. [If I had told the man to leave the boy alone,] I would have been asking for [*comprando*] a briga, because he really would have let the guy alone [he laughs] and would have turned around with the intention of fighting with me.

[During all this] I was thinking that I really didn't want, really I didn't want there to be a briga. Something about it was bothering me: Why does a man want to lay the responsibility for all his problems on another man who isn't doing anything at all to him? That's really something very disagreeable.

I forgot [about the girl]. She was terrified, and she was also a strong reason why there was no briga, because she was always pleading with her boyfriend, or husband, for it not to happen. [He laughs.] [She was holding on to him while the man was provoking him,] asking the boy to not connect, asking him not to do anything, in sum, asking that there not be a briga.

[I wasn't exactly satisfied with my behavior] because I really wanted to do something, because it was very disagreeable to watch something like that and keep quiet. But it's the kind of

thing where you . . . either keep quiet or else decide to assume
the role of defender. [He laughs.]

The main point of the story is that the boy made an error of judgment
that briefly threatened disaster. Unlike the others at the bus stop, he chose to
respond to the drunk by echoing the final word in the drunk's declaration,
"I'm really stoned." Inadvertently the boy connected with a provocation.
His subsequent behavior, delayed but energetic attempts to not connect
anymore to what the drunk was saying and doing, shows that he had never
had any intention of fighting. We can imagine the boy's discomfort, perhaps
alarm, upon realizing, as the drunk walked over and began kicking his leg,
that he had been unknowingly provoked by, and had heedlessly connected
with, someone looking for a fight.

The notion of being provoked without knowing it sounds a little strange.
It is less mysterious if we recognize that a provocation, although it refers
to a prodding, an inflammation of an adversary's inner state, is subjectively
defined. In Tito's story there was, on the boy's part, a subjective reconstruction of the meaning of the drunk's desabafo, which converted the act in
retrospect from an innocuous venting to a provocation. The reconstruction
amounts to a frame switch. For that matter, the boy must have reconstructed
his own behavior (repeating the drunk's comment) as well, recognizing
suddenly that it had signified connection. The drunk in effect managed to
impose his own definition of these behaviors on the boy by walking over
and kicking him, a metamessage instructing the boy how to interpret what
had gone before—informing him rudely that the frame for their interaction
was now briga.

The boy's subsequent lack of resistance was an effort to escape this definition, to break the frame. To Tito it was obvious that the drunk was seeking a
pretext; the boy needed to disqualify even that by a radical refusal to connect
further, by an act of self-abasement. Here we can guess that the audience was
important: everyone understood who was in the wrong and that the boy
was refusing to collaborate in the reframing of the interaction. His abject
passivity undermined the drunk's pretext.

This incident suggests the difficulty of backtracking once a connection
has been made. Not connecting, except in unusual cases (a pathologically
aggressive provoker or provocation by a gang, for instance), is considered
excellent protection against physical aggression because it rejects the momentary alliance usually required to erect the briga frame; conversely, connecting—accepting the invitation to fight—opens the door to violence.
Shutting it is difficult: here it took the boy's determined refusal to respond
to insults, aggressions, and even lethal threats, as well as the girl's intervention (she restrained the boy with an embrace and positioned herself between
him and the drunk), to forestall a violent exchange.

The most common response to a provocation in São Luís is probably to do nothing, to give no indication of having seen, heard, or felt anything— as people say, "I'm not even there" (*Não estou nem aí*). We can understand why the boy originally connected—an error of judgment—but why, if not connecting offers such good protection, should anyone consciously and willingly connect?

Provocation's Dilemma

Occasionally in São Luís two boys who are angry with each other nevertheless feel reluctant or afraid to fight. A third boy, who has been observing their argument, comes up to them and draws a line in the dirt with his foot, saying, "Whoever rubs out this line is rubbing out the other one's mother."[6] Almost inevitably one of the two does so, an act followed by a punch from his adversary, and the briga begins.

Although this is a special (but culturally recognized) instance of provocation, in that a third party (the diabolical figure conventionally known as a *pivô*) sets it up, providing the spark that ignites the briga, it shows that an effective provocation is essentially a challenge. That the reference is to the boy's mother, and that if the boy does not respond to the provocation the other will claim to be his "father" with the right to order him around, may indicate that some of the force of the challenge has Oedipal roots. But the line in the dust is more than a symbol of the mother. It represents the boy's integrity, his honor or sense of dignity; rubbing it out is a symbolic erasure of the person himself, a humiliation that, if let stand, can symbolize an encompassing claim of domination. To be humiliated in São Luís is to be reduced to a nullity, through domination or disregard. If unchallenged, the humiliation is redoubled owing to the provoker's impunity, the victim's acquiescence a confirmation of the aggressor's claim to command.

In its essence, then, a provocation is not about mothers or manhood or any of the symbolic devices it uses to, as Tito puts it, "drag you from a stable to an unstable [state]." A provocation tests your will and power to defend yourself against another's infringement, to refute another's declaration, through word or act, of your insignificance. The outcome defines the dyadic relationship, as measured along a vertical axis of power, between you

---

[6]This ritualized challenge is weakly reminiscent of "sounding," also called "playing the dozens," described by Roger Abrahams (1964). "Signifying" (1964: 212–13) also has a Brazilian analog in the actions of the *pivô*, one who instigates a briga. In São Luís, as in the ghetto, this is reprehensible behavior. But Abrahams's analysis, which emphasizes the problems faced by black American males growing up in matrifocal families, would not seem to apply to the Brazilian case, where social and cultural factors differ so markedly, except in one important respect: the phenomenon appears most often in São Luís, as in South Philadelphia, among those who reside in the social basement.

and your provoker. A provocation pushes you to the point that violence is your only means of self-defense. Otherwise, you must accept your submissive position, whether to a playmate who will thereby become your new "father," to a stranger who bumps into you roughly on a bus, or, perhaps, to a boss who has just fired you.[7]

Sometimes humiliation is explicitly linked to an assault on one's virility. But women too experience infringement on the self or symbolic nullification as humiliating, so sensitivity to humiliation cannot be thought of as merely an aspect of *machismo*.[8] The reverse may be closer to the truth: that for some of the symbolically nullified men at the bottom of this hierarchical society, machismo becomes the debased coin in which power or efficacy can be negotiated. A man infatuated with machismo, a *machão*, can defend his deformed version of honor or integrity by brute force, a resource accessible in some measure to all. Personal force becomes his illusionary measure of power; slights to his masculinity become symbolic of his daily diet of indignities. Hence the cult of machismo and socially generated symbolic nullification feed off each other.

Brazilian gender constructions and categories of sexual practices clearly manifest this symbolic link between power and masculinity. As Peter Fry (1985) and Richard Parker (1987, 1991) have pointed out, Brazilians identify activity and command with the masculine, passivity and compliance with the feminine. The active sexual partner "eats" (*come*); the passive one "gives" (*dá*):

> *Comer* describes the act of penetration during sexual intercourse. Used in a variety of contexts as a synonym for verbs such as *vencer* (to conquer, vanquish) and *possuir* (to possess, own), it clearly implies a form of symbolic domination, as played out through sexual practice. In contrast, *dar* describes the role of being penetrated in either vaginal or anal intercourse. Just as *comer* suggests an act of domination, *dar* implies some form of submission or subjugation. (Parker 1987: 160–61)

A man (*homem*) is a biological male who "eats." Someone who "gives" can be either a biological female (*mulher*) or a biological male (known most com-

[7]Although cross-class brigas are not common, certain situations are especially volatile. In firing an employee, for example, a boss becomes a "bad *patrão*": this can lead to trouble. A sensational case of this type was the murder of John Harold Kennedy. See p. 22, n. 4. The attack on São Luís's city hall by fired municipal employees in January 1986 fits the same pattern.

[8]I did not, regrettably, delve deeply into how a similar concern with frontiers of the self gets culturally elaborated among women, a topic that would be a fascinating area for further study.

monly as a *bicha*, worm, intestinal parasite, female animal) who takes the passive role during intercourse. A biological male who penetrates a bicha during intercourse remains essentially a man: he does not thereby become a bicha. This is not, in other words, a homosexual interaction. The English-language category "homosexual" has a Brazilian equivalent in the medical model of sexual classification adopted in Brazil around the turn of the century; "gay" has an equivalent among middle-class southern Brazilians involved in or influenced by the gay liberation movement; but the opposition homosexual/heterosexual is not particularly salient for most Brazilians. Essentially, maleness is identified with activity, penetration, domination: no wonder then that hyper-manliness, machismo, becomes a mode of expressing personal power and that the machão reacts violently when "invaded" by a provocation.

Not many men in São Luís, however, are machões, and commonly both men and women view the hair-trigger readiness to fight, the sexual bravado, and the hypersensitivity to insult that characterize machismo as foolish and even ridiculous. Nevertheless, most find it difficult to ignore the issue of power raised by provocations. They tend to view the situation not with the aggressive arrogance of the machão, but with ambivalence, for they seem strongly pulled in different directions.

The following story, recounted by Tito, involves perhaps the simplest form of provocation—the accidental-on-purpose physical infringement—and it occurs in a quintessentially anonymous public space, a city bus. The incident is a paradigmatic anonymous confrontation that reveals some of the fundamental inner workings of these events. In this case, unlike the young man at the bus stop who connected by accident, Tito perceives that he is being provoked and deliberately connects with his antagonist. Nevertheless, he wants to avoid briga, and his connection is designed to terminate the confrontation immediately.

GETTING SHOVED WHILE RIDING THE BUS

an interview with Tito

T: [It happened] on the bus, I think it wasn't really a provocation on his part directed at me, exactly, maybe he must have been annoyed at something and he passed by me in the bus in quite a violent way, and he pushed me in a manner I didn't like and I looked into his face and asked him what it was that he wanted. He lowered his head. I looked at him from head to foot with a traditional look [that I have]. I think people get scared when I look at them like that. I remember that he was a guy a lot older than me, and much stronger and much bigger than me, but I noticed that he was afraid, maybe it wasn't fear of my physical type, but, I don't know, a way that I have learned to look at people to instill a certain terror in them [he laughs].

DL: What did he do [then]?

T: He fell silent and lowered his head. He didn't apologize, but it was really a posture of apologizing.

DL: And so with this posture he denied having provoked you?

T: That's right, yes, yes. [But] when I gave him that kind of look, I was already thinking about some way to escape, right? I would have to escape, I couldn't create that kind of scandal on a bus.

DL: But then why did you look at him like that?

T: Exactly not to demonstrate weakness, because if you show strength and very great security, it's easier to make the other person renounce [*renunciar*]. It's a weapon that I used. So it was the kind of thing, a kind of weapon of self-protection, knowing how to look at somebody and how to confront that type of case. [But this wasn't a case] in which I could see that I would really run the risk of losing my life, in those cases no, in those cases I simply renounce, completely ignore the thing.

DL: But then why not simply not connect with this incident on the bus?

T: Not connect? Ah, I've got my problems too, I've got my annoyances, my frustrations clash with other people. I'm there mad as hell [*puto da vida*], he arrives there mad as hell too, [thinking,] "Look at that clean back," and gives an elbow.

DL: Would it be better to not connect?

T: It's really hard to not connect, it's really hard to not connect because your heart is about to explode from the desire to give so many punches [he laughs]. So self-control is necessary; also, I can't stand brigas, I don't like brigas.

DL: But you connected, you gave him a really evil look.

T: It's like I told you, the look is a way to intimidate the enemy, it's self-protection and a message of firmness and sureness that I give him, showing my willingness to do anything, go to any lengths, let the blood run as much as it will, but I'm here. It's clear that it's false but it's [he laughs] self-protection that works and has already worked a number of times. I have to do this kind of thing because in reality, well, it's my willingness to fight, right, but also to . . . of nonviolence, to not seek violence and also fear of running the risk of losing my life. It's looking for a way out in which I get out without any kind of degradation or humiliation.

DL: If he wanted to continue, what would he have done?

T: I think he would respond, he would insult me.

DL: And then you . . .

T: Well, I, that's the problem, isn't it, I would have to insult him, [and] it could stay in that business: he insults me, I insult him, I insult him, he insults me, and one of us waiting for a stronger attitude on the part of the other or else one waiting for an attitude of renunciation of the other. But I know very well what kind of person I can do this kind of thing with, I don't do this with just anybody.

DL: So he indicated by his attitude that he didn't want to continue and even that he was renouncing.

T: He even left me in a very high position, because he was afraid.

DL: He was humiliated?

T: Yes, [but] just between the two of us . . . between the two of us because the thing, even on the bus, wasn't public. I spoke in a low voice, near him, nobody heard, he heard and I looked at him. Ah! Another thing is that if the thing becomes public it can get much worse, because then it isn't just between us two, then you've got the *obligation* [his emphasis] to give some satisfaction to the people who are there watching.

DL: [So] you tried to limit [the situation]?

T: Exactly, it was a tactic, I tried to limit it, to come out the winner but through ability and not by force, because even he would have a lot of work to beat me up even though he was big, he would end up really hurt too but he would beat me up easily, no, not easily, he would beat me up but only after getting really hurt himself.

DL: So if the thing becomes public or if he runs the risk of being publicly humiliated, that isn't acceptable?

T: No, that's very, very difficult to accept that kind of thing, it's the kind of thing where you get home and can't manage to sleep right. In a way, I think he didn't exactly want to [provoke me], but did it because of an impulse. Well, the person who's affected doesn't care whether it was an impulse or whether it was something premeditated.

Tito's plight is clear in his stated objective, to "get out without any kind of degradation or humiliation." Owing to his own turbulent inner state, he cannot overlook the elbow thrown, whether maliciously or not, by the other passenger, but he recognizes that connecting poses physical and moral dangers.[9]

This is the devilish and inescapable dilemma set up by a provocation. You can "renounce" (*renunciar*) the confrontation, thereby avoiding briga, but then you must swallow the dose of humiliation that comes with not connecting (or infinitely worse, connecting and then deciding to back out). Alternatively, you can "accept" (*aceitar*) the provocation by connecting, thereby defending the self ("I'm here" is Tito's message), but as a consequence risking an unpredictable, potentially disastrous, and morally reprehensible slide into briga.

Tito's solution was a form of brinkmanship. Although the provocation was ambiguous, Tito fell victim to his emotional state ("I've got my problems too"), as his aggressive connection demonstrated. His consciously menacing gaze put the other on notice that Tito saw his adversary's act as provocative—whether this was the other's intention or not—and that they were now engaged in the briga sequence, with Tito ready to go in deeper ("let the blood run as much as it will").

Tito's gaze, a metacommunication, is reminiscent of the drunk's kicking the boy's leg at the bus stop: both actions warn the adversary that his actions have been interpreted as part of the briga sequence. The aim in this case was to avoid violence, for underneath the gesture Tito was apprehensive. By threatening a disproportionate, irrational, violent response, Tito frightened his adversary into submissive behavior designed to break the frame immediately. (One is reminded here of MAD, the mutual assured destruction strategy of nuclear deterrence.)

Two major factors account for Tito's aggressive stance in the bus episode. Tito boarded the bus in a foul mood ("I've got my problems too. . . . I'm there mad as hell"), ready to expel his frustrations should an appropriate provocation (pretext?) occur. And he immediately sized up the man in the bus as not posing a mortal threat: this was not a situation "in which I

[9]Unless one belongs to a very restricted subculture in which machismo is really worshiped, the best solutions to physical confrontations are nonviolent: exits in which you use your wits or in which a lightning bolt of good fortune removes the enemy from the scene, breaks up the fight, or allows escape.

could see that I would really run the risk of losing my life, in those cases no, in those cases I simply renounce, completely ignore the thing," swallowing the humiliation and keeping life and limb intact, as the boy did when confronted by the drunk at the bus stop. In this case, Tito's strategy of deterrence produced a victory: he suffered no humiliation, no violence.

If Tito's narrative is a reasonably accurate description of an actual event, it seems unlikely that anyone but those directly involved was aware of the confrontation. The emotions and calculations involved in such seemingly trivial incidents are amazingly complex. Tito reveals various, sometimes conflicting, goals, emotions, and preoccupations that guided his behavior. When the man pushed past him, Tito construed this act as a provocation both because of his knowledge about what may constitute a provocation in an anonymous encounter ("accidental" shoves, foot-stompings, elbows, and the like) and because of his emotional state, which he admits colored his interpretation of an act that may have been, if not exactly benign, more of a desabafo than a provocation. Similarly, Tito's intimidating response grew out of his angry mood and threatened the adversary with a violent loss of self-control on Tito's part ("let the blood run as much as it will") but was tempered with a caution that seems remarkably calculated, although it was based on fear of injury, fear of shame, and perhaps pangs of conscience. The gaze was menacing, but "when I gave him that kind of look, I was already thinking about some way to escape, right? I would have to escape, I couldn't create that kind of scandal on a bus."

Indeed, Tito took a crucial measure to give his adversary a way out and therefore to reduce the possibility of escalation: he spoke in a low voice to prevent others from hearing. For if the encounter were to become public, "you've got the *obligation* to give some satisfaction to the people who are there watching." In private one can swallow a little humiliation, but to be seen doing so, or to be known to have done so, is intolerable. Tito's adversary's renunciation, by way of a signaled apology, permitted termination of an event that otherwise could have escalated to verbal insults and then possibly to blows. Insults and blows are almost necessarily public acts, and hence escalation to these stages implies not a stepwise increase in the difficulty of retreat from the event but a quantum leap.

These incidents suggest that são-luisenses see anonymous confrontations as arising from directed desabafos in which one individual provokes another in a more or less ambiguous manner, presenting the person who is provoked with the highly unpleasant dilemma of either refusing the encounter (ignoring the provocation by not connecting) and suffering a degree of humiliation or else acknowledging the provocation (connecting) and risking briga. In the decision to connect or not, both emotional factors and reason profoundly influence the individual's course of action.

Tito's presence of mind in these uncomfortable and unpredictable situations, at least as he replayed them verbally, was remarkable, as was his anticipation of possible hazards. His ability to calculate dangers and steer his way around them indicates that there is a model that he knows quite well. But part of his, and others', understanding of briga consists of the conditions under which safe navigation becomes difficult or impossible and the person loses control of the situation. Control fails when psychological equilibrium vanishes. Not everyone, Tito included, can always harness or successfully manage the vengeful feelings aroused by a provocation, regardless of the known possible consequences of releasing them. These feelings can be overwhelming, erupting in a powerful, involuntary desabafo that makes retreat from briga impossible.

The Basic Stuff of Brigas

Connection as Desabafo

A provocation is a malign desabafo directed at a human target rather than, as is normal and healthful, vented (in Joana's words) "into space." Provocations relieve psychological pressure through aggression and are therefore condemned. But connection, too, is a sort of desabafo, one that often has a dangerously self-righteous cast. This is not because connecting is something good—it is not—but because it is emotionally comprehensible and thus viewed (with reservations) as justifiable. As a desabafo that responds to the reprehensible actions of another, it has a quasi-legitimacy that provocation lacks.

A connection can sometimes trigger a briga by redefining an innocent act as a provocation, thereby freeing the connector (in reality, the provoker) of the moral onus of having initiated a briga sequence.[10] In the following passage, Tito describes an imaginary incident in which a desabafo-connection has exactly this intent.

JOÃO ACCUSES PEDRO OF HAVING PROVOKED HIM

Tito

Let's say, João goes out, he had a fight with his wife, or he fought with his mother, or his father. He lost his job last week and he's up to here in debts. He's really very annoyed, very angry, not on the surface, but inside he's very hurt. All

---

[10]I sometimes got the impression that the storyteller distorted events so as to portray his own provocation as a connection. This would be, of course, the more acceptable public stance. But it seems to me that this is also a necessary self-deception: people intent on fighting often engineer provocations to enable them to attack.

right, and here comes Pedro, who accidentally steps on his
foot. And he says, "Don't you look where you're going, you
idiot?" Pedro says something like, "Look, I didn't really mean
to do it." And so [João] starts to insult him, and insult him,
and Pedro also starts to get really angry, and afterward a big
argument begins and [now that] both moods [*temperamentos*]
are altered [*alterados*] a briga begins.

In this hypothetical example, João leaves home looking for a pretext to
fight. His connection, hardly an error of judgment, is a malign desabafo, an
effort to find a way into a briga. Briga, in this case, is João's way of expelling
his frustrations. This is the same motive ("I noticed a very great resentment
in him, looking for the first person he could find so that he could obtain
relief") that Tito attributed to the drunk for his aggressive provocation at
the bus stop. In the end, because the moods of both men eventually become "altered" (i.e., out of control: the interaction becomes what Bateson
[1972b (1935)] would call "schismogenic") through the exchange of insults,
they find themselves in the cycle of vengeance that is briga.

A connection, like a provocation, can therefore be a perverse, highly
problematic desabafo. People generally seem to feel that responding aggressively to a provocation is illegitimate and inadvisable; they connect with
provocations in spite of a reluctance to do so rather than out of a desire to
find a pretext to fight. For são-luisenses, wisdom and conscience dictate not
connecting, but people also accept in a matter-of-fact way that an emotional
explosion may drive one to respond anyway.

Tito puts it succinctly:

It's not good to respond to a provocation. I think this opinion is unanimous. The problem is that there is a necessity
to respond to a provocation, an *organic* [his emphasis] necessity, because you feel the thing deep down, you feel a kind
of fury, your heart speeds up and your teeth clamp together
and your hands want vengeance [*vingança*]. That's where self-
control comes in: if you don't have self-control you really
respond to this kind of thing. You really respond. The people
around here are always saying they don't know how to argue
[*discutir*] about things. Why don't they know how to argue?
Because different kinds of emotions take them over, [such
as] an emotion [caused by] the insult that offended you, vengeance, right? and your very desire, your organic necessity to
hit, to throw punches, to crush if necessary, to beat someone

without stopping, without stopping. That's why I say that reacting to a provocation isn't good, but you feel a very strong
necessity.

This "organic necessity" to avenge oneself, a desabafo in the form of a
connection, is revealed clearly in Tito's description of a confrontation that
went to the very edge of briga, involving himself and the conductor of a
city bus. I quote at length because the case in all its particulars underlines the
impulsive, irrational, desabafo-like nature of some connections, which risk
briga to provide psychological relief. In this story, Tito boards a bus with a
false student card—students, upon presenting this card, can pay with a special ticket, which costs only half the normal fare, a concession won during
several days of citywide riots in 1979—and is challenged by the conductor.
His connection with what he interprets as the conductor's provocation is
a desabafo that expels a mountain of frustrations and problems but almost
ends in violence.

TITO IS CHALLENGED BY A BUS CONDUCTOR

Tito

If I paid for all my bus fares I would simply spend more than
half the month at home. A lot of people are using the student ID card, but a false one, and so, sure, I was using this
method. The only thing was that one day my photo fell off
the card, and like a good Brazilian, like a good maranhense,
I never bothered [he laughs] to get another one to put in its
place. I just left it like that. The card was my brother's, [since]
I couldn't prove in any way that I was a student.

One day about four or five months ago, Waldyr and I caught
the bus for the center of town. At that time I had a lot of problems: the problem with Celeste [a girlfriend], the problem
with my grandmother [who had just died], and the problem
with my father [who was in the hospital], and really I was in
a state of nerves such that at any moment I could explode. I
was bearing up under a lot of things, so that I had a very great
tendency to explode at any moment, right, but always controlling myself to avoid something like a suicide [i.e., getting
involved in a potentially lethal situation] or something that
would bring me very disagreeable problems. When we caught
the bus of course we were afraid that the conductor would
ask for Waldyr's student card, because he didn't have one. I

at least had the card with the missing photo. I would always show the back of the card and pass by the conductor [who sits at a counter in the rear of the bus] stone-faced, somewhat cynically, and very serious, and he would never ask for the card, right.

We were in the "kitchen" of the bus [i.e., the area behind the conductor, by the rear door]. Just before arriving at the praça in Monte Castelo [a bairro adjacent to the Center], Waldyr goes up to the turnstile. As he does, the guy asks for Waldyr's card, and Waldyr says, "Oh, rapaz, you know what happened? I was robbed and all my documents were stolen," [he says] with the face of somebody pitiful and wretched who doesn't really want to fight because he [just] wants to go through [the turnstile to the front of the bus], you know, [as if saying,] "For the love of God, let me go through," and that's it, [but] the guy was very crude. He didn't see that side [of Waldyr's performance], I mean, the typical thing is if you go limp or if you cower, like Waldyr cowered, then the other guy very well [can say to himself], Porra, let the guy go by, right, because there's no use fighting with this guy. But the conductor, who maybe had a lot of other shit in his head, started to say to Waldyr that what he said was a lie and so on, treating him crudely, even right when Waldyr was going through the turnstile the conductor grabbed it and rolled it over and it hit Waldyr. All this offended me [*me agrediu*], it offended me too, because the conductor was doing this to the guy, it wasn't right, and on the other hand now it was my turn. He knew that I was with Waldyr, [and] I knew he was going to ask for my student card. How could I show him my card with its missing picture? There were people I knew riding that bus, it would be a terrible shame [he laughs], a terrible shame, how would I explain? How was I going to show my student card that isn't mine and doesn't have a photo? Porra, I saw what things were like, the miserableness of the situation. So I said [to myself], You know something? I'm going to find an excuse to get mad at this guy and the excuse is going to be his having mistreated Waldyr, right. Honestly, though, even if Waldyr was my friend I wasn't going to get mad to the point of inviting a suicide, because the guy was strong, big, I wouldn't have the least chance against him in a briga.

So when I went to pass through the turnstile, since I knew he was going to demand my ID card I took my card and showed him the back of it, without any inhibition. [But] just when I gave him the student ticket and was about to pass through, [he did something] that really wounded me [*me magoou bastante*]. He put his foot up like this, [barring my passage through the turnstile,] as if he was dealing with an animal [*bicho*], right, and after he had already done all that to Waldyr. I thought quickly, No, this isn't right, this is already *sacanagem* [devious, illegitimate behavior], this is an insult. And then [I thought], How am I going to have the nerve [*ter cara*] to show this ID card, when some people who I know are going to be watching? And what kind of situation am I going to be in?

So then I said [to myself], I'm going to let this guy really know what an angry person can be like. And then I really acted the thing out. My theory was the following: to show myself to be as fierce as possible to get him to back down, and to a certain extent it worked. So he said, "Student card." So I looked at him, [and] I said to him: "I'm not going to show it to you." I *couldn't* [his emphasis] show it to him [he laughs]. So he said, "No, without a student card you can't pass." So I say, "But I'm not going to show it to you, if you want to fight, we'll fight, if you want to go to the police, we'll go to the police, if you want to shed blood, we'll shed blood," right, "anything, I'll agree to anything [he laughs] except to showing this student card, because I'm not going to show it to you, in the first place because you humiliated my friend here, you can't do that to anybody." I started to appeal [to the passengers], right, in a certain way it was already sacanagem [on my part].

I think maybe I would know how to get out of it in the same way as Waldyr got out of it, but I was looking for someone to insult me, so I could avenge myself for [all those problems I had,] really I had a terrible disgust [*revolta*] inside me, not knowing, not understanding anything that was happening [in my life]. I was becoming more and more lost, I was just letting time go by and not resolving a fucking thing [*porra nenhuma*].

The conductor was surprised, [not only] by my size but [also] by what I was saying to him. Obviously I didn't really want [to fight him], obviously I was afraid, deeply afraid, but anyway I did what I did. He was kind of shocked [*meio assustado*], [and] he said, "Would you do me the favor of showing me your student card?" He was polite, very polite. This was a kind of blackmail [payment] for the other people who were watching, right. I say, "No, I won't give in" [he laughs], I say [to myself], I'm going to talk really crudely to him because I can't show my card. He said, "No, no" [i.e., "you have to show it"]. So then I altered my voice and got the attention of even the driver. I said, "No, I'm not going to show my card and that's it and I'm going through, it's time for me to get off, I'm going through one way or another, with your foot there or not, I'm going through."

So then he pointed out that traditional sign [they have there in the back of the bus] saying, "Students, please [note that] your ticket can only be accepted with the presentation of your student card" and so on, he pointed to it and said, "Look at what it says here." So [I said,] "What the hell does that bullshit [he laughs] mean [*que que essa porra significa*], what does that bullshit stuck up there mean," I said, "that bullshit stuck up there, I don't know what it means, but it doesn't mean you can shout at people like you're shouting at them," and he said, "No, the one who started shouting [he laughs] was you, you're the one who started shouting."

[And then] I pushed his foot aside and passed through [the turnstile]. So then he said, "The problem with you two is that you're a couple of clowns [he laughs], you don't want to listen to anything and just go passing right through, you don't want to obey anything," [and] I say, "I'd obey you if you knew how to treat people but you come on with that kind of crudity, who do you think you are, you're a, a, a shit!" I said, loud and clear, and then he started to get up a little bit. I was saying a bunch of things all at once. Just then I got really furious. When he got up, I went over there. I don't know, cara, what was in my head. He rose up, an enormous black man

[*um negão enorme*]. . . . He would crush me with two punches.
He got up as if he wanted to react [to what I had said], as if he
wanted to hit me. What was my reaction? I was two meters
away from him, [and] I moved toward him, I went right up
to his face, I went right up to his face and said, "If you came
to hit me, hit me right now, hit me and you'll see something,
you'll get hit too."

And then came the bus stop. I remembered that we were
near the PM box [a post of the military police] and that there
was something [i.e., marijuana] in my pocket, [and] that there
was really not the slightest chance of getting rid of it. So
when the bus came to the stop I said to the driver, "Stop
this thing here, please, I'm going to get off," but always egg-
ing on the guy and the guy insulting me, too. Waldyr stayed
motionless, he didn't say anything, watching the whole business, sitting there terrified, he couldn't figure out what was
going on [with me], and everyone inside the bus kept silent,
serious and praying that no knives would appear, or wanting
knives to appear, I don't know. Just then the bus got to the
Praça Deodoro and I asked the driver to stop. I had gone up
there intending to fight with him, [too,] but he deceived me
because he treated me very well, and the fury I felt toward
him for not doing anything [during the quarrel] I directed
again at the conductor. So I was at the front door, the conductor called me a clown and I also called him a clown, and
the driver said, "My friend, psst! my friend," speaking softly,
"my friend, I've got to get going, I can't wait here [for you
to finish your] fight [he laughs], I've got a schedule to meet."
So then I looked at him [and said], "Sorry, *rapaz*," and got off
the bus.

But just when I got off the bus, the first feeling I had was
that I had been able to say something to somebody. To have
said something to somebody. You repress yourself so much,
you see somebody cut into a line and you have to keep quiet,
somebody cuts into a line in a devious way [*de uma forma
sacana*], cuts in right ahead of you, [and] you have to keep
quiet so you don't get into a *briga*. You see a person provoking you in a bus, you have to keep quiet, because he might be
armed and he might kill you. [But] at that moment [on the

bus, with the conductor] I didn't want to know about any of that, I really vomited, I vomited all those problems that I was having, and when I hopped off the bus I was a very happy guy. I even said to Waldyr, "Rapaz, what a relief I'm feeling [he laughs], from having been able to say all those things, for having said all that. I'm even happier because I didn't hit anyone or get hit myself, but I spoke, discharged [*descarreguei*], kicked, he shouted at me, I shouted twice as loud at him. He asked me to stop, I didn't want to stop: it was when he asked me in the most polite way to show my ID card, and I didn't want to stop." Really, I was feeling very good with that freedom, as if I had thrown off a huge weight from my back, my problems got better and I felt able to resolve them, and also to feel myself able to resolve something, to have shouted out for a right that isn't legally mine but at the bottom is: there's a half-baked rule that you have to follow [i.e., the student fare rule] and [so] you've got to find a way [*dar um jeito*] to get around it to survive. So I said to Waldyr that I was feeling really good, really good, much better, that I could see things better after that desabafo.

Even [during this quarrel] I was controlling myself, I was already looking for ways to escape, to avoid the worst, because my real goal was to expel. Deaths occur, in my view, when you build up a very great anger [*cria uma raiva*], when the conscious or unconscious objective is to expel [but it] goes too far, and you lose control of the briga and really end up killing somebody [even though] your intention wasn't to kill him. I didn't have any weapon with which to kill, I didn't have any power to kill the guy, but he could have killed me. Generally [conductors] go around with weapons, with knives, etc., etc. I was wishing that the Quit-It Gang [*turma do deixa-disso*, persons intervening to separate antagonists during a briga] would appear, I was thinking, Porra, nobody's showing up to end this thing.

I want to emphasize a single crucial point about this passage—Tito's connection with the conductor, after the conductor had provoked him by barring his way, bears all the hallmarks of a desabafo:

1. *Previous accumulation of problems.* Tito remarks on the circumstances that combined to produce his explosive "state of nerves"—problems in his

relationship with a girlfriend, his grandmother's death, his father's hospitalization, his implied financial difficulties, his general feeling of confusion: "I was becoming more and more lost, I was just letting time go by and not resolving a fucking thing."[11] He summarizes: "I was bearing up under a lot of things, so that I had a very great tendency to explode at any moment."

2. *Irrepressible urge to expel these problems.* "I was looking for someone to insult me," says Tito, "so I could avenge myself for [all those problems I had]." Tito was primed for a situation in which he could expel his load of problems. The directed nature of this act, which he describes as one of vengeance, is what distinguishes it most clearly from a simple desabafo.

3. *Lapse of self-control.* Although he takes into account the possible danger of expelling in this way, Tito's need to expel is stronger than his fear: "Obviously I didn't really want [to fight him], obviously I was afraid, deeply afraid, but anyway I did what I did." And again:

> Just then I got really furious. When he got up, I went over there. I don't know, cara, what was in my head. He rose up, an enormous black man. . . . He would crush me with two punches. He got up as if he wanted to react [to what I had said], as if he wanted to hit me. What was my reaction? I was two meters away from him, [and] I moved toward him, I went right up to his face, I went right up to his face and said, "If you came to hit me, hit me right now, hit me and you'll see something, you'll get hit too."

Tito himself seems surprised at his actions here: this is not the same person who responded so deliberately and carefully during the shoving incident. Although this encounter, like the others, never becomes violent, Tito here is teetering on the edge.

4. *Relief.* Tito's description of the relief he felt afterward is graphic. He finally "said something" instead of "keep[ing] quiet," he "vomited" all his problems, and he left the bus a "very happy guy." This is the relief that comes with desabafo, with expelling. The actions Tito celebrates (speaking, shouting) and the images he uses to describe what these actions mean (vomiting, discharging, throwing off a weight) are isomorphic with the notion of casting away an evil or unloosing something oppressive—ideas at the heart of desabafo. Tito himself acts a bit like his mythical João, seeking an outlet for his problems by means of a directed and potentially violent desabafo disguised as a connection.

[11] This disturbing state of motionlessness is a culturally recognized condition sometimes described as being "stopped" (*parado*). To be stopped is to rot or fester spiritually and emotionally, and to be incapable of resolving personal or other problems.

Tito is not unique. Other individuals seem to have similar understandings and sentiments, although they may couch them in slightly different ways. The testimony of Jair, Rubem, and Genival, for example, also displays the notion of the irresistible desabafo-connection: a failure of self-mastery leads to the uncontrollable expulsion of stored-up resentments in response to a provocation, providing relief.

Speaking of a particular briga he was involved in, in which he faced off against a man he describes as a "giant" and apparently came off the worse for it, Jair explains why a provocation is unbearable:

> How could I have avoided this briga? The guy ridicules me, says that he's going to hit me, grabs a piece of wood, I've got to do something, right? Sometimes you can't [ignore these things], there are times when you've got to, you've really got to blow up, because if not you take it home [and] keep thinking about it. Why didn't I [ignore it] and so on? [Because] the guy is going to ridicule me to my face [*debochar da minha cara*], that's it, [and] you'll be stuck with this in your head, so you've got to explode right away, when I'm like this I explode right away, because that way my head will be all right [*legal*], because you've got to have your head free of problems to be able to dream, that's it, because the man who doesn't dream isn't alive.

The notion that a provocation imposes an insufferable burden—"you take it home . . . you'll be stuck with this in your head"—and therefore gives rise to an extraordinary fury, which seeks to cast it off or cast it out, also crops up in the reflections of Rubem, when describing a briga that occurred during a Sunday afternoon pick-up soccer game, a prime setting for arguments and fights. Self-control is the remedy Rubem sees for avoiding brigas (cf. Tito's comments above), but it is not always possible to contain the rage that is inflamed by being put "under something," in Rubem's phrase, through a provocation:

> It's hard not to respond [to a provocation]. I don't know, it's something that wells up from inside, suddenly, like that. I think it's an anger [*exaltação*], I think that people don't like to be under something [*ficar por baixo de uma coisa*], and so the person responds, [and then] begins that blah, blah, blah, and then come punches, kicks, sometimes not, but it's more likely that they come. [In the briga at the soccer game] what annoyed me most was when I bent down to pick up the ball

and he came up to kick me in the face. That angered me inside [*me contrariou lá por dentro*]. [After the briga] I thought I shouldn't [have tripped him up, after the kick,] but I did it. It was all so sudden. . . . You have to control yourself, but it's hard. Not everyone has total control, I certainly don't, some people have a stronger control, they have a stronger head, but meanwhile a lot of things offend you, it's that the person is weak.

Tito's report of catharsis is echoed by Rubem, who describes how he feels after "throwing everything on top of" a provoker, especially if the provocation was particularly offensive:

Sometimes I control myself like crazy but there are times when I blow up. You put up with things [*o sujeito segura uma barra*] every minute, every minute you're bearing up [*segurando aquela barra*], *poxa* [an exclamation], you're irritated every minute, controlling yourself, but irritated as hell, and [if] you [can] expel that stuff [*botar aquilo pra fora*] for at least a few moments, you feel relieved. You were irritated and suddenly someone starts up with you and you throw everything on top of that person. But it's good to do this when you're in the right.

Rubem's statement that "every minute you're bearing up" would seem to refer to that same burden of frustrations, tensions, and anger that motivates the grand communal desabafo that is Carnival. Once again, the evidence points to the same emotional and cognitive origins for both briga and Carnival. In these comments são-luisenses express their anxiety over violence, in particular an anxiety over their *own* propensity to explode, which I suggested might be at the root of Carnival's annual ritualized experimentation with aggression. The problem underscored by both Carnival and briga is the management of the interior world and, by extension, society: how to engineer desabafos that equilibrate rather than devastate.

Living in a "Neurotic Atmosphere"

The overall picture of the world as (at least intermittently) experienced by those quoted here is one of a tense, frustrating life punctuated by explosions, large and small, whether festas, drinking bouts, sexual escapades, or brigas. Tito introduced the phrase "neurotic atmosphere" to describe this tense everyday state, and in the following quotation Genival, giving a somewhat sociological interpretation, conveys vividly the feeling of what he also calls "neurosis":

> There's a factor that can't be underestimated, in my point of view: that's the question of real neurosis, of dissatisfaction, of not succeeding, I'm not even talking of professional life but your personal life. Feeling good about life. If you go and ask this to people, almost nobody feels good about himself, about life, he's always feeling exploited, he's always feeling . . . maligned [*vilipendiado*], isn't he? He's feeling violated [*violentado*]. The person who isn't clear about this, who maybe even doesn't know this, expels [*põe pra fora*] at these times [situations of briga]. He's like this, he doesn't know why, but suddenly he is transformed [*se desfigura*]. Something banal, and *pa!* he explodes. This explosion is the result of a sum of exploitations, a sum of frustrations.
>
> A briga always starts with a provocation in the general sense, there has to be that thing that unleashes it. So the thing that unleashes it is the provocation. But I don't know, this type of provocation doesn't always happen. For example, one time I heard on television that a guy came up and hit the rear of the car in front of him, he only broke the tail light, the other guy jumped out of his car, with the jack handle already in his fist, came up to the first guy's car and destroyed it: *ta! ta! ta!* And the first guy ran away, because if the other guy had grabbed him he would have turned him into paste. So there was a provocation, colliding with a car, [but] there has to be that neurosis of the other guy that unleashes the liberation of tension, of frustration.
>
> But notice: there has to be that aspect of dissatisfaction with life. Who is satisfied with a son-of-a-bitch society like ours, where everybody is a part in a machine, producing money for someone else's pocket? Spending eight, eight? who spends eight? ten, ten hours working to receive a starvation salary, but it isn't even this. . . . The guy isn't free, the guy is something wasted [*um estrago*], we're still slaves, except that today instead of going home to slave quarters we go to our houses. What a fucked-up life [*que vida fodida*] this is, you leave home at 6 A.M., take the bus, full of people, after a day of working in the bank, in the factory, people summoning you, the inspec-

tor calling you, the production manager calling you, chewing you out [*dando pito*], and for what? For something that's not going to give you any profit, that you're not even going to use. And so a guy like this, us, I don't exclude myself, because sometimes I also feel myself sort of expelling [*botando pra fora*] this. We've got to expel, if not we'll die of a heart attack. So this is it, the basic stuff [*matéria prima*] of brigas, of conflicts.

It seems that anything resembling a provocation symbolizes the generalized feeling of being exploited, maligned, and violated that (in Genival's view) characterizes contemporary Brazilian life, at least for the lower and lower-middle classes. A provocation is the "drop of water" (*gota d'água*) [12] that causes the cup of resentment to overflow. Genival sees the society as figuratively still mired in slavery. Under these circumstances it is not surprising that many anonymous confrontations seem to be rooted in the rancor spawned by life in the lower reaches of the hierarchy, or that desabafos are sometimes directed at persons and seem to be fueled by a diffuse desire for vengeance.

A briga cannot begin (unless the antagonists are already enemies) without a preliminary ritual of provocation and connection. The dilemma is this: one can either connect with the provocation, thereby avoiding humiliation but chancing briga, or one can not connect, avoiding briga but accepting a dose of humiliation. The choice between connecting and not connecting depends both on a calculation of risks and on the conflicting emotions triggered by the provocation.

Being provoked sometimes presents one with an opportunity to discharge anger and frustration—to avenge oneself for conditions that may have little or nothing to do with the immediate situation—by means of a desabafo that takes the form of a connection. Such a desabafo-connection is likely to be an exaggerated response that stimulates a desire for vengeance on the part of the adversary and therefore sets in motion an exchange of insults (which can escalate to violence) or else jumps directly to physical aggression. The confrontation, in short, escalates, entering the realm of briga proper. Someone does not want, or is not able, to control the emotions that unleash a cycle of mutual vengeance. This breakdown of control that gives rise to briga and thus to ever-increasing levels of violence is the subject of the next chapter.

[12]The "drop of water" that causes all hell to break loose is nicely consistent with the image of accumulating frustrations that require periodic venting. *Gota d'água* is the title of a play by Chico Buarque and Paulo Pontes (1975), an adaptation of Euripides' *Medea* set in contemporary urban Brazil, which examines this phenomenon from a political as well as a psychological perspective.

7

EXACERBATIONS

Alteration

There is a Brazilian saying, "I'll give away a bull not to enter a briga, but if I do enter, I'll give away a whole herd not to leave it."[1] The phrase captures neatly the discontinuity that occurs when an antagonist becomes "altered" (*alterado*). Revealingly, alteration (*alteração*) is a synonym for briga. To become altered is to lose control of one's emotions and therefore of the interaction. The urge to wreak vengeance on the adversary overwhelms reason and conscience. Suddenly the exits available at earlier stages—not connecting, apologizing, or leaving the scene—close down, and only physical injury, the intervention of third parties, or death can end the confrontation.

Thus far I have looked at aborted brigas, situations that did not go past an exchange of insults. I now turn to confrontations that spill over into physical aggression, events that are properly termed "briga." The focus here is on culture-specific answers to the question, Why is it that some brigas escalate? Why, that is, do people sometimes become altered, so that a violent schismogenic exchange (a vicious circle of aggression) occurs? ·

Provocations attack the self by infringing on one's personal space, treating one as a negligible human being, consigning one verbally to a category

[1] "Eu dou um boi para não entrar numa briga, mas se eu entrar, eu dou uma boiada para não sair."

of human rubbish, and so on. But são-luisenses consider such provocations likely to produce a violent response only under certain conditions. Much of what we hear in a briga story is a description of such conditions.

The folk scheme that emerges locates the causal factors of escalation both outside and inside the antagonists. São-luisenses identify certain incendiary factors that tend to inflame emotions or subvert control. So-called "fighting words" (Taylor 1979: 81–83) need not lead to fighting: it is not so much *what* the person says that determines the force of a hostile statement as it is *under what circumstances* and *how* he or she says it. I can call my friend a *fuleiro* (no-account, worthless person) in jest, and we laugh and order up another bottle of Brahma beer; if I say the same to João, a stranger who has just lost his job and is out looking for a fight, I am surely asking for (*comprando*) a briga. In other words, são-luisenses recognize a number of circumstances under which words or acts tend to alter the antagonists. But as we shall see in Chapter 8, an important culturally constituted intrapsychic variable—the antagonist's intrinsic capacity to maintain his or her psychological equilibrium—is perhaps the most crucial determinant of the fate of the briga.

This chapter explores the external causes of escalation, the factors that são-luisenses see as exacerbating the destabilizing psychological effects of provocations and other aggressive acts, thereby tending to elicit and intensify physically violent exchanges. São-luisenses first take into account the *effects of intoxicants*, the degree to which alcohol (or drugs) has impaired self-control. They also consider the *situational context*: a public interaction is dangerous, for the presence of an audience can aggravate feelings of shame. The effectiveness of a provocation depends on the *metamessage* appended to it: an offense marked as flagrant and deliberate poses a direct challenge difficult to ignore. In the case of accusations, *truthfulness* (perceived correspondence to a "fact" about the self) matters: if the accused feels unmasked, he or she is more likely to respond with physical violence. Finally, confrontations occur in a *relational context*: their meanings and possible consequences depend substantially on the relationship between the antagonists. A provocation may, for example, signify betrayal, an important component of the illegitimate behavior known as sacanagem. Or the antagonists may have a relationship of belligerence (rixa) that makes both liable to a sudden, violent physical attack, thereby bringing fear, and the volatility that accompanies it, into the equation.

Alcohol

The bar and the festa are the classic settings for brigas. Most people believe that alcohol inflames aggressive impulses so that they break through the psychological structures that usually contain them.[2] This is the axiom embedded, for example, in Eduardo's analysis:

> It's that people [who are drinking] are not in their normal states. That's what generates violence, the probability of a disagreement and of an immediate reaction. Alcohol is a vehicle, in the beginning, of all violence. Even among friends. So we're friends, real friends, but when you don't share my feelings, this gives me something against you and you against me, so we're friends, we're talking about some matter, but from the moment you wound my feelings, I immediately feel revolted [*revoltado*] with you. It's as if you [had] stabbed [me].

Alcohol makes one's feelings vulnerable, so that when injured they overflow their normal boundaries, making reaction immediate rather than deliberate, a reaction to a "stabbing" rather than to a dissenting word. Reason, normative constraints, and even usual emotional bonds are rendered ineffectual. This situation is nicely summarized by Eduardo's use of the word "revoltado," suggestive of desabafo, to describe the outpouring of disgust and anger one experiences under these circumstances.

The Audience

The audience plays a central role in briga by raising the emotional stakes for the participants. As he awaited the conductor's request for his student identification card, Tito anticipated the intense shame he would feel if his subterfuge were exposed:

> How could I show him my card with its missing picture? There were people I knew riding that bus, it would be a terrible shame [he laughs], a terrible shame, how would I explain? And then [I thought], How am I going to have the nerve to show this ID card, when some people who I know are going to be watching?

The presence of the audience, then, mobilizes shame (*vergonha*) as one of the feelings associated with briga.[3] Shame usually increases danger. Referring

---

[2]People use alcohol *consciously* to free up impulses—as an aid in making desabafos—in these same settings. A problem arises only when the desabafo is hostile. Most são-luisenses argue that drugs, especially marijuana, have a potentially dangerous effect. Many, but not all, users of marijuana deny the validity of this theory.

[3]The excruciating hurt public humiliation can cause shows clearly in this account by Rubem, in his mid-teens at the time, of an incident at his aunt and uncle's house: "Rapaz,

to another confrontation on a bus, Tito explains why he spoke softly to the man who pushed him while passing through the aisle: "If the thing becomes public it can get much worse, because then it isn't just between us two, then you've got the *obligation* to give some satisfaction to the people who are there watching"—that is, to respond aggressively to any challenge or slight. If not, "it's the kind of thing where you get home and can't manage to sleep right."

This insight into the feelings aroused by the presence of an audience helps us to understand stories that provide no direct line into the inner worlds of the antagonists. In the following story, Jair was an observer rather than a participant. The briga he recounts begins with a provocation that seems designed to shame one of the adversaries, giving rise to a violent, extended briga.

JACA TAKES HÉLIO'S KNIFE AWAY

Jair

Right when the Roma bus company started running to Cruzeiro do Anil [a bairro of São Luís], it had only new buses. I used to go to the bus stop sometimes just to make a round-trip to the Center, just for the pleasure of riding, right when the line began. So I was there waiting for the bus, talking there with the other people. There were two guys there drinking. [The name of the first was Hélio, and] the other, a *moreno* [i.e., a black man], Jaca [Jackfruit] was his nickname. The first guy had a knife. This Jaca insisted [*cismou*] that Hélio had to give up the knife and hand it over because nobody was allowed to carry a "white weapon" [*arma branca*: a knife, as opposed to a firearm]. So Hélio said, "Rapaz, but I'm not doing anything." [And Jaca replied,] "No, but you can't keep that knife." Mainly I thought Jaca really wanted to show off. So then *pa!* he took the knife from the guy and gave it to someone else there. [Hélio] got furious [*revoltado*] and started to

my presence made [my uncle] uncomfortable. So he said to me, 'Rapaz'—right in front of [Aunt] Luisa—'would you do me a favor, a real favor, cara, don't come around here anymore, because I can't stand your presence,' all this in front of Luisa, cara. So I just walked out of there and never went back. So then Aunt Luisa came one time to our house. [She said to me,] 'Why don't you come visit us?' and so on. Rapaz, I sat there looking at her. Porra, the guy says a thing like that at the top of his voice, cara, so that the neighbors stand there looking at me, porra, what could they have thought? I pretend that I'm not even there in front of them [*eu não tô nem aí pra eles*], but at the same time I am, it's hell [*é fogo*, it's fire]. You say you're not there but at the same time you are, you try to force that thought [of humiliation] out of your mind, and then she asks me to come back there, oh, bicho."

fight. But [Jaca] was a tall black man, and his body, for his height, was satisfactory, and Hélio was of medium height, but fat. Hélio got the worse of it, because the big black man would raise his leg, and when he would lower it it was in Hélio's face. So then a half hour went by and the guy who was beaten up [i.e., Hélio] went off to drink a beer. I was at the bar counter, and this Jaca had his back to the guy. Hélio grabbed a bottle, and, I don't know how that black man had the agility not to get hit with the bottle, even with his back turned he felt something coming at him, [and] he ducked, [and] the bottle hit against the railing. Then it started all over again. When I left there, everything had calmed down. But the next day I got the news that the fat man had cut Jaca's arm with a knife.

Here, Jaca disarms Hélio in front of what is probably a good-sized group of people—the bus route is still a novelty. Jair thought Jaca was "showing off," obviously at Hélio's expense. In São Luís, gratuitous disarming of this kind by someone with no authority to do so is an affront, in this case a deliberately public affront.[4] Hélio's response is, predictably, to attack Jaca; despite suffering a beating in the first installment of the briga, he later attacks him again—this time with a bottle, a clear escalation—and then again, with a knife, a further escalation. This kind of briga, which occurs over and over in the narratives, might be called an extended briga. Extended brigas resemble broken spirals of violence; each episode builds on the last. In this case, Hélio, the person responsible for the escalations, appears to be seeking vengeance for the public humiliation, the shaming, he suffered at the hands of Jaca.

Both Hélio and Jaca were drinking at the time of their confrontation. In this, as in many other cases, the narrator mentions more than one inciting factor. The stories do not usually isolate a "most important" factor, but the storytellers, by including what they see as salient details, point toward a set of factors that recur in various combinations, causing (in this culturally defined system) antagonists to become altered and hence brigas to escalate.

The "In-My-Face" Metamessage

Bocado, a 24-year-old unskilled casual laborer, tells the following story of a confrontation with an acquaintance.

[4]Sometimes the sponsor of a neighborhood festa will check those entering his home for weapons. He has such authority within his private space. Jaca had no such right in a public place like a bus stop.

HOMERO CALLS BOCADO A THIEF
Bocado

I was in front of Dercy's house, I'd already smoked a joint and drunk two shots of cognac, and then Homero comes up, right. [He said,] "How's it going, rapaz?" [and I said,] "Fine" and so on and talked with him. And then the guy came up and needled me to my face [*veio cismar da minha cara*], saying, "Rapaz, you and Milson [Bocado's brother] are two *thieves* [his emphasis]." [I said,] "What, rapaz?" He said, "You're two thieves." Then he went down, toward Elizete's bar. Rapaz, I went down in the dark, feeling really crazy [*doido*], and then I really went at it with him. We fought like madmen, I bit him, he slugged me. When you're furious, biting a guy so that you tear off pieces, rapaz, you're crazy! I really bit him, and then slugged him, he hit me but I really hit him, crazy punching. Afterward I was kind of pissed off [*meio invocado*] because I was unlucky because he scratched me all around here [indicates his throat]. The next day I got up and this here was all swollen from his fingernails, because he had me down and then he grabbed me around here and scratched me. Then after I got free from him he grabbed me and gave me a punch in the nose. Rapaz, it was a good punch and all I saw was stars. Then right away I went crazy. I attacked him and clamped my teeth on him, you know, like those fierce dogs [*aqueles cachorros valentão*] who really tear off pieces, I grabbed him with my teeth and there it went—I really bit him. Afterward he left town and never came back. I don't know what's going on with him, but he said he was going to return for us to have another rixa [i.e., briga].

Homero, after a friendly approach, suddenly bursts out with a direct insult right in Bocado's face.[5] Bocado's connection ("What, rapaz?") takes the form of a request for clarification. Does Homero really care to throw

[5]Homero's "You're thieves" is suggestive of what Taylor (1979) calls "fighting words." Fighting words are insults that precede physical violence. Taylor found that in the Mixteca Alta of Oaxaca fighting words ordinarily alluded to cuckoldry, whereas in central Mexico the insults were more varied. My guess is that in São Luís the range of dangerous insults is wider yet. Taylor was looking specifically at cases of homicide. But to say that fighting words preceded fighting is not to say that these insults *always* triggered fighting. Probably são-luisenses have it right: it is not words per se that precipitate violence, but rather words *as spoken in a specific situational and relational context* (Stoller 1978).

down the gauntlet, as a "right-in-my-face" insult does? Homero confirms his intention, and after an interlude during which Bocado stews and becomes "crazy" over this interchange, Bocado attacks Homero. That Bocado at this point was altered is demonstrated by his own choice of an image to describe himself—he was "like those fierce dogs who really tear off pieces." Also, as people sometimes say after a briga, "things are not going to stay like this" (*as coisas não vão ficar assim*): this briga threatens to generate a sequel.

In sum, "right-in-my-face" provocations offer a challenge that is hard to resist because they send a metamessage confirming that the provocation is deliberate, intended to attack the victim and defy him or her to respond. In São Luís, a "right-in-my-face" provocation justifies a physically aggressive response.

Unmaskings

An unmasking does two things that enrage the one who is unmasked. First, it brings a shameful, concealed character trait to light, either directly or by implication. Second, it tends to stamp the accused with this trait, as if to say that this negative quality summarizes his or her essence.[6] This reduction of a complex person to a single, highly negative image, often a stereotype, is felt by the accused to be an infuriating distortion, even though in a narrow sense the accusation may be true.

Sensitivity to unmasking has a long history in São Luís. The newspapers of the 1820's, the earliest to be found in Maranhão's public library, are studded with refutations of "calumnies." These rebuttals were sometimes distributed as elaborate supplements and beautifully printed on fine paper. A citizen defends himself from accusations that he is a debtor, a businessman denies that he has cheated another, a military commander refutes a report that his troops were cowardly or rebellious, and so on.[7]

Such protestations do not, however, provide much insight into how unmaskings *feel*. For this, let us turn to a first-person account in which Tito describes a briga with his brother, kindled by an exchange of insults that penetrate to the quick.

This briga has a history. Tito went through a very difficult period during his early adolescence. He was forced to wear a corrective vest to remedy a spinal problem, and he was ridiculed by his peers. "I was considered," he

---

[6]Velho (1981) looks at *drogado* (drug addict) and *subversivo* (subversive) as common examples of such "globalizing" or "totalizing" accusations.

[7]A more recent case that points up clearly the effects of an unmasking is the murder of Olegário Lima by Manoel Neiva, a cause célèbre in 1933 (Linger 1987: 262–65). Lima had accused Neiva's family of corruption in a signed newspaper article. Neiva admitted killing Lima, but the jury accepted Neiva's contention that the offense to his family's honor had caused him to lose his senses, and it acquitted him.

says, "to be a person from another planet, I mean, I was serving as a clown the whole time, [a target] for chuckles and even provocations, and, incredible as it seems, one day they almost threw stones at me." Though talkative as a child, he became introverted and shut himself up in his room. Eventually, however, he began to make forays to the city center, where he fell in with a group of teenagers who hung out on the Rua Grande, São Luís's main shopping street. He entered into their world, which was also a world of drugs, where he found a greater sense of self-esteem and autonomy. They smoked marijuana together and went to unscrupulous pharmacies where they could get other drugs injected, probably amphetamines.

Then one day Tito accompanied a friend to Turu, a distant bairro, to fetch some boots, without telling his father. When he got home, his father angrily demanded to know where he had been. He tried to explain the nature of his innocent errand, but his father cut him off and struck him. Tito swore at his father, which no one in the family had ever done before. Tito's brother Rodolfo, who is twenty years Tito's senior, admonished him: "You'd better shut up, because in this house a *maconheiro* [habitual marijuana user] has to keep his mouth shut!" "How that really hurt me," comments Tito, "that hurt me a lot, because I was crying out, I was asking for help, and instead of understanding the message, they were throwing me in a hole, or else they were simply indifferent." Tito could not forget his brother's stinging accusation, and relations between him and Rodolfo frosted over. Even by the time of my fieldwork, five or six years after this incident, it had not been forgotten.

Subsequently, Tito resolved to intensify his drug use. He lived for drugs and "bacchanals." He grew thin; his veins resembled "plastic pipes," and his arms hurt so much from the injections that he could not bend them. He was keeping company with a group of disreputable people who stole cars and falsified documents, "the poor Mafia of São Luís" as he calls it, although he did not participate in their schemes. But he knew something was wrong: he felt desperate. About this time a new school opened near his house, and he took to posting himself by the wall that surrounds his front yard to watch the students go by on their way to night classes before heading off to his own evening activities. He fell in love with a young woman, Jandira, who passed in front of his house every night—"the only person who didn't smoke marijuana who would talk to me during that time. We became addicted to conversing with each other." When she said to him one day that friends of hers had seen him with people who took drugs, he said it was not true. But the lie bothered him, and he resolved to break up with her. He confessed that he could not give up drugs or his friends, and she replied: "I want to stay with you. But I don't know how my mother will react when she finds that I've fallen in love with a maconheiro." "Porra," laughs Tito, recalling this scene, "it was really awful to hear that word again."

> And I said, "Really [he laughs], we have to break up now, really, once and for all." Well, and we did break up. So then she walked away crying, right. . . . So she was walking away, it was so sad, I remember, I was crossing the street, I couldn't stand it anymore, I started to cry, and I called her, I looked at her and she looked at me [he laughs], she came back and we embraced and I said to her, "Look [he raps the table], I prom- ise you one thing: I'm going to change my life completely, from now on I'm not going to use any drugs, and I'm also going to change my friendships, I'm going to change com- pletely." And I did, really, we spent three years as boyfriend and girlfriend and I changed myself completely.

Tito's family began to respect him, something that (except for his mother) they had not done before. Although the intense affair with Jandira eventu- ally ended, and Tito resumed moderate use of marijuana, he gave up most of his drug-using friends and did not return to the harder drugs. Moreover, despite problems at school, where he was disgusted by sacanagem such as the sale of high marks by his teachers, Tito had embarked on a project into which he poured his hopes for the future. He had begun classes at one of São Luís's ubiquitous private English-language schools, at a great financial sacrifice to the family, and had become one of the top students. He had also obtained steady employment as a clerk. In short, although he still faced many problems and had periodic crises of self-confidence, he felt that he had dragged himself out of the gutter and that, difficult as it might be, he had a chance to make a future for himself.

In the meantime, Rodolfo and his wife had begun to fight, owing (says Tito) to Rodolfo's drinking and neglect. She eventually left Rodolfo and their two children, going off with another man. That is where we join the story.

TITO FIGHTS WITH HIS BROTHER AFTER EXCHANGING INSULTS

Tito

My father began to complain about Rodolfo's behavior. He was becoming irresponsible, and my father couldn't stand it that a man of almost 40 was doing this kind of thing. He would complain to me, since I was already somebody who

he listened to. So he always asked my opinion, and I was beginning to get disgusted [*começava a me revoltar*] with this kind
of behavior [i.e., Rodolfo's], because Rodolfo was making
mamãe and *papai* [Mom and Dad] worried. And I can't deny
a little bit of, of, of, of anger [left over from] that other time
[i.e., of the fight years ago], right?

So I was thinking: Well, well, where is the guy, so secure, of
many years back, who was ordering [me], "Maconheiro, shut
up, because you have no right to speak." But I said absolutely
nothing to him. Well, one day I was taking a shower, and my
brother had stepped outside the house, and there was a serious
argument. I thought, What's going on here? It was very unusual for this to happen at home. I was in the bathroom when
I heard the argument outside between my father and him.
So then I walked out of the bathroom, naked, with a towel
wrapped around my waist. And then I got very disgusted [*revoltado*]. He [Rodolfo] was speaking in a very aggressive tone.
So I said to him that he didn't have any right to speak like that,
that he was acting like a *moleque* [a pretentious, irresponsible
young man; a punk]. So then he got furious and he said—he
said again—"Who do you think you are? . . . Do you think
you have the right [*que tu tens moral*] to tell me that kind of
thing—maconheiro, marginal?" At that I became completely
devastated [*arrasado*], with a total loss of structures [*com per-
didas de estruturas mesmo*], right. I said, "Look, you remember
that time," I spoke really harshly [*bravo*] with him, and very
loudly, "you remember that time when you said the same
thing to me, and I didn't do anything?" He said, "No." "Well,
now I'm going to shut your mouth, with punches, because I
can't stand this kind of thing." He had got hold of a target to
get at me, to get at my conduct, in front of my parents and
the whole family. So I said, "Then . . . I'm a maconheiro, but
you're a *corno* [cuckold]." Of course, I don't have this kind of
prejudice, but I just went as low as he did, right, I hit him just
as low, I had to strike back at him, right. My father pulled us
apart, and I was going into my other brother's room, taking
off the towel, when he tried to jump in through the window. I
said, "You don't have to jump through the window with that
enormous belly of yours, because I myself am going to jump

through so I can beat you up there," and I went [through], I
threw the towel away, and we traded some blows. Although
he's older than me, he doesn't have as much staying power. It
was a horrible thing, and we attacked each other a lot in terms
of saying things to each other. And today we live in the same
house, but although we're not angry at each other we avoid
interacting so that the same thing won't happen again.

The word "maconheiro" sounds like a shot three times in this account.
Twice, coming from Tito's older brother, it is a devastating accusation;
once, pronounced by Jandira, it is a matter-of-fact summary of what Tito
has already told her. For Tito, "maconheiro" has two fundamental, negative implications, themselves bound together: the maconheiro is the person
without respect and therefore without the right to speak.[8] To be called a
maconheiro, says Tito,

> means to be put in a position of inferiority, that you are worth
> absolutely nothing. It's very complex, really, because I think
> that "maconheiro" doesn't decipher, it's not an expression
> that takes care to express what a maconheiro is, exactly. It ex-
> presses a person's state of . . . moral and physical decadence.
> People see this as the end point of demoralization, as the point
> of being useless, as a final consequence. So, since people see it
> this way, it's a very serious kind of aggression toward another
> person. The person really feels his problems in his skin.
>   It [means] the total failure of a person. What is this word ex-
> pressing? A ruin of a human being, useless, right? A person
> who is malevolent because he has a cloud of false information
> and . . . I don't know, many other things. [The word says]
> that you are guilty, just as a thing of guilt, right, that you're
> guilty, that you should . . . you know, keep quiet [he laughs],
> you understand, it plays with a kind of guilt. Now, don't ask
> me about what, because I can't manage to understand it. Just
> that it's something that hurts, and a lot, anyone, whether or
> not he uses [marijuana].
>   I can't tell you how deep [this word goes]. Because I don't
> know that, I feel threatened. It surpasses the limits of your

[8]There is a connection here with desabafo. A desabafo is a speaking, a shouting, as we have
seen. Not to be able to desabafar is to be disrespected; conversely, the desabafo, as in Carnival,
is itself a way of asserting one's worth as a human being. (Gilberto Gil and Chico Buarque
make the point tellingly in the song "Cálice," some verses of which I quote on p. 223.)

[understanding], you simply stand there automatically expecting the worst, the worst of the beasts [*bichos*]. It's something you don't know, and so you simply become terrified, it
threatens you because you can't reach where it is. It's something unknown, it's a *beast* [his emphasis] that sits there always
threatening. You feel something that you don't know how
to describe. You obviously feel very hurt, that's logical, but
you can't get an answer to what that hurt is. All right, if you
have a headache, you know that [you got] that headache [be-
cause] you must be tired, and so on. Well, when you have a
pain in your arm, for which you don't know the cause, that
pain grows psychologically, in the sense that when you don't
really know where it came from, what its cause was, it increases because of the . . . I don't know, because of the lack of
information about its source, right?

So it's that kind of thing, it's hard to say how it is, I can
say that your heart gets really very squeezed, that you . . .
simply . . . say, maybe in a very hurt way or sometimes without saying a word at all, that the person [who called you that]
is wrong, that it's not like that at all, that in reality it's something completely different. The pain is even greater if you
use [marijuana], you feel a guilt, the word has an additional
sweetening of accusation, of a . . . of a conclusion. You've lost
all respect, and losing respect you no longer have any right
to speak, because you won't be believed, or you won't be respected. That's the way you are, you know, it's this kind of
thing, hey, you're black, you can't marry my daughter, right?
because [you're] black.

If you are a maconheiro, you don't have any right [*moral*] at
all to say anything to me or else I don't have any obligation
to listen to anything you say because I am superior to you.
[But] if you try to deepen [your analysis] and discover what
is the exact meaning [of the word] you will simply stop in
the middle of the road, and you will have a wave of thoughts
[but] you will get lost, you won't have any more words to
describe or express your feeling.

Tito is struggling here to try to express ideas that he has trouble grasping. The accusation that he is a maconheiro has the effect of casting him
down a black hole. His reference to a "beast," or bicho, is probably an

allusion to the Bicho-Papão, a formless, featureless, devouring monster, a shadowy nightmare creature familiar to maranhense children. There seems to be a double image of the bicho in this passage. The accusation itself is a bicho: it hurts you, squeezes you, instills a terror of obliteration. At the same time, the bicho is *within* you: the accusation makes you feel guilt in your skin, as if you have come face-to-face with your own primitive malevolence. The word "maconheiro" at once penetrates and undermines the moral and rational structures, the civilizing elements of the person that restrain unacceptable, dangerous desires and feelings. In his recounting of the briga with his brother, Tito uses a graphic expression that captures this sense of moral annihilation. "I became completely devastated," he says, "with a total loss of structures."

Maconheiro is precisely what Tito does not want to be, what he most *fears* to be. The accusation cancels his struggle to construct a self that he and others can respect. Suddenly he feels overwhelmed, consigned once more to the trash heap, nullified. And vengeful emotions break through the demolished "structures," the ruins of the Tito he has fashioned, materializing in the insults and the blows he rains upon his brother.

Sacanagem

The word "sacanagem," in its most restricted meaning, refers to sexual acts that, however common they may be, carry a hint of the forbidden—oral sex, anal sex, in short any variant, the more imaginative and unusual the more *sacana*, of, as Tito puts it, the "Mom-and-Dad style" of intercourse. Tito's commentary would not evoke universal agreement or sympathy (some people do not share his tolerance for sexual variety), but it captures the essence of a generally held view of sacanagem:

> Sexual sacanagem has for me something of the prohibited, and because it's prohibited it's also very full of pleasure. Sexual sacanagem [is] when two people go to bed, a woman and a man or a man and another man or a woman and another woman, [and] usually when one of them tells [his or her friends] about what happened in bed with this other person, they ask: "How was it, did you do sacanagem?" Because lying down, screwing [*a trepada*] in the Mom-and-Dad style, isn't sacanagem; sacanagem starts with oral sex, goes on to anal sex, and all the ways and proportions and positions that you can find to satisfy your sexual fantasies. Sacanagem is doing something in sex that you haven't done yet, sacanagem is fucking [*comer*, literally "eating"] a bunda, right, which is the

favorite national dish, from the north to the south of Brazil. Sacanagem is important, sacanagem is breathing, you know, sacanagem is having the right, at least in bed, to something that is castrated from you every day, something that it isn't permitted to do. And in sacanagem you have a vast field in which you can, in either a true or illusory way, find a better, less anguished heartbeat. I have a friend who says, "Look, cara, when I don't screw for, let's say, a month, I feel sick. I feel sick, I feel neurotic, I feel completely irritated [*chateado*]."

I don't want to be too radical, but when you hear a Brazilian say, "Look, I went to bed [with someone]," he's saying that he went and did sacanagem. When he doesn't do sacanagem, he doesn't say anything. I don't see this [talking about what he did with somebody] as a form of disrespect to that other person; it's saying that he "ate" [*comeu*] something, that he had a certain satisfaction, and I have to talk about this satisfaction to tell you how happy I am. I have to give the smallest details. They say, "Yesterday I had a happy thing happen to me, yesterday things got better, yesterday I, we, exchanged negative energies and I put all my vomit in the other person and she gave me her vomit too," and since her vomit doesn't affect me, and mine doesn't affect her, we played [*brincamos*] together. Doing whatever you can in relation to your fantasies makes you happy and satisfied, and also dresses you in fresh clothes. For example, I don't feel really satisfied going to bed [with someone] if we don't have big *sacanagens* [plural of sacanagem] and laughs, [if we don't] laugh at each other, and screw and screw and screw and screw, finish screwing and screw again, and after a very great exhaustion your prick gets hard again and let's screw again and screw and screw and screw and screw until we reach the conclusion that we're tired and that we should screw again, but not today [he laughs].

For Tito, sexual sacanagem is a vehicle for desabafo: sacanagem is "breathing," "vomiting," it is having the right to do what one is not usually permitted to do.[9] As Tito portrays it, sacanagem involves the use of another person (consensually, in the scenarios he sketches) for one's own psycho-

[9]The conscious identification of sacanagem as a kind of desabafo may be particular to Tito. But in any event, it shows how desabafo serves as a metaphor for understanding intense personal experiences.

logical benefit. The individuals engage in a private act that has an element of creative illegitimacy—there is something original, yet in some way "dirty," in successful sacanagem. In sum, sacanagem, when it is well done, is an imaginative, consensual, more or less prohibited or unusual sexual act, the purpose of which is momentary pleasure or relief. (For a more extended discussion of sacanagem as a component of Brazil's "erotic ideology," see Parker 1987: 163–65; 1991: 101–4.)

The term "sacanagem" is, however, extended into other areas of human relationship than the sexual. Sacanagem in this sense refers to egoistic, counternormative, self-aggrandizing behavior, with a base objective (power, greed, vengeance, or sheer malice), carried out in a devious manner. As in sexual sacanagem, one uses another to satisfy one's own desires, and one does so in an illegitimate (or "rebellious" [Parker 1987: 172]) way. Here, however, the suggestion of reciprocity that is often present in sexual sacanagem vanishes. Sacanagem in this extended sense is one person taking advantage of another. Moreover, the creativity of sexual sacanagem sours into deceit and inventive exploitation. The contortions become truly perverse, and there is a victim.

Everyone in São Luís hates to be a victim of someone else's sacanagem. It is to be an *otário*, a fool, a sucker. A person who is the victim of sacanagem therefore reacts strongly. Sacanagem in this sense occurs in personal confrontations, between people who have relationships that carry certain obligations. Sacanagem provokes by betraying, by exercising duplicity in the service of self-interest, as the next story illustrates.

ZÉ BARALHO STEALS GATO'S MARIJUANA

Denilson

Everything started because of the smoke. Gato had Cr$300,000 worth of smoke, and was there in the [billiards club], he and a guy who lives with him named Wagner. I was there shooting pool, and he had the stuff under his arm. But because it was bothering his playing, he gave it to [Wagner] to hold. Wagner threw it behind a latrine they have there. So then Mr. Zé Baralho saw where the guy hid the smoke. He went to the street and said that a guy out there had taken it, and then he grabbed the smoke [from its hiding place] and left. Gato didn't know who had robbed his smoke. So then Gato went home; he was mad as hell [*puto pra porra*]. He was saying that if he found out who had stolen his stuff he would kill him.

So then a few days went by. Cabo [a military policeman]

said that it had been Zé Baralho who had robbed his smoke. [Cabo told Gato this] because he realized that it was sacanagem, since Gato had been going there every day to get [Zé] stoned. And also because Gato wanted to beat up Rubem, but it wasn't Rubem who had stolen his stuff, it was Zé Baralho. [At this point Rubem, who is present at this conversation, interjects: "So then Gato [spotted Zé and called out]: 'Ah, compadre, it was you who took my smoke, wasn't it, *safado* [wicked one], come over here.'"] And then Zé Baralho took off running. He went to his house and grabbed a shotgun. So then Gato took off running, and went into a house.

When Zé Baralho came back he had this friend of Gato's, this Wagner, and [Zé] hit him hard [several times] on the head with the butt of the shotgun. So everybody thought that this Wagner was soft, because he [had] a [big] knife, sharp on both sides, [and] when Zé Baralho was hitting him, he could have pulled out the knife and stabbed him. I was as offended [*injuriado*] with Wagner, who was soft with Zé, [as I was with Zé,] who hit [Wagner, even though] Wagner didn't have anything to do with this affair. I got emotionally involved with the thing [*eu fiquei ligado com aquilo*]. [I said to Wagner,] "Compadre, give me that knife." I took his knife and went after Zé Baralho. Zé Baralho was going down the street where he lived. I called to him, called to him loud and clear: "Hey, Zé Baralho, come here, let's talk about something, it's something really serious."

So then this Wagner comes running down from above and says [to Zé], "Ah, compadre, this is how it's going to be, I'm going to kill you, I'm going to shoot you with a revolver," porra, and at this Zé flies home and doesn't come out again. He had already been coming over to talk with me, I mean, if he had come I would have given him a few good ones with the knife. So I said to Wagner, "You really screwed up, cara, besides the fact that when you had the knife you didn't do anything to the guy, now you come and [scare him away]."

[We were looking for Zé when] Gato showed up. So then [a bunch of us] went to smoke a joint. [After walking around for a while,] a long way off we saw Zé in [a] doorway. When

Zé saw me with a knife ready to get him with, he took off and
hid himself. And that's how it ended, just like that.

The person who provoked this *briga* was Zé, who stole
Gato's smoke. This isn't something you do to a guy who has
been good to you. [Rubem: "Gato comes all the way from
Anil to get the guy high, he sells smoke on credit to him."] I'll
tell you something. [If I were Gato,] although I couldn't manage to do anything to him that day, he could be sure that the
next time I saw him, I would. I don't know what [exactly],
something like stabbing him a few times. He deserves more:
he deserves to die. What he did isn't something that you do.

The story can be summarized as follows. Gato has been supplying Zé
Baralho with marijuana on credit. Despite this favor, Zé devises a plot to
steal a packet of marijuana from him, blaming the robbery on someone else,
a plot that evidences the typical shiftiness of *sacanagem*. Cabo, the military policeman, "realized that it was *sacanagem*, since Gato had been going
there every day to get [Zé] stoned"—the linkage between betrayal and
sacanagem is clearly marked here. This act of *sacanagem* offends a number
of people, not just Gato. It was a serious moral transgression that involved
not only a violation of an ironclad rule among marijuana users in São Luís—
not to steal someone else's smoke—but also an offense to someone who was
treating the offender especially well. "What he [Zé] did isn't something that
you do," says Denilson, explaining why in his opinion Zé Baralho deserves
to die. Cabo informs on Zé, Wagner ineptly gets into the act, and Denilson,
who portrays himself as the most outraged of all of them, tries to attack Zé
with a knife and vows to try again if he gets the chance. This incident gave
rise to at least one episode of physical aggression—Zé's attack on Wagner
with the butt of the shotgun—and threatens to generate reprises as well.

The final story in this section is such an extreme case that it probably
stretches the boundary of what can be called *sacanagem*. Here, the act of
sacanagem leads directly to a murder. Killer and victim appear to be disturbed individuals—disequilibrated individuals, as *são-luisenses* would put
it—and the circumstances are altogether unusual and tragic.

Bartolomeu, the narrator, was at the time of the murder (April 1985) the
owner of a small bar facing one of São Luís's beaches. Amália, the eventual
victim, ran this bar on a day-to-day basis. Amália was a single mother living
apart from her children, who were scattered among other households, probably those of relatives. Amália had sought employment from Bartolomeu
so that she could save money to establish her own household and bring her
children back to live with her.

Into this scene came Paulo, a boy of seventeen who also had a dolorous story to tell. Paulo said that his father had died some time ago, apparently of natural causes, and that his mother, three siblings, and uncle had all been killed in a car crash. He appeared at the bar, asking Bartolomeu for employment so that he could make enough money to continue his studies at a *colégio*.[10] Bartolomeu agreed to hire the boy, providing his meals as well. Soon, however, conflicts arose between Paulo and Amália.

AMÁLIA REFUSES PAULO WATER, AND HE KILLS HER

Bartolomeu

[These were] normal arguments [*discussões*], for example, he would complain when she told him to do something, anything, he would complain and call her names. He would get obnoxious, and so I would always reprimand him: "Rapaz, have respect, have respect for Amália, because Amália is the same age as your mother." [I said this] because previously she had given this rap that the first child she had been pregnant with would have been his age, so there was this rap of hers, adopting him really.

It was a day when we had a round table and we talked about the team, right. And she said, "Look, Paulo, Bartolomeu is my father, my brother, my friend, he adopted me, he's helping me, he gives me strength [*me dá uma força*]. You don't have either a father or a mother. If I'd had a child your age, you would be in reality my child who was never born, so I'm going to be your mother, [and] you and I will be the adopted children of Bartolomeu."

[And with this] we went back to work, [but] afterward there was all this arguing, he saying that she was being stingy with the food [that she gave him]. All the name-calling [*esculhambar*] was creating so much anger, creating that state of nerves, that disagreeable [atmosphere] that many times when I arrived there, [when] they would start complaining, I would imagine: Can this be some kind of farce [designed by] the two of them to drive me crazy? A thing like that is ridiculous, be-

---

[10] A colégio is either a primary or secondary school, public or private. Paulo told Bartolomeu that he was afraid to go to night school, his only public-school option at age seventeen, and therefore wanted to attend classes during the day, which he could do only at a private school. (Schools in São Luís generally run on triple shifts: morning, afternoon, and night.) Most colégios in the city are privately owned and vary widely in quality and expense.

cause right when I get there, wanting to know how things are going, they don't tell me, they don't come up to me telling me how things are going in the bar, I'd like to know how my business is going, [but] right away they come up with personal problems of the one and the other, and so it went on like that. But I always cut it off: "Look, tolerate him, look, tolerate her, you have to be humble, things can't go on like this, you have to be humble," I said this a lot to him, "I can't fire her and leave you here, lose her and put another person in her place, because I know her, and I think that she needs [me] and I need her" and all the rest of it. And I would go up to her and say, "Look, this boy is deprived, his story is sad, let's put up with him, that's the way they are, the youth of today." And it kept on like this, you understand, she's a mother and he's like a son and none of this helped.

After I fired him, he came back [two days later]. I still think she was illogical with respect to this problem she had with the boy. She, as a woman who said she would be a mother, at an age to be his mother, could have been understanding: "Look, my friend, treat me better." I mean, there was a way to get his attention and capture the friendship of that boy, she even allowed him to become like a son to her—so what the hell kind of mother is that [*que diabo de mãe é essa*]? So I say that everything happened rashly, in his case because really he was of an age, 17, I've been 17 and I know that at age 17 you don't think a single thing that's worth anything, you don't even have a "formation" [*formação*: a structured character], a personality to defend yourself from a danger like this one, avoiding a murder. So depending on the torment, on the torture, a person of 17 does things that even he doesn't know what he's doing. Now she, at 33, already has [achieved] this condition of [being a] human being, I think that a person of 33 already can have their head more in the right place. We shouldn't play or fight [*brincar ou brigar*] with the feelings of others. I think this [incident] was really a war between the [two] people, in his case because he didn't yet have enough education and wasn't old enough, and in hers because she was old enough but also didn't have the formation.

So what happened was that one confronted the other one.

According to him, he defended himself, it was she who attacked first. He came in asking for water and she didn't give it to him. There were three guys there in the bar at the time, and she ordered them to beat him, and one really went so far as to give him a kick and they grabbed hold of each other and later he ran out to the beach. He [hid himself] at a distance, in the bush, waiting for her to be alone. So then he came [back] into the bar [and] asked for water; she didn't give it to him and told him he was prohibited from coming in there, [which wasn't true]. She should come up to him and say, "Do you want water? Here's some water. Have you eaten? Here's a plate of food." It wouldn't have cost her anything to do that because she knew he needed it. He asked for water, she didn't give it to him, she said he was prohibited from entering, and then he said she hit him in the face, he asked her not to do that, she hit him again, and that was when he sticks the knife halfway in. I imagine that at the moment she hit him twice he hit her, so then she must have gone running for the knife, grabbed it and headed for him. He [must have] disarmed her and killed her.

I was trying to arrange a room for him in the Casa dos Estu-dantes [i.e., the Student House, a dormitory for those who are studying in São Luís, away from their families who live in other areas of the state]. Meanwhile, he could have stayed where he was, eating rice and beans in the bar. Then I was going to find a job for him, so that he could be independent of me. But he didn't consider her, and she didn't consider him. Violence and poverty lead people to meet death in a ridiculous manner.

This pathetic story is replete with irony and symbolism. Amália keenly feels the absence of her children; Paulo has lost his entire family. Paulo is the age Amália's first-born would have been had she not had a miscarriage. Their desperate, complementary needs throw them together in the roles of mother and son. But not only are they unable to fulfill these roles in any mutually satisfactory way, they act perversely toward each other. He refuses to obey and insults her. She shows no tolerance for his behavior and indirectly (via Bartolomeu) puts him out on the street. When he attempts to return, she refuses him water, tells him that he is no longer permitted in the bar, and orders other young men to attack him. (The symbolism could hardly be more dramatic: this is the antithesis of good maternal behavior—providing nourishment, intimacy, and a safe haven.) He has been expelled from his home, publicly, by his mother.[11] When he returns, to petition her privately for water, she again refuses, strikes him, and possibly threatens him with a knife. Bartolomeu supplies few details of this final encounter, but clearly its central theme is betrayal. Having assumed a maternal role vis-à-vis Paulo, not just implicitly but also overtly, Amália now turns on him— "What the hell kind of mother is that?" Abandonment at a time of need, a failure by the "mother" to abide by even a primal moral imperative (giving water to another human being), would seem to have been, Bartolomeu suggests, what drove Paulo to the denouement of this tragic relationship.[12]

Amália's actions have the essential elements of sacanagem—treachery, with the malevolent twist represented by the denial of water—but in this case, the emotions were so profound, the matter so grave, that the story evokes none of the grudging, ironic amusement that so often flavors tales of sacanagem. This case is, in short, sacanagem's outer limit.

Rixa

Enemies

Of the four murders tried in São Luís during 1985,[13] one ended in acquittal. By a 7–0 vote of the jury, José Benedito Ferreira ("Biné"), 23, a manual laborer, was absolved from the charge of murdering Raimundo Gomes Veiga, 38, also a manual laborer. The main facts in the case are not in dispute. Biné and Raimundo met by accident in a street in São Francisco, the bairro in which they lived, on the morning of June 4, 1981. Raimundo was carrying two pieces of wood. The two men exchanged words. Raimundo may or may not have assumed a threatening position, and then Biné took

[11]This incident can be compared to Rubem's banishment by his uncle from Aunt Luisa's house (note 3 above), but that event, which was so mortifying to Rubem, is insignificant by comparison.

[12]Some other details of this case may be of interest. Bartolomeu found Amália's body and was arrested and briefly held for the murder before being released. (There is no doubt that he is innocent and that the murderer was Paulo.) Paulo did say that Amália had attacked him with a knife just before he killed her (*OI*, April 20, 1985). Paulo is reported to have stabbed Amália first in the vagina, then in the abdomen, and finally in the heart (*JH*, February 7, 1986). Given the logic of the case, I think Bartolomeu was lucky not to have been in the bar at the time of the murder. Indeed, according to Bartolomeu, Paulo had told him during a visit to the jail that "he would be capable of killing even two people." Bartolomeu thinks he would have been in danger, but that he might have been able to prevent the crime. Because Paulo was a minor, he spent only eight months in the Children of God juvenile detention center. Two months after his release, he was picked up once again, during a pre-Carnival police sweep, in early February 1986, for armed robbery (*JH*, February 7, 1986).

[13]The local criminal justice system, starved for funds and without a permanent site for trying serious crimes, was just about moribund.

out a six-inch fishing knife and stabbed Raimundo once through the heart. Biné fled; Raimundo said, "José Benedito killed me," and died.

Why, then, was Biné acquitted? His defense lawyer was skillful, but even a skillful attorney needs to have a client whose motives can arouse the sympathy of the jury. (The same lawyer failed, the next day, to save another client from an eighteen-year jail sentence.) Biné's great advantage was that Raimundo had been his enemy, and a dangerous one. Whether, as Biné claimed, Raimundo had cast down the larger piece of wood and secured the smaller, threatening and perhaps swinging at him, or whether (as an eyewitness's testimony suggests) no such menacing actions had taken place, is in the last analysis irrelevant. The defense succeeded in establishing that Biné and Raimundo had a relationship of rixa, so that at some point Raimundo would unleash a treacherous attack on Biné. As the defense attorney put it during the trial, "Biné didn't need to wait until the club fell upon his head to defend himself."

The rixa began about half a year before the killing, at a festa in São Francisco. Biné and Raimundo had argued (over a piece of coconut, according to one newspaper); there had been some pushing; and Raimundo, who was drunk, had pulled a knife and chased Biné. When Biné's younger brother tried to intervene, Raimundo cut him in the hand and on the ear. From that moment, according to Biné and other witnesses, Raimundo, who (unlike Biné) had a reputation in the bairro as a drunk, a maconheiro, and a *brigão* (a person who provokes and participates in brigas), insulted and threatened Biné every time they met.

The jurors evidently viewed the stabbing as Biné's response to the *promise* of a treacherous, lethal attack. This promise lies at the heart of rixa. A rixa can endure for years with undiminished mutual hostility, generating a series of truncated brigas, which, like the fatal meeting between Biné and Raimundo, dispense with preliminaries.

The Truncated Briga

Rixa, explains Cravo, means

> we've been "bad" [i.e., enemies] for a year and when we meet, today we're going to settle accounts [*acertar os parafusos*, literally, adjust the screws]. I [try to] kill you, you [try to] kill me, so whoever is able to, kills first. Then they say, "Poxa, that guy never fought with anybody" and all that, but not knowing that we've had this briga [i.e., rixa] for a long time.

The closest English translation for rixa is probably "feud," but rixa has a more intensely personal ring. Rixa is essentially a dyadic relationship, and it is serious business.

Cravo, who is about 50, is a gambler who lives in a poor bairro out toward the port of São Luís. He says, and there is no evident reason to doubt him, that for years he worked as a pistoleiro, a hired gunman, in the hinterland of Maranhão.[14] Here he describes an encounter with an enemy, in a rural region of the state:

CRAVO'S ENEMY STRIKES HIM WITH A HOE

Cravo

I've had many longtime enemies who wanted to kill me. I had a friend who always taunted me when he saw me [*sempre passava com deboche*], until one day I passed by and he was in a field and he said, "Look here, rapaz! Hey!," and he grabbed the hoe he was using and hit me with it. I turned, tethered the horse at the side of the field, and then I said, "Hey, rapaz, what is it that you want? Come up a little closer." Then he looked at me, I put two bullets over his head, *pa! pa!*, and then he ran into the bush, tearing through [the bush], I mean, you don't call this a man, you call it a coward, I mean he thought I was some kind of soft-ass [*bunda mole*] who didn't have the courage to look a man in the face, but I'm a man, I looked him in the face, the one who wasn't a man was the one who ran away.

Any encounter with an enemy can lead to violence.[15] On this occasion, with little ceremony, Cravo's enemy attacks him with a hoe. Cravo escalates the

[14]The hired gun is a common figure in Maranhão, especially in rural areas. Often these gunmen help landlords expel peasant owners, whose lands are then appropriated by the landlord, a practice known as "grilagem" (see Chapter 2, note 19). The level of rural violence, virtually all of it aimed at small landholders, landless peasants, and organizers of these groups, is extraordinarily high in the state.

[15]But there is a suggestion that the relationship of rixa has a paradoxical component of erotic attachment. Tito describes a man from his bairro, a "surreal maranhense *caboclo* [rustic person]" from Pindaré in the interior of the state, a machão named Galinho, who, when he gets drunk, always wants to jump into a taxi to go back to Pindaré to fight with an enemy there. "I've fought with Mr. So-and-So 50 times," Tito quotes Galinho. "I'm sure he's waiting for me there, he's going to kill me. We really fought, brigas between *machos* [real men], we threw our knives away and slugged it out." The only problem, Tito discovered, is that the enemy died years ago. "His longing for those brigas is enormous," says Tito. "He's not going to fight anymore in Pindaré, because he isn't going to find his partner there." It can also happen, according to Cravo, that two men with a rixa become close friends. It is as if they decide they are worthy of each other's friendship. Note that Cravo calls the enemy who ran from his bullets his friend.

confrontation by firing twice over the enemy's head, sending him scurrying—a resounding victory according to the code of machismo that Cravo clearly espouses.

Brigas in Series

Although Cravo's macho ideology is unusually pronounced, the explosiveness of this encounter with his enemy, which virtually skips preliminaries and goes straight into physical violence, is typical of confrontations between enemies. One reason that such brigas are so explosive is that, strung together over a long period, they make up a gigantic extended briga in which the aggression that broke off the last encounter serves as the starting point for the next. One need not repeat steps taken earlier. The briga between Juca and Marcelo, reported here by Waldyr, who was a spectator, illustrates this phenomenon.

JUCA AND MARCELO FIGHT WITH KNIVES

Waldyr

Denilson and I were talking to each other as we came down the hill. We looked and saw two guys in the middle of the street, jumping around [he laughs], passing knives from one hand to the other. When we got closer, I recognized the two guys who were fighting, Marcelo and Juca [the owner of a house of prostitution]. Well, each of the two men has a knife, passing it from hand to hand and seeing which one would kill the other first. So they were there fighting, Juca was thrusting the knife at Marcelo, Marcelo was thrusting the knife at Juca. Marcelo managed to cut Juca's hand, right, oh, brother, Juca got mad as hell [*ficou puto da vida*], he was saying to Marcelo, "I'm going to kill you now, you cut my hand, I'm going to kill you, you cut me, you spilled my blood, I'm going to eat you with the point of my knife [*vou te comer na ponta da faca*]."

Well, at that instant Cuica shows up. He went to the fence and broke off a piece of wood and said to them, "Let's go, stop it, stop it." Juca stopped, I think Juca thought that Cuica was going to club him with the piece of wood he ripped from the fence. Well, Juca looked at Cuica, simply looked at Cuica and dropped his hands and Marcelo went to a bar where he was having a few. Juca went home. When he came back, it was with a machete [*facão*], a machete about a meter long.

So then the bunch that was there watching the guys fight went and warned Marcelo. There were about fifty people watching, and they said to Marcelo, "Marcelo, here he comes with a machete in his hand, a huge machete, Marcelo," and Marcelo, instead of wanting to know what Juca's problem was, said, "Let him come, we're really going to go at it now." What did Marcelo do, he goes to the fence and rips out a piece of wood, one he could hardly lift, and a thin stick.

Juca comes toward Marcelo, when he's at the right distance, brother, Marcelo throws the piece of wood at his chest, it made a *buc* [he imitates the sound]. So then Juca didn't give up, Juca came at him with the machete in hand, he came with the machete in hand, Marcelo running around the cars, he even struck Juca twice with the stick [he laughs], on the ribs, Marcelo ran with Juca behind him, Marcelo tripped and fell down, and then everyone closed his eyes. But he didn't quite fall, he didn't fall, by luck he didn't fall. [Juca was] running after him, snorting, with the machete. His eyes were glassy, the only thing that could happen was a disaster, right, since the only thing he wanted at that moment in the whole world was to kill Marcelo.

The fight continued, Marcelo running, he pushed aside that mountain of bricks that's over there, [and] Marcelo goes into the house of I think his sister-in-law. Marcelo's sister-in-law spoke like this to Juca, "Seu Juca [a respectful form of address], please don't do this." Marcelo had already gone in, Juca is standing outside, Juca looks at her, obeys her a little, and Marcelo is prodding Juca with the stick from inside the house.

Rapaz, Juca kicks the door, breaks the door down, and goes in. He invades the house. While Juca is raising the machete to bring it down on Marcelo, Marcelo hits the light fixture and everything goes dark inside. Everything goes dark, and everybody there outside, you could only hear the cracking sounds, *ba! ba! ba!* the machete hitting the furniture [and] the television there inside, and the people outside shouting, right, and of the men who were killing each other inside you only heard the racket of the machete, the quebra-quebra, it was terrible, bicho.

Those guys stayed [inside like that] some seven or eight minutes. Less, five minutes fighting inside there, then they came out with their arms around each other. Juca didn't have the machete, he'd dropped the machete. When the crowd came up Juca let go of Marcelo and Marcelo lay spread out on the ground, and it was then that the story got ugly. The people shouted, "He killed the man, the man is dead," and so on, "Let's help him, let's—" and so on, it was . . . even macabre. And when they went to see Marcelo he had his hand dangling. He caught a heavy blow in the hand, right in the wrist, it cut it [so] that it almost chopped off the hand and he said that he had lost [feeling] on one side and the other had become stiff.

People said that they had been enemies for a long time. They had a rixa. Pedrinho had already saved Marcelo from dying before this. Juca was going to stab Marcelo, [and Pedrinho] shouted to Marcelo, "Watch out for the knife, cara!" So then Marcelo jumped out of the way, but they didn't fight that time. [But] Marcelo is maladjusted, everybody knows that. Marcelo goes out to drink, he sits down at a table, drinks, drinks, drinks, and gets up and leaves and doesn't pay the check. He did this several times in Juca's house and, poxa, Juca got pissed off with him. Marcelo [provoked this rixa], Marcelo is . . . dangerous.

It is only at the end of this story, recounted with flair and a nice sense of drama, that Waldyr provides the pieces that make sense of it. He sees Marcelo as the culprit, a surprise in light of Juca's aggressiveness during the briga, but a conclusion that follows logically once we learn that Marcelo had been drinking at Juca's bar on credit and not paying. Marcelo provoked the rixa, and what happens thereafter becomes his responsibility. The immediate cause of the briga he witnessed does not even seem to interest Waldyr, since this briga is just one more episode in the rixa. It is more significant that, in a previous installment of this rixa, Juca attacked Marcelo from behind with a knife, apparently without warning. As in the case of Biné and Raimundo or of Cravo and his enemy, preliminaries are dispensed with, and escalation occurs rapidly. This is why rixas are so dangerous.

The Region of Paranoia

That rixas are dangerous is also another reason why brigas are dangerous. A violent briga threatens to generate a rixa, and then one is condemned to the insecurity of awaiting the enemy's sudden attack. Here, Cravo describes a briga that gives rise to a rixa:

CRAVO IS STABBED DURING A CARD GAME

Cravo

One time I went to play cards with some other guys. I was losing some Cr$20,000, so when I [finally] won a hand, the other guy [*o caboclo*] grabbed the money and kept it. [I said,] "Rapaz, put the money back," [and he said,] "No, I'm not going to put this money back, I won't put it back for anybody," and so on, and then I drew a twelve[-inch knife]. I said, "Rapaz, you're going to put the money back," and he put the money back, he turned yellow [*se acovardou*], but behind the curtain he had a knife. When I put my knife away, he stabs me here a good one in the arm. It missed my heart, but this guy lives on the run, I've been after him for a long time. Later on he was a porter in the Praia Grande [a warehouse district of São Luís], then he was out of work. He robbed a warehouse, stole a lot of merchandise, and robbed even the warehouse safe, *preto safado* [literally, wicked black man, harsher in Portuguese than in English], and then the earth opened up and he threw himself into it, I've never seen him again in Maranhão.

Cravo has never forgotten the stabbing at the card game; his enemy "lives on the run," as Cravo tracks him. Rixas sometimes have this fixed, engraved quality, especially once the cycle of physical violence has been set in motion. Jair explains:

Papai told me something when I was a child that I've never forgotten: you don't beat up a man, you kill him. I think I agree with my old man, because if you hit a man in the face, he'll never forget it, *never* [his emphasis]. Every time he sees you he checks you out, he's going to get his vengeance on you, you better believe it. To see somebody in the street getting hit in the face, *pa! pa!*, that's a guy tearing out a piece of the life of the other guy. I don't know, this is my opinion, the guy better not do this [to me] because I'll go wherever I have to, but I'm going to avenge myself.

Tito complicates the scenario:

> An enemy can do any kind of malevolent thing to you, even cowardly, treacherously. Even though you want the day to arrive when you can come face-to-face with him to resolve your hatred and your fury, you worry a lot about that day when you'll face him. You feel that this [confrontation] is necessary, but there's another thing that says, porra, what a drag to do this, to face the enemy and settle accounts. I know a lot of people who have enemies. The lower-class [guys] always leave school with a knife. I even asked a guy who I know, "Why do you need to use that thing there, that knife?" So he said, "Listen, cara, this is my guarantee [*garantia*]. There's a guy out there who wants to get me and this thing here is my security." A person goes somewhere but is always worried, he's always awaiting some possibly unpredictable reaction [from his enemy]. Because it's unpredictable, it transforms itself into the region of paranoia [*no campo paranóico*].

This is why special moral allowances are sometimes made for people in a rixa. Recourse to violence is bad, but the jittery fear engendered by a rixa can understandably cause one to react disproportionately to a threat, as Biné may have done when he stabbed Raimundo.

A rixa is in many respects a briga stretched out over a long period of time. There is an underlying emotional rationale for this equation of rixa with a protracted, episodic briga. Both briga and rixa are fueled by vengeance.

A connection or even a provocation sometimes avenges a situation having nothing to do with the person provoked. The urge for vengeance incites escalations, be they penetrating insults or blows. Once the plane of physical violence is reached, vengeance as an irrational, uncontrollable impulse comes into its own, and winding the situation down becomes extremely difficult. The briga may seem to end—but then one of the antagonists returns, armed with a broken bottle, a knife, or a gun, and attacks without warning. A new and more dangerous level of violence is reached. The emotion of the moment hardens into a desire for vengeance that can endure for years.

Accounts of brigas by people in São Luís reveal an elaborate set of understandings about what causes a briga to escalate. Such escalation depends in part on what I have called exacerbations, that is, conditions that inflame, but do not originate in, the inner world of an antagonist. But são-luisenses consider yet another variable: the antagonists' ability to withstand such exacerbations. Whether a *briga* escalates—whether the antagonists become altered—depends therefore on a complementary internal factor, the vulnerability of the actor's psychological equilibrium.

DISEQUILIBRIUM

São-luisense Folk Psychology

People in São Luís assign great importance to the inner, or psychological, side of briga. They bring to confrontations, as they bring to Carnival, an internal capacity for self-regulation. Playing Carnival requires a sense of balance, a knowing when to stop. As vengeful emotions blossom in briga, one's equilibrating skill faces its severest test. Much of the drama of briga is played out in this invisible struggle, for if self-control fails, a briga speeds toward disaster.

The issue of psychological equilibrium is at the center of a folk psychology that posits an uneasy interior world of dangerous impulses and accumulating anxieties and frustrations. These are more or less tenuously prevented from expressing themselves in behavior by a moral and rational personality structure, sometimes called one's formação (literally, formation), a product of childhood training (educação), reason, or religious belief.[1] From time to time, ideally in a controlled way, pressures that build up inside oneself are permitted to escape, as during Carnival, festivals, or other culturally defined or privately devised occasions for desabafo. Difficult situations, however, can challenge one's exercise of dynamic self-control. (I have suggested that Carnival may be a sort of rehearsal for facing such challenges.) A person

---

[1] The resemblance of this folk model to certain elements of the Freudian model is striking: id and superego seem nicely represented here. One wonders whether Freud's model is a systematization and elaboration of a European, or even more widely held, folk theory.

who is equilibrated (*equilibrado*) does not succumb and manages to negotiate his or her way through hazardous events without engaging in uncurbed
aggressive or self-destructive desabafos.

São-luisenses have different ways of formulating this theory, though
similar components are almost always evident. Typically, Tito gives an exceptionally vivid rendition of a general cultural model. He once told me:

> I think that for us ourselves we are a real confusion, a real
> multitude [of people] who we don't know. We confuse our-
> selves [so much] with all the many persons we were during
> the day that . . . I think we could reason and analyze and reach
> the conclusion that, that we are . . . we are deep down what
> maybe we wouldn't want to be. People are really what they
> don't want to be, I mean, deep down, when they are . . .
> alone, right, for example, with their head on the pillow, or
> with a certain insomnia, and when they stop to think about
> something. I don't know if we could classify ourselves as a
> real pile [*monte*] of flesh, rotten, without even hope, and want-
> ing to have the strength to express a hope that maybe [we]
> don't have, or to believe in something that doesn't exist, be-
> cause of the need to believe in something, I don't know, to
> fight for something. I don't know if this is really it.

The pessimism in this statement may or may not be idiosyncratic, but the
images Tito uses to elaborate it are not, roughly coinciding as they do with
evidence from less articulate individuals. He continues:

> The brain can become very dangerous if you don't control it
> [he laughs]. That's what I think. So it's like this: you're always
> policing yourself, always controlling [yourself], saying that
> such and such isn't all right, or [such and such] is all right. But
> I think—I don't think, I *know* [his emphasis]—that the pillow
> part also exists, the part you don't know, the part you won't
> admit. I attribute [this part] to human nature itself. Above all
> else we're human beings.

The brain, for him, is an "uncontrollable machine" (*máquina incontrolável*):

> In a human being . . . there is an uncontrollable machine
> [that is his] brain, his imagination, and he can't control it [he
> laughs]. He can control his actions, in a limited way. But . . .
> the brain . . . the brain, no. I think that [the brain] has [an

evil side] because you can see and feel a bloodthirsty side within each human being. A certain appreciation [*admiração*] for violence, too. These are impulses that obviously should be controlled, should be trained [*educados*], because you run the risk of breeding [*criar*] a monster inside yourself. It's much easier to breed a monster inside you than to breed a man.

This uncontrollable machine is universal, and any person is capable of malevolent acts:

To know profoundly [what is inside a person] is impossible, since neither you nor I know ourselves exactly. We're unpredictable. I don't know what I'm capable of doing, I don't know exactly.

But a person who has what Tito calls (in a phrase of his own coining) an "affirmed personality" (*personalidade afirmada*) is less likely to surrender to the uncontrollable machine. "The worst," he says, "is much less likely to happen in the case of an equilibrated person [i.e., one with an affirmed personality] than in the case of a person who doesn't have an emotional equilibrium." This is because

if you [have an affirmed personality], you can see and understand that this [bad] thought you had is simply a thing of human beings, but doesn't have any practical value, and your scruples [*escrúpulos*] will react right away. But when you don't have an affirmed personality, you can simply be carried away by an emotional thought, and do things that might harm not only yourself but also other people. [If you don't have an affirmed personality,] inevitably any person, or any thought, could influence you to do anything, obscene things, despicable things [*coisas abjetas*].

For Tito, the elements of an affirmed personality include a "philosophy of life," conscience, foresight, and reason. Many, perhaps most, são-luisenses would include religion in this list. Regina, a woman of 35 who is a Spiritist and a Catholic, tells a tale of a man whose Protestant religious "formation" restrains him from violently attacking his wife. Regina and two other women have been discussing a case in which a husband murdered his adulterous wife—unfortunately, a not infrequent occurrence in São Luís.[2]

[2] I read the women a fictional story I had concocted out of some actual murder cases in São Luís and let them discuss it. I presented the same story on another occasion to two men,

THE PROTESTANT PARALYTIC WHO DID NOT MURDER
HIS ADULTEROUS WIFE

Regina

[Murdering his wife] was a weakness; if he had a certain degree of religious formation he wouldn't do a thing like that, because there are a lot of stories around here, not stories, true cases, of people who find their wives having sex with another man and they leave her, without a *briga*. At least here's a story [like that].

The brother [of So-and-So] was married to a girl. So when they were courting, he did everything to test her, like going around with other women, dancing with other women, he did everything. They say that one day she was doing I don't know what and he was there and her sister came and cut her with a knife and she bled and she didn't do anything [i.e., react] at all, and he said, "That's the woman that I want." So then they got married. He was a Protestant, I don't know if it was after they got married that he became one. He was always saying that the day he found his wife messing around [*fazendo safadeza*] on him he would kill her on the spot.

[But] the story happened completely differently. He got some kind of problem with his spine, it seems that it was spilling a liquid, and he had to go right away to São Paulo. She had a sewing machine, so the doctor told [her to sell it for the fare], because if not, his legs would be paralyzed, the way they still are today. She said she wouldn't sell the sewing machine and that he should try to get there on his own. Ah, what that man suffered. It came to the point that when he was taken from the place where he lived [and moved] to another place, he traveled there on top of the truck, getting rained on,

---

Eduardo and Gabriel. They produced analyses that made use of the same model. Eduardo commented, for example: "Tomorrow you see her kissing another man, puxa, if you don't have a formation, if you don't have equilibrium, an equilibrated mental state, you can arrive at a tragic end. Now, if you are a 'formed person' [*pessoa formada*, similar to Tito's 'affirmed personality'] who can dominate yourself, and if you know that there are others who can take her place, you can't commit a crime like this." Gabriel remarked that it is hard to evaluate the man's situation unless it happens to you—"until [your own] feelings are provoked like that or [until your own] reason is challenged like that." In other words, Gabriel and Eduardo, like Tito and Regina, see the danger as feelings that are provoked and reason (or religious formation) that is challenged to contain those inflamed feelings.

while she was down in the cab with the driver fooling around with him.

They say that he cried like a child, she didn't give him meals, he was dirty, lying in a hammock, without eating. Then one day he was crawling like a child on the ground, and his tears, oh! He called out, he was needing her so much, calling her at night, he awoke wanting I don't know what, and that was when he realized there was a guy with her in the hammock, in his room, [right] where he was sleeping. So from that day on she was terrified [that he would do something to her], he would call her, asking, "Maria! Give me such and such," and she wouldn't go [near him] for anything in the world. He said to her, "You can come as close as you want to my hammock and I won't do anything at all to you." Just look at that: if [what she did] isn't a humiliation for a man, and he had said that if his wife did that he'd kill her on the spot!

That's why I say that sometimes religion helps. That man has suffered until today. He's a Protestant. He went to São Paulo to see if they could fix him up but they couldn't. He said it was obvious that she didn't want a man who was sick, she wanted a man who was healthy, he was crying, they say that he cried tears like . . . a child . . . and a bunch of little children laughing at him, with him crying like a child!

That's why I say that sometimes we're weak, sometimes there are situations that leave us in such a mess that when we think about it we've got a hole right on top of us and we need to have a lot of guts [*muito peito*] to confront it because it isn't easy. This is a true story, something real, he's still alive. These kinds of things are the best proof that there are a lot of people who manage to overcome these cases of betrayal, men and women, on the basis of prayer [and] religion.

Regina constructs here an extreme case, in which the man declares himself predisposed to respond violently to a betrayal—he puts his wife on notice that he will kill her—and then is confronted with a betrayal (indeed, a primordial form of sacanagem) of the "in-my-face" variety, which he is forced to witness owing to his infirmity. Yet this terrible humiliation fails to provoke violence because the man's religious formation contains his turbulent emotions. Regina is not promoting Protestantism: she herself is not a Protestant.[3] What is important is that religion, perhaps any religion, provides a structure to contain dangerous impulses, in just the same way that reason or moral training does so.

Tito tells a story about himself that bears resemblance to Regina's morality tale and points up even more clearly the basic correspondence of the cognitive schemes of the two individuals, despite their dissimilarities of gender, class, age, and religion. Although he claims not to have an affirmed personality, in the following passage Tito describes an incident during which he feels he acted in an equilibrated manner. The events took place in a modest bar in a poor neighborhood of the city, where he was working as a waiter.

TITO DOES NOT THROW THE BAR OWNER'S
BROTHER-IN-LAW OUT THE WINDOW

Tito

I was over there [at the bar] Friday night. A man came in, it looked to me like he was a little lost, accompanied by another guy. So I came up and I said "Good evening" to him, and I asked him if he would like to sit at a table. So then he looked at me and said, "What is it that you want?" [*O que que tu quer?*— a provocative remark], as if he were someone who wanted to get me to say [*quisesse roubar*] a few offensive words so that he could immediately give me about ten slaps, twenty punches, and ten kicks in the face. I said, "No, I really don't want anything, I'd just like to know what you [*o senhor*, a formal, polite locution] would like me to do for you, with all the pleasure in the world." I said, "I really didn't have the pleasure of meeting you, but who knows, if you would be so kind as to introduce yourself, I would be very pleased." Well, [he said,] "Listen closely, I'm the brother-in-law of the owner of this bar." I said, "Excellent. Very good. I'm also his friend, I'm not his brother-in-law, but I'm his friend."

All I know is that later he thanked me a lot. All right, I did all that, but what I wanted to do was to hit him with a chair,

[3]Protestants are a small but visible minority in São Luís. Most are affiliated with evangelical sects. In general they are viewed with both a touch of respect (as "serious" and relatively free from vices) and a touch of derision (as humorless, Bible-toting, and sanctimonious). They are often called *crentes* (believers), a word that carries a hint of slightly amused derision. Some regard Protestantism as a cure, albeit a radical one, for alcoholism, criminality, or similar spiritual ills.

right after he asked those questions. What I wanted to do was to give him ten punches and after that hit him a lot of times with a chair and throw him out the window, not the door, [but the window,] which is about fifteen feet off the ground. I don't mean to describe myself as a guy with an affirmed personality, because I don't really consider myself to be one, I think I'm still lacking a lot of things, but as a guy who is concerned about thinking [things through] so as to avoid certain types of problems.

Tito's emotions are clear. The man's arrogant behavior produces in Tito a rage that he smothers with his reason, much as the Protestant man's rage and hurt at his wife's behavior are subdued by his religious belief.

By contrast, when one is disequilibrated, dangerous impulses break through the structures of reason, religion, and upbringing that normally contain them, and wreak havoc on oneself or others. This can be a temporary state, as when the person is experiencing severe personal problems that demand to be expelled (e.g., Tito's desabafo directed at the bus conductor). Alternatively, lack of equilibrium can be a permanent character trait. Bocado is an unskilled laborer aged 24, a volatile individual who is inclined to get mixed up in quarrels and fights. His testimony about himself is suggestive. He gives a hair-raising preview of a rematch with an enemy:

> I've got a rixa [i.e., briga] today at 6:00, a moleque [punk] who I've already fought with, but when he shows up I won't freeze, we'll fight right then. If he's got a knife he might even cut me but I'll kill him wherever he is. I'll really kill him. I don't have a child to feed, I don't have a fucking thing [porra nenhuma], I'm not married, wherever I am, fine, I'll grab the shotgun and let fly right in his chest so he can't even cry out, right in the heart and bust up everything. I'm "invoked" [invocado, filled with fury], I'm crazy, I'm invoked as hell.

The disequilibrated person is explosive, invoked, harbors a fury that does not find an outlet in normal and harmless ways but erupts chaotically and violently against friends, enemies, family, strangers, or self. To expel in a controlled way is desirable and salutary; to explode is disgraceful and potentially disastrous. The disequilibrated person is like a bomb, and the biggest danger in briga-like situations is inadvertently to run up against such an individual. This is why Tito has developed a sort of radar to advise him about the person he is dealing with, and why são-luisenses exercise care in anonymous encounters: a face-to-face confrontation with the wrong person can, with lightning rapidity, turn into a lethal encounter in which apologies and even self-abasement are of no avail.

Disequilibrium and Escalation

The next two stories, first-person accounts of brigas that occurred in small, informal neighborhood bars, involve Pato, 22, unemployed, known in his bairro as a relatively benign sort of *malandro*, or scoundrel, and Bocado, whom we met above. First, Pato tells how an invitation to drink turned into a fight with knives. It is early morning, and Pato is coming from an all-night umbanda session at the house of Salomão, located on the hill above Pato's own house.[4] Pato often attends these rituals as a spectator, drinking cachaça, sometimes smoking marijuana, and enjoying the mesmerizing dance of the adepts and the percussive music.

PATO IS "INVITED" FOR A DRINK HE DOESN'T WANT

Pato

I was really kind of bombed [*meio chumbado*], completely drunk, I was coming from the festa, right. I was passing by [a small neighborhood bar] and a guy there called me inside. So I went in, in a good mood, I talked with him and so on. When I get inside the guy insists that I have a shot of cachaça, so I did, right, and suddenly right away he ordered me to drink another one, calling me names, ridiculing [*esculhambando*] me. So I said, "Hey, compadre, porra, I don't feel like drinking any more, I'm OK right now, I'm going home." He starts to ridicule me, so I say, "OK, OK" [i.e., "that's enough"], so then he pulls a big knife, [the kind you use] for cutting bread, so I said, "Oh, yeah? All right, wait here," and I [went down the hill to my] house. [It was] early in the morning, around 5:40 or so. I get home, put a beautiful machete [*um facão porreta*] in my belt and go back up.

When I get there on top the guy is coming down from the

[4]Umbanda is an Afro-Brazilian religion that combines elements of African creeds, Catholicism, and Spiritism. See Brown (1986) for a discussion of the origins, ritual, and political significance of a major branch of umbanda called *umbanda pura*, pure umbanda, in southern Brazil. I would underscore, however, Brown's observation that umbanda is highly variable in practice. Although umbanda was not a main focus of my work, I visited a number of umbanda centers in São Luís working-class neighborhoods and was impressed by their diversity and innovativeness.

festa, right, and then, poxa, I'd gone through all that agony
with him, right, so then I leaned back like this, with Waldyr
[a friend of Pato's who had accompanied him back up the hill
but a short time later ran away] on the other tree trunk that
was there. And then he comes up to me calling me fuleiro,
pulling his knife on me, [so] I pulled my machete and threw
myself at him, [I tried to] cut him [but] my machete fell behind me. So then I turn to grab the machete, right, the guy
comes at me and I grabbed the machete and hit him with the
blade on his back, *pa!* My machete had a point like this; I say
to him, "Now I'm going to stick the point [of this machete]
into you all the way, because of your wickedness [*safadeza*],"
and that's when he runs, back toward [the bar], and he goes
inside.

I left [and went a short distance away], and then he and his
sister come toward me, his sister holding on to him to keep
him from fighting, and he [objecting]. He grabbed two big
rocks, and then he came toward me wanting to fight with me
in the middle of the street. I just said this: "Watch out, rapaz,
I'll stab you or you'll hit me with a rock and one of us will
die," but the guy didn't want to hear this, he followed me, me
with the machete, but then, listen, to dirty yourself with shit
like this [*uma porra daquela*] is nowhere [and that was the end
of it].

That Bocado, unlike Pato, sees himself as a dangerously mercurial person lends his briga, despite the absence of knives and machetes, a more
sinister tone:

SOMEONE DRINKS BOCADO'S SHOT OF CACHAÇA
Bocado

The briga was like this. I'm a guy, you see me [being] quiet
[now], but at the same time I'm, you know how it is? I'm
crude [*grosseiro*]. I was *drinking* [his emphasis] in Abreu's house
[which serves also as a neighborhood bar]. [I said,] "Abreu,
pour a shot for me here." He pours it. "Pour another one,
Abreu." He pours it, *pa!* His wife calls him to the kitchen:
"Abreu, come here." I'm drinking and smoking my cigarette,
and then the guy drinks the shot, [another guy who was there]

drank it. [I said,] "Hey, rapaz, I poured that shot for me, not for you." So then he came at me with all this stuff [*ele veio com onda comigo*]. Ah, rapaz, I don't know what . . . I gave him a punch in the eye [and] a real hard kick. When I kicked him, he said, "I'm going to get you now." I said, "Come on, porra." I grabbed a bottle, broke it on Abreu's counter like this, *pa!* and held the bottle like this and said, "Come on, porra, now, you son of a bitch [*filho de uma égua*]." I really gave it to him. He was some guy named Miguel. We really went at it, but later he came to apologize to me. I said, "Nothing doing, there's no apology, cara, you don't even know me, [and you come and] drink my cachaça right in front of me. Are you paying for it?" He said: "[It's OK,] rapaz, I'm paying for this one, not you."

Both Bocado and Pato paint themselves the victims of provocations, Bocado of a classic bar provocation—someone availing himself of someone else's beer or cachaça, without asking or being invited—and Pato of a kind of inversion of this situation, an attack masquerading as generosity. These are "right-in-my-face" provocations, neither subtle nor artful. Pato's host rapidly revealed the aggression momentarily concealed behind his ostensible hospitality. Accepting the second drink would have been no solution because the scene would have simply repeated ad infinitum until, barring some stunningly inventive maneuver, Pato was forced to decline— the connection the provoker was waiting for. Similarly, the man who drank Bocado's cachaça under his very nose, whether he fell victim to an act of momentary madness, blithely ignoring the possible consequences, or whether he actually wanted to provoke Bocado, was certainly going to evoke a connection. Both provocations were blatant challenges aimed more at creating the necessary preconditions for a briga than at scoring quick points in a game of humiliation.

But these brigas developed differently. When Pato refused the second offer of a drink and excused himself, his provoker could have let him leave and things would have gone no further. Instead, the man launched a stream of insults, the effect of which was to verify that the "offer" was a provocation, in effect throwing it in Pato's face. When this too (according to Pato's version) failed to get a reaction, the man pulled a knife. This act finally sent Pato scrambling home to get a knife of his own, and the briga turned violent shortly thereafter.

Pato's story gives the impression that his opponent was determined to start a fight by moving from sacanagem to insult to armed threat. The story may not be literally true, but it is culturally credible that some people look for a fight by insistently provoking others. Joana explains:[5]

Sometimes a lot of people leave home with bad intentions, like during Carnival, people playing and everything, [and] a person comes up and provokes [you], pushing, stepping on you and pinching so that you'll make some kind of response so that they can fight with you. I think that a person like that wants to fight with anyone else, to desabafar, to expel something [*botar alguma coisa pra fora*]. Many people drink because they want to desabafar with the liquor, [and] all of a sudden, either he or she gets angry with something or other and provokes someone, anyone, so as to start [*arrumar*] a briga, just like that [*sem mais nem menos*]. When the person gets there they're ready to fight—hitting, wanting to avenge themselves [*querendo se desforrar*] for something that the other person has nothing to do with. Sometimes it's because the person has a lot of problems and can't manage to figure them out alone and wants to take vengeance on anyone. There are a lot of people who leave home with the intention of fighting. Like this: "Today I'm going to the praça, there's a festa in the praça, I'm going to look for a briga." [The person might have] problems with her mother, or a problem with unemployment. Many people [fight because they] have a weak mind [*mente fraca*]. A person who goes out, let's say, every day looking for work, every time he goes to a place he gets a "no," he's going to think he's inferior: Hey, everyone works, everyone finds a job, it's only me that doesn't. So then he goes out, goes and drinks, gives himself up to despair . . . this happens with really a lot of people. [And if he gets into a briga,] I think it gives him relief. [But] it doesn't really help, he can't

[5]Compare Joana's statement here with Tito's hypothetical case in which "João" engineers a fight with "Pedro" ("João Accuses Pedro of Having Provoked Him," Chap. 6). Cf. also Dionísio's observation: "There are [some] people who are frustrated. They don't do this or that because everyone might think badly of them. So they get frustrated. And sometimes they expel this frustration that they feel and generally hurt others. And this causes the thing that people call briga. He's afraid to do this, and ultimately he thinks it's wrong, [but] after he lets loose those frustrations he feels like a new person, a renewed person." On another occasion Dionísio qualified this last comment, noting that "briga wounds you physically and at times psychologically. [A briga] leaves you renewed [but] unhappy, because it hurts people." Joana also sees discharge through briga as leaving a bad residue.

really manage to get rid of [that problem], he can't forget it, it gets worse. Because tomorrow is another day, he sleeps, in the morning if he gets over the drinking [of the previous night] he's going to remember what he did, [and] he's going to get even more disgusted [*revoltado*].

Both Pato and Bocado were victims of flagrant provocations. But whereas Pato laid the primary responsibility for the escalation of the briga on his antagonist, Bocado prefaced his story with the admission that he himself was "crude." Pato claimed implicitly that only repeated, gross, public provocations could induce him to fight; Bocado admitted that he had a short fuse. In these two cases, something happened that são-luisenses know to be true about briga—brigas escalate when at least one of the antagonists (Pato's host, in the first case, and Bocado himself, in the second) is disequilibrated (*desequilibrado*). Pato, the benign scoundrel, needed a push to make him go deeper into the briga sequence. Not so Bocado; invoked, he (more than his provoker) urged the briga onward into violence.

Plunging into Briga

At times a person who is disequilibrated seems, in briga stories, determined to provoke and then push a briga to its ultimate consequences. The motive of such an individual is hard to evaluate with confidence, but it often looks like enraged self-destructiveness.

Pato witnessed a briga bearing the stamp of a single disequilibrated person that occurred in one of the hundreds of terreiros that pepper the poor bairros of the city. The house of Salomão, a residence also devoted to the practice of the syncretic religion umbanda, sits on an unpaved hilly street in a poor area of the city ironically called Brasília, after Brazil's gleaming capital. This is a small terreiro whose *pai-de-santo* (ritual leader) is, as the name of the house indicates, a man named Salomão. Salomão draws his followers mainly from Brasília and nearby neighborhoods. One evening a small penny arcade, just a few booths, was set up at Salomão's as part of a religious festival. To this festival came Gato, a young man with a reputation in the bairro for being disequilibrated. The story is told by Pato, who witnessed the event.

GATO'S BRIGA

Pato

We were all playing at Salomão's house, when Gato showed up. They had a shooting gallery set up there and Gato paid to play. It was that kind of brincadeira where you shoot at bottles trying to make them fall down. [There was a shot] and the lights went out. The man at the shooting gallery blamed Gato, and it *was* really Gato who had shot at the bulb. Gato was saying, "It wasn't me" and so on, and the guy [was saying], "Ah, it was you" and so on, that kind of argument that always goes on, and then Gato pulls out a knife this big, twelve inches. [He was] altered, really altered, he had become transformed, and then he began swinging his knife through the booth, knocking over bottles and breaking everything. When he began hitting the bottles and knocking everything over, the man ran toward Salomão's house, [shouting,] "Let's call Salomão," this, that, and the other thing. At this time Salomão didn't even appear, he kept far away, just observing, just looking, inside his house.

Then Gato left. Later, here comes Gato again, then he slaps the guy with the blade of the knife, then he breaks up everything again. This was when Salomão came out [of the house, but] Gato had already left again.

Then everybody was enjoying themselves and everything. I was there outside the house, when here comes Gato again with a knife in his hand, comes in heading for the room [*barracão*] where people dance, right, and Salomão came upon him there inside the dance room. Then Salomão came out, bringing Gato with him, talking to him, [trying to] calm him down. At this moment they were outside the door, and it seems like one of Salomão's friends was standing nearby. Gato pulled the knife from its sheath and asked, "Come over here, boy [*garoto*], what do you want here? Is this conversation any of your business?" and so on, this, that, and the other, then the guy said "But—" and at this Gato pulled the knife and gave him a slap with the blade on the side of the face near the ear, like this, *ta!*, and then the guy went away, [holding his face] like this from the pain. This was when Salomão tried to take the knife, right, he fell upon Gato and managed to take the knife, except that when he went to take the knife, Gato cut Salomão's finger. Then Gato tried to plunge the knife [into Salomão's stomach]. Then everybody jumped on Gato, more or less eighteen people on top of him, making a circle around him. They beat him until he passed out.

Gato seems to insist on this *briga*. There is a clear progression in his provocations and aggressions, as if he is aiming for the confrontation with Salomão, a confrontation that, under the circumstances—it occurs in Salomão's house, and Salomão bears the ultimate responsibility for order—must lead to a dramatic climax. Gato's actions are punctuated with absences; after each absence he escalates the provocation.

The first episode begins with shooting a light bulb (a marginally, if not convincingly, deniable action) and escalates to a *quebra-quebra* (literally, break-break: breaking up a residence, shop, bus, or whatever). The second combines a quebra-quebra with physical violence against the man at the shooting gallery. The third begins with an armed invasion of the dance floor during a sacred ritual—an absolutely prohibited act, guaranteed to generate a response. Gato hooked Salomão. Previously, Salomão, probably sensing a briga coming, had acted with restraint, avoiding intervention, but now Gato gave him no alternative. Salomão's attempted disarming of Gato bears a resemblance to Biné's stabbing of Raimundo: both are preventive measures. In this case, however, there is no evidence of a *rixa*. The problem is that Gato is altered, disequilibrated, determined to push the confrontation to a limit for obscure, possibly self-destructive, reasons of his own. His escalations are prompted by his own inner drive to plunge headlong into briga, come what may. Such an unrestrained plunge is bound to have a disastrous outcome, as it does here when Gato is beaten by the mob, a predictable ending for someone who creates a violent disruption in a terreiro during a religious ritual.

Disequilibrated persons, of course, have their reasons. Bocado expresses his poignantly in an account of another bar fight, this time between him and a waiter, occasioned by a classic source of brigas, dispute over payment for a drink.

A WAITER INSULTS BOCADO'S MOTHER

Bocado

One time I was with my brother and my sister-in-law Roseane at a festa, and then a friend of mine [named Josué] showed up and asked the waiter for a beer. So the waiter brings it, and [Josué] says, "I don't want it anymore, put it on Bocado's table," and so I asked him, "Rapaz, is this already paid for?" and he said, "It's already paid for," and so the waiter *pa!* puts the bottle on my table. When I finished off that beer my brother says, "Rapaz, go over to Abreu's house and buy a liter of Velho Barreiro [an inexpensive brand of cachaça] for us to drink here at the festa," so I went there and bought the liter and came back.

So then the waiter came up and said, "Rapaz, look here, who's going to pay for this beer?" I said, "Who ordered the beer?" He said, "It was Josué." I said, "Did he pay for it?" He said, "No, no he didn't, you're the one who's going to pay for it." I said, "Rapaz, you heard what he said and he said he had already paid for the beer and I'm not going to pay for any beer, I didn't order beer." He said, "Rapaz, you come in here broke [*liso*], if it was your mother who was broke I'd give her a beer." And then he sat down.

Then I sat there and thought, porra, the guy insulted my mother. So then I got up and asked him, "What was that, rapaz?" He repeated it, and then I went after him [*eu me meti*]. Rapaz, it was a punch that knocked him over along with the table and everything, *pa!* we're going to go at it now. I hit him, then my brothers came over and grabbed me, and I said, "Porra, let me go." When I'm fighting I don't like anyone to grab me. And then there was some fucking ugly fighting [*aí foi pau feio pra porra*]. There was [blood], they [the waiters] cut us.

And then I said, "The problem was that he insulted my mother, and my mother's got nothing to do with this business here." When my mother died I was one year old, I didn't know my mother and I hardly know my father. I really don't even know my mother, I even wish I had a picture of my mother so I could look at her face, but I don't have one. I don't even know what she looks like. Rapaz, I prayed to God that better my father had died than my mother. Everyone says that I look a lot like her, and then I say, "I never knew my mother." [They say,] "Your mother was a very good person, a very fine person [*era legal*]." There are people who ask me, "Which one would you want to die, your mother or your father?" I say, "Better my father than my mother." Rapaz, if I had my mother I wouldn't be the way I am now. In the middle of the living room I used to ask for my mother's breast. When I think of this story, which my grandmother told me, I cry like hell [*eu choro pra porra*], I'm serious. I'm the most messed up [*lascado*] person in the world, but not my brothers and sisters. Vily works in [a federal agency and] makes a lot of money, Ilona works for the Caravelas Coffee Company, she's a book-keeper, all the money passes through her hands. The one who is fucked [*fodido*] is me, I'm the one who's really fucked.

The circumstances that tend to excite violent emotions (Chapter 7) tell only half the story of briga. People in São Luís also ascribe fundamental importance to the antagonists' psychological equilibrium. Psychological equilibrium depends on the relation between passions and formation—the moral, religious, and/or rational structures charged with containing those passions. In the chronically disequilibrated person, easily inflamed emotions tend to overwhelm a weak formation; readily altered, such a person pushes a briga toward a disastrous climax of serious injury or death.

9

EXITS

Briga's Deadly Climax

angerous passions draw a briga toward a deadly climax. To abort the briga sequence, one must fight off the "organic necessity" to connect with a provocation. If that effort fails, and the real fighting starts, options close down. The antagonists become altered, wanting nothing other than revenge for offenses and blows already received. At this point, in Tito's words, "You can hit, or be hit, or kill, or die."

The prototypical briga ends in an unpremeditated murder. This is the appropriate dramatic resolution of a briga, its "natural" consequence, much as the gun on the table in act 1 must go off in act 3. The event is improvised, subject to the cultural constraints of the briga model, around the specter of violent death. An intrinsically unpredictable event, briga leaves open the question of who (antagonist, witness, peacemaker) might kill, who might die, and how.

This drama is obviously compelling: brigas always attract crowds suffused with excitement and apprehension. After a violent briga, people describe themselves as having been transfixed, torn between fascination and terror. Some told me that although watching brigas made them feel sick, they found the spectacle gripping. During the briga that culminated in Sérgio's murder (see Chapter 10), Léia was sitting with friends at a sidewalk table of an adjacent bar. She describes painfully, with exceptional candor,

174

her emotional response to this briga, which had a powerful and disturbing effect on her:

> My first reaction was to get up and get away from the chairs that were coming in our direction. My tendency was to protect myself, to get behind a car, something like that. But when I saw the gun I turned around, I couldn't believe that they were shooting all of a sudden, and I really couldn't manage to move myself from where I was. And the only reason I didn't see what was going on any better was because there were people in front of me. I couldn't manage to move, either to flee or to get closer. My initial impulse to get away got bottled up [*ficou trancado*] and I stopped as if I couldn't believe that this could have happened. . . . I don't know [why I couldn't move]. I wouldn't know whether to tell you if it was . . . to stay to see what was going to happen, curiosity maybe as a spectator at this scene, or if it was really . . . I don't know, the terror of not knowing where to run. . . . I wouldn't know how to explain it to you, thinking about it right now, maybe it was wanting to see what was going to happen. Basically, what I felt was fear. . . . It was fear and it was . . . anticipation of something serious [*grave*] . . . a fear of this, what might happen. What I would like is really that nothing had happened, not even that the tables and chairs had fallen over, all that interfered brutally in a pleasant moment that we were passing. But I can't, I can't, I can't refuse to admit that that paralysis, suddenly it seems that a fascination over something that could happen, an anticipation of something [that might happen] could be touched with a desire that perhaps it would happen, but at that moment I think that this didn't occur to me consciously.

Tito, in another candid statement, summarizes:

> It's hard to say that people really like to fight, but I can say that they have a very great thirst [for briga]. You can see it in all their faces, in the streets, in their body movements, in their provocations, in their reactions. It's that side of people that likes blood, to see blood. What makes them curious is really the result, not exactly briga [itself], but the result. If

the result doesn't lead to anything, let's say, if some more sensitive [*sensíveis*] people break up the briga, well, I think people feel frustrated, because I think that deep down they want the two to kill each other, or one to kill the other.

Whether in fact people want (in any usual sense of the word) to see the antagonists kill each other is doubtful: the emotional mix stirred up by briga is too contradictory and too complex to be characterized so simply. But Léia's introspection and Tito's analysis point to death as the "result" that does not "frustrate," although it produces revulsion, outrage, and horror. A sense of awful dramaturgical necessity, based in understandings about the nature of briga and its psychological underpinnings, collides with the strong emotions, themselves often conflicting, aroused by the spectacle of violence.

Briga means danger—physical, psychological, moral, existential danger. That is why the threat of briga triggers restitutive mechanisms. This chapter describes são-luisenses' understandings of how brigas can end short of the tragic resolution prefigured in early aggressive exchanges. An expected pattern emerges: as a briga develops, exits become less and less voluntary. The further into briga the antagonists descend, the greater is the impairment to psychological equilibrium. Increasingly, therefore, third parties, themselves potentially violent or even out of control, must intervene if the briga is not to follow the disastrous course dictated by the logic of runaway passions.

Voluntary Exits

Especially during the early stages of a briga, the sequence may be broken off voluntarily by one or the other antagonist to prevent a move into more dangerous territory. Three such exits are available: not connecting, apologizing, and abandoning the scene of the interaction.

Not Connecting

Not connecting with a provocation is, as we have seen, one of the principal strategies used to interrupt the preliminary ritual during which an encounter gets redefined as a briga. As Dionísio, who has long hair and a frail appearance, passes in the street, certain individuals call him a "faggot" (*veado, qualhira*), intending to provoke him. Dionísio suffers from a heart condition and cannot fight them; his solution is to not connect, that is, to act as if nothing is happening and continue on his way.

Physical separation follows not connecting. For Dionísio or his harriers to engage in chitchat after a provocation would be awkward: the resulting frame confusion would make interaction difficult if not impossible.[1]

Apologizing

Any impression that São Luís's praças are mainly battle zones is an artifice of my subject matter. The people of São Luís, despite the material burdens of poverty, poor health, and sometimes disgraceful living conditions, and despite less tangible but no less oppressive spiritual frustrations, coexist by and large in a civil, even congenial, fashion. Bumping incidents are likely to evoke apologies, smiles, and reassuring pats on the back, displays of courtesy and concern that justifiably give Brazilians a reputation for cordiality upon which they pride themselves and for which foreigners habitually praise them.

The homem cordial, the cordial man, is a Brazilian self-image that has become an internationally held stereotype of the Brazilian. One can be too cynical: very few who have lived in Brazil would claim that the homem cordial is a fraud and that Brazilian warmth in face-to-face relationships is a deceitful mask. Yet it would be a mistake to ignore the social context of the homem cordial, a context that conspicuously includes briga. The man who graciously apologizes for jostling you in the Praça Deodoro at 3 A.M. on the last night of Carnival may glow as much with communitas as with cachaça, but he is also reassuring you that the accident was not on purpose. Where does goodwill stop and caution begin? Knowing that brigas start with provocations, that provocations are subjective events, and that brigas can be fatal provides a powerful incentive for courtesy. To argue that the apology is one or the other—an act of consideration or of prudence—would be, I think, to miss the point that consideration and prudence dovetail in an act that is perhaps consciously neither.

Apology, then, can prevent a briga by redefining a possible provocation as an accident. Further into the sequence it can also serve as an exit strategy, but, as is equally true of not connecting, apology rapidly loses credibility or acquires the taint of humiliation once the adversaries have conspired to erect the briga frame. In the shoving incident on the bus, for example, dur-

[1] But sometimes even leaving the scene seems like a connection. I remember another provocation (at the same bus stop, near my house) involving a drunk, this time aimed at a woman who was waiting there with a child. This drunk, who was carrying a stout length of sugarcane in one hand as he staggered from the direction of the market, stopped in front of the woman and fixed her with a menacing gaze. She gave no indication that the man existed: she altered neither her own gaze, her expression, nor her posture. For her, walking away was clearly out of the question. After several moments, the drunk moved on up the avenue. At this, the woman—and the rest of us who were waiting there—visibly relaxed; she moved rapidly past me to the market end of the bus stop, as far away from the drunk as she could get.

ing which Tito with a glance advised the man that he considered the shove to be a provocation, the man responded by hanging his head in an attitude of apology. This was not a preventive apology: there had already been a provocation and a connection. The man's after-the-fact apology was a retraction, as if he were saying, "I provoked you and I'm sorry about it." Tito emerged a winner in this interaction.

Once insults have been traded, apology is usually ruled out on both logical and emotional grounds. Both participants have agreed to fight; why now subvert the briga frame with an apology? Moreover, insults threaten the equilibrium required to make an apology. Apology at this stage therefore seems either insincere, irrelevant, or cowardly. After the briga has terminated in some other way, however, apology once again makes sense. After the briga between Bocado and the fellow who drank his cachaça, the latter came to apologize. The motive for his apology was obviously not to end the briga but to forestall the development of a rixa.

Abandoning the Scene

Two people cannot physically fight unless both are in the same place at the same time. A third way to break off a briga sequence is therefore for one of the antagonists to abandon the scene of the interaction. This exit can occur at any stage of the briga, but leaving after aggressions have been exchanged is not the same as leaving beforehand.

Moving off is usually a relatively painless and effective way of terminating the briga sequence during the preliminary phase. Leaving will also end the sequence—at least temporarily—during later stages, but the use of this tactic becomes increasingly problematic. First, moving off begins to look and feel like running away: if abandoning the scene takes the form of flight, it is humiliating. This consideration weighs more heavily on those who attach great importance to masculine honor, like Santos, a clerk in the police department:[2]

> When I go out at night I go out armed. I'm not going to come home with my face swollen, saying that someone beat me up. If someone provokes me with words, all right, I just go away. But there are guys who provoke you with knives, with revolvers. I have three children; how can I come home with my face swollen, demoralized, telling them that someone beat me up? If someone comes up to me like that, attacking me, I'll send him right to Gavião [the chief cemetery of São Luís].

[2]This quotation was reconstructed from notes rather than (as is the case with other quotations) from the transcript of a taped interview.

Cravo, the former hired gun, adheres to a similar view—only a coward runs away—but softens it a bit:

> It's cowardly [to run from a briga]. I've never run, sometimes I've been stabbed or shot but I've never run, no way, and also I've had mobs after me to hide from but not to run from. My friend was saying [to me, while I was hiding], "Are you scared?" [and I said,] "No, I'm not scared, no, rapaz, I'm just avoiding a misfortune." . . . Because life is good, I wouldn't like either to kill or to die, life is good, if you die it's the worst thing there is, you've fucked yourself [*você se fodeu*], but if you kill, your soul becomes burdened, your spirit becomes burdened. . . . From time to time you dream of that guy you killed, if his name was Manoel, well then, you dream of Manoel, of João.

Cravo's subtle (but perhaps unconvincing) distinction between running and hiding reveals a dilemma: fleeing from a briga is bad, but so are killing and dying. A similar observation, although weighted more on the side of flight, is embedded in a simple maxim that Pato attributes to his father: "Better to run from a briga than to stick around for a death." The words of both Cravo and Pato reflect, albeit in different proportions, conflicting concerns with honor and safety. The point is that going away during the preliminaries does not necessarily compromise honor, at least not deeply, but later on it can. Prudence works in favor of running away; honor requires one to stay put.

This leads to a second observation: much apparent running away from brigas is not running away at all, because it interrupts but does not end hostilities. A violent briga is subject to resumption, either as a renewal of the initial briga after a short interval (as a new episode in an extended briga) or as an entirely new briga within the context of a rixa. Once physical aggression has occurred, one of the most frequent reasons why a person leaves the scene is to secure a weapon. Thus under certain circumstances—if there is a rixa between the antagonists, or if serious physical aggressions have already been exchanged—abandoning the scene may portend resumption of the sequence at a more dangerous level of violence.

Interventions

When brigas reach the point of physical violence, that is, when the preliminaries have been concluded, voluntary exits tend to shut down. By the time blows are exchanged, challenges have already been issued and accepted, relatively painless options for disengagement have been bypassed, and honor has been consciously placed on the line. It is not just that some strategies no longer work; rather, they have already been cast aside, and to resurrect them at a later stage would contradict the expressed intent of the person who has rejected them. To revive these strategies would expose one to shame and ridicule, which could have been avoided by not connecting, abandoning the scene, or apologizing at an earlier stage. An example was the case of the boy and the drunk at the bus stop, when the boy tried to not connect after he had already inadvertently connected. The tactic worked, but it was an awkward and barely successful effort requiring a degree of self-abasement, an improvised remedy for a bad error of judgment.

Given what everyone knows about briga, then, certain exit routes have their moment during the preliminary ritual but do not remain viable beyond it. This is, as I have indicated, partly a logical phenomenon—not connecting after one has already connected seems senseless and unconvincing—and partly a consequence of the emotional dynamics of briga. Once a person has been challenged and accepted the challenge, especially if the transaction is public, he or she is trapped cognitively and emotionally in a new situation. To back out now will be humiliating because one's honor is at stake. Moreover, as personal testimony indicates, the feelings of having been challenged or in some way violated by the adversary often create a powerful desire for vengeance. Apology cannot satisfy this need. The emotions require a strike at the adversary, who experiences it as a challenge and a violation likewise requiring vengeance. And so the question arises, How can the retaliatory cycle end short of incapacitating injury or death?

When blows begin in earnest, a briga will careen toward disaster unless someone intervenes. People in São Luís understand that there are three possibilities. Third parties may step in and separate the adversaries: this is known as an intervention by the "Quit-It Gang" (*turma do deixa-disso*). Allies of the adversaries may enter the briga, transforming it into a battle. And in what is often perceived as a worst-case scenario, the police may arrive to pacify the situation.

The Quit-It Gang

The Quit-It Gang is one of the great institutions of briga. Drawn from the crowd of onlookers, the Quit-It Gang steps in at the critical moment, after the two antagonists have had a chance to go at it for a while but before things get too serious, that is, before life and limb become imminently endangered. The timing suggests ambivalence on the part of the Quit-It Gang, but by stepping in at this point it performs a crucial function, giving the antagonists enough time to preserve honor but not to kill each other. In a briga in which the antagonists are defending honor but are not yet altered, they sometimes later confess that they were anxiously awaiting the intervention of the Quit-It Gang before things got out of hand. That is, they could not honorably run away and did not want to get seriously injured; the Quit-It Gang is the solution to this problem.

The Quit-It Gang, however, does not always materialize, for the reasons suggested in the following comments:

[When a briga starts,] what I want is distance. First, because I'm almost positive that it isn't anybody I know. And second, because I think it's bad vibes [*baixo astral*], and suddenly it could spill over onto whoever's there watching, a blow with a bottle or chair, a bullet. [If I knew the people fighting,] I think I would try to separate them, but if you entered in a confrontative way, it's better to stay out of it, I wouldn't . . . force things. As long as I wasn't risking my skin, I think I'd try to separate them, but the second I felt I could get involved in the briga, I get away. That's what I would do, that's what I *do*. (Genival)

Rapaz, if I don't know the person, if he isn't a friend, I don't mix into brigas. Let's suppose I'm coming up the street, there are two guys fighting, I don't know them, [then] I'm not even there [*não tô nem aí*, i.e., I completely ignore it]. It might even be a case of human solidarity, but I'm not going to try to calm them down, it's got nothing to do with my life, does it, I don't know them, I don't know who's right, [or] who's wrong, so you've got to mind your own business [*você tem que ficar na sua*]. Let the two of them settle it, or others who know them. Because often, when you mix into a briga, you grab someone, calming him, right, he comes at you sort of stupidly [he laughs]. Sometimes there's a knife . . . and the one who gets cut is the one in the middle of things. (Rubem)

The Quit-It Gang is very important, because the Quit-It Gang [both] wants and doesn't want to see a disaster [*desgraça*]. It gives permission for a while for things to get heavy [*pro pau rolar*], and at the same time it decides to prevent [the worst from happening], I mean, it avoids a disaster. [But someone in the Quit-It Gang] can die without [even] being involved in the briga. He's got nothing to do with the fight, he enters [to urge], "Quit it. Quit it, stop it, it's OK, it's OK, you two have already fought enough." Well, he can get stabbed, shot, can't he, and die, that person died but he wasn't fighting. Why, [if] he wasn't fighting? Because he went to break up the briga. For example, I wouldn't mix in with two people fighting with knives or clubs, I could be beaten or stabbed. (Waldyr)

I don't think I'd break up a briga [between people I didn't know], because it's very risky. At least for me, if I'm fighting [and] a person wants to break it up, however much I'm getting beaten up . . . I'm not going to like it. So then right away I want to start hitting the one who's breaking it up. But [in the case of] two friends who I know, it's easier to break it up. . . . I [would] break it up. For example, in the [soccer] game I play in every Saturday in Maiobão, almost every Saturday there's a row. But the others come and break it up. (Jair)

Stepping in to try to calm down a briga can be risky. The general rule is not to do it if you don't know at least one of the people fighting, if the antagonists are altered, or if weapons have appeared. Rubem's nod to "human solidarity" is the only evidence of a general moral obligation to stop a fight, and even for Rubem concern with solidarity takes a back seat to the practical consideration of saving his own skin.[3] In some briga stories strangers attempt to intervene, but usually from a position of strength or authority, as when a man steps into a briga between boys, or when the third party, unlike the antagonists, is armed (although this can lead to unforeseen consequences). Nevertheless, intervention in violation of the general rule is universally condemned as dangerously foolish.

Hence for our storytellers the Quit-It Gang tends not to materialize when those in the crowd do not know those who are fighting, when the fighters are altered, or when they are using arms. Even when it does intervene to break up a briga, however, a by now familiar situation arises: the possibility of a later resumption. The Quit-It Gang pushes the briga toward an exit but cannot ensure that further episodes will not follow.

[3]Witnesses to brigas often complain of a deeply disturbing feeling of impotence: they wanted to do something to stop the fighting but felt incapable of taking any useful action that did not pose unacceptable danger for themselves.

Allies

Third parties do not always intervene to separate the antagonists. In some cases they actively enter the fray, thereby converting a dyadic struggle into a general melee. In the following narrative of the first part of a *briga*, Pato takes a girlfriend to a neighborhood Carnival *festa* where an enemy provokes him. Both Pato and the enemy have come to the club with their respective *turmas*,[4] groups of neighborhood friends, and the confrontation rapidly escalates into a small war.

PATO FIGHTS WITH HIS ENEMY DURING
A CARNIVAL FESTA (beginning)

Pato

It was during Carnival. I arrived at the festa about four in the afternoon, with a girl. I was dressed as a fofão, [in a costume made] with really enormous quantities of cloth. [I was saying,] "Let me pass through here" [as I entered]. One [of the guys inside the club] pulled me one way and another pulled me the other way. I say, "Rapaz, stop that, I don't like it," and so on, [and they said,] "Ah, what are you talking about" [*que nada*], they're really crazy, right. They were drunk, so they were carrying on, pulling [me] one way and the other, and I was also kind of bombed [*meio chumbado*], right, and I got annoyed [*fiquei grilado*], right, really annoyed, [but] I didn't say anything, and went through to the *quintal* [the rear courtyard].

So then I asked for a beer, the girl sat down, and then she asked me, "What did that guy want [with you], pulling [on you] all the time? I can't understand it, [what was happening] with you there inside?" and so on. I told her [what had happened], and then they came up, acting crazy. Two stayed at the door, watching, [and] two came to my table and grabbed the bottle of beer, each one with a glass. One already had a rixa with me, so he came up to me [and said], "Look here, cara, aren't you going to buy me a beer?" [And I said,] "What, rapaz? What money am I going to buy you a beer with? But

4"Turma" means gang, but the English word has connotations that would be misleading in this context. Pato and his friends constitute something more akin to an age-set: a group of young males of roughly the same age who have passed together through a set of comparable experiences and exhibit a pronounced solidarity.

if you want, I'll buy one beer and you buy the next," [and he said,] "Hey, you're going to buy me a beer, if you keep on like this you're going to be in trouble" [*assim tu vai se dar mal*].

I looked back behind me, Cuica was there and a bunch [of other friends] in reserve. There was that big black guy, Romeu, there was Urubu, there was a whole turma back there in the rear of the quintal, everyone with a liter of cachaça.

So I got up from the table [and said], "Hey, what's your problem? [*Ó, meu, qual é de vocês?*]. I come in here and you guys come at me with all this bullshit [*vêm com maior onda comigo*], you want to mock me [*quer curtir da minha cara*], I come here now [to the quintal and] you come and drink my beer, oh, bicho, you're going to pay for this beer." I got up and really told him, "You're going to pay for this beer for this reason: not a cent is going to come out of my pocket," [and then I turned and said,] "Look here, waiter, this guy is going to pay for the beer," [and he said,] "Hey, but you ordered it," [and I said,] "But he drank the whole beer and came here to my table wanting to fight with me." At this the guy grabs a stool and comes after me, so then I ran, I was expecting him to hit me with the stool. I ran to the back of the quintal, oh, cara, I went right to the fence and broke off a piece of wood. [My friends back there said,] "What is it, Pato, what is it, what's going on there, Pato, what's going on with you over there," and then [I said], "It's that guy who comes over here with all that stuff" [*com maior onda*], and then everyone went after him, and then came his whole turma, all of them, everybody fighting at once.

Just then the girl gets slugged, ah, compadre, porra, everything came down on that guy. Renato, when he saw [the punch to the girl], grabbed a bottle [and] hit him a few more times, butted him with his head, and gave him a beautiful jab with the bottle. The guy has [still] got some cuts here on his face that Renato gave him in that briga. So then the other people inside the club calmed down the briga, but not without getting punched themselves, and threw [the rival turma] out.

This briga begins with an ambiguous provocation, the jostling that occurred when Pato entered, which under the circumstances could perhaps be attributed to the carnivalesque atmosphere of "Anything goes!" This action annoyed Pato but did not evoke a strong reaction. The subsequent incident at the table in the quintal, however, was an "in-my-face" provocation reminiscent of what happened to Bocado at Abreu's, when the man drank Bocado's shot of cachaça under his nose. Pato does more than simply connect: he unmasks the situation by accusing his enemy of trying to provoke him by drinking the beer and then orders him to pay for it.

In the usual course of events, when Pato's enemy comes after him the Quit-It Gang would intervene to separate them. This does not happen in Pato's story: instead, the two forces join battle. Pato paints the event as a confrontation both between two enemies and between two turmas. Pato's friends saw that Pato was being persecuted by a hostile turma: this was not a simple one-on-one face-off. They rallied to his defense rather than pulling him away. In general, the local chauvinism in the bairros of São Luís is quite remarkable; it can even attach to a particular street within a bairro. These feelings are still more pronounced in age-mates. At least in the more established bairros, such friends may have grown up together from infancy. They share intimate details of each other's lives, as well as significant life experiences. If (in Rubem's words) human solidarity has a place in briga, it is in defense of a compadre[5] of the bairro.

This first episode of the briga ended when Pato's rivals were evicted from the club. It is not clear who threw them out, but usually hired guards or waiters deal with such situations. Social clubs and neighborhood associations seem to expect fighting during São Luís's great collective celebrations, but they never tolerate it. When allies enter a briga, a further intervention becomes necessary: the police (or an analogous superior force) wait in the wings, prepared to deal, often drastically, with free-for-alls. The following chapter examines the murder of Sérgio, a result of exactly this kind of briga followed by a lethal intervention by the policeman Cosme. Sérgio's murder was an unusual event in many respects, but for people in São Luís police intervention is always a frightening and dangerous development in a briga.

Police

If the police came for him, says Jair,

> I'd die right there [on the spot], because the police, these days, the person who's a marginal, even a good citizen, is risking death. For example, I'm here playing ball, everybody watch-

[5]Strictly speaking, the relationship comadre/compadre, comadre/comadre, or compadre/compadre is that between parent and godparent. These terms are extended, however, to refer to close friends.

ing me play ball, not doing anything, and the police arrive
and want to arrest me. I wouldn't go, I really wouldn't go,
if they want to kill me, let them kill me right here, and let
everyone see it, at least someone will say that they were the
ones who killed me, right. Look at that student they killed
on the Beira-Mar. [He is referring here to Sérgio.] Porra,
that's inhuman, that's something that disgusts you, nobody
did anything, that's why I say that the people of Maranhão
are very passive [*acomodado*]. . . . They're afraid.

Indeed, it would be difficult to underestimate the degree of confidence, or
overestimate the degree of apprehension, with which the people of São Luís
regard the police.[6] The police, say são-luisenses, impose a respect based on
fear: one avoids them if possible, or falls silent in their presence. At best, the
police are seen as necessary but on the whole ineffectual; at worst, as corrupt
and vicious. The latter is probably the dominant view, especially (but by
no means exclusively) among the working-class people who make up the
vast majority of São Luís's population. "The poor man's hotel is the jail,"
goes one saying. "The poor man's taxi is the paddy wagon," goes another.
Young men are often reluctant to walk long distances at night, not so much
because they fear being mugged (though this is an ever-present worry) but
because they dread being accosted and harassed by a police patrol. Persons
arrested often suffer beatings and, during my stay in São Luís, a number
of prisoners were beaten or shot to death by police—even within the jail.
São Luís's human rights organizations regularly denounce occurrences of
torture and murder; the accusations are trumpeted in the newspapers, but
significant disciplinary actions, much less criminal proceedings, are almost
never undertaken. The outstanding popular image of the police officer,
based substantially in fact, is that of an arbitrary, violent authority who can
and does act with impunity.

As Pato describes it, the briga did not end with the rival turma's expulsion from the club. The briga resumed outside, in the street, and ended with
a sudden visit from the police. Pato continues the story, as the enemy group
prods its champion into a duel:

[6]Officially there are two police organizations in Maranhão: the civilian police (*polícia civil*)
and the military police (Polícia Militar, or simply PM). Both bodies fall under the jurisdiction
of the state government, and both are charged with enforcing criminal laws, although the
military police takes a more conspicuous role in the maintenance of public order during large-
scale disturbances, such as strikes and riots. Street arrests can be made either by agents of the
civilian police or by PM's. The two organizations have equally negative images.

PATO FIGHTS WITH HIS ENEMY DURING
A CARNIVAL FESTA (conclusion)

Pato

So then the festa ends and we're all leaving. Just when we're
leaving, his turma [says to him,] "Go on, go on," [and he says
to me,] "Come here, compadre, you want to fight with me,
just the two of us, you want to?" [and] I say, "Rapaz, I don't
know, it's up to you [*tu que sabe*]." Right away he came at me,
right . . . I say, "Come on, cara," really crazy [*louco*] too. . . .
I wasn't dressed as a fofão anymore, I had taken off the costume and was dressed in the shorts I was wearing beneath
it. [I said,] "OK, cara, come on," he came on and then we
punched each other like we were crazy, porra, I was kicking
the guy and the guy was kicking me, we rolled over and over,
we got all hurt just from bumping into the ground, rolling
around, and no one separated us or anything.

So then [comes] the police van. When they arrived we were
clinched, and the whole bunch was around us. When they arrived they came without that business, *au-au-au* [the siren].
They gave no fucking warning at all [*não avisaram porra nenhuma*], and they went in hitting us with their clubs. . . . In
the midst of this they found the two of us rolling around [and
said,] "Get up, sacana!" They had surrounded everybody,
[but] pulled just the two of us from inside. I was thinking a
thousand things, I even thought about God, I thought of my
mother, I thought, porra, about so much stuff [*tanta transação*],
because I was in the hands of the police.

They threw us in the rear of the van. So then we arrived
[at the station, to talk with the delegado]. I explained I was
dressed as a fofão and everything, [and the delegado asked,]
"How did this briga start, cara?" [and the guy said,] so on and
so forth, "It was a rixa because of one of my sisters," and then
I said, "What sister, cara?"—in front of the delegado—"What
sister?" [and he said,] "Ah, my little sister who you're always
flirting with, you messed around with her [*tu mexeu com ela*]." I
say, "I messed around with your sister? What, rapaz? Are you
telling me that that girl who slept with me [*foi transar comigo*] is
a virgin, cara? Look at my face, rapaz, ah, compadre, call her

here, and I'll prove in her face [*na cara dela*] if she's a virgin . . .
call her, moleque." And then I said, "The girl sleeps around
[*anda transando*], the thing is that this guy has a rixa with me
and it's ended up here."

Compadre, just then I was praying I'd be able to get out
of there, [I was] talking seriously with the delegado, cara,
seriously, looking straight at him like this, porra, with faith
that he was going to let us go. Around four or five o'clock,
[he said,] "You're going to be let go, and so make peace, and
give each other a hug." So then we hugged and [he said,] "All
right, see that you don't fight anymore." I said, "No, cara,
everything's all right."

As usual, Pato tells his tale with a light, slightly self-mocking air. Nevertheless, the dramatic highlight of the story—the arrival of a van full of club-
wielding police—is steeped in dread: "I was thinking a thousand things,
I even thought about God, I thought of my mother, I thought, porra, about
so much stuff, because I was in the hands of the police." Later, face-to-face
with the delegado, he sweats out his release, and we can imagine that, distasteful as it must have been, he embraced his enemy with immense relief.
Beneath the somewhat humorous surface of this story lies a fearful truth immediately recognizable to anyone in São Luís: one cannot count on leaving
the police station with body and soul intact, or, to be sure, on leaving it
at all.

Police do sometimes intervene benignly in disputes, and the delegado
in Pato's story is ultimately a sympathetic (if godlike) figure, but examples
of violent police intervention are so common and so well known to everyone that the perception corresponds closely to Pato's description: a swirl of
clubs followed by rude arrests and a tense journey to an unknown fate at
the station. Jair puts it bluntly: "[When the police] arrive [at a briga], they
frighten people, beat people up, arrest them, this is what they're for, to beat
people, to kill them there inside [the jail], and that's it."

This exercise of terror has a certain parallel with a tactic encountered
earlier. When Tito was shoved on the bus, he fixed the man who had provoked him with a stare that announced, "Let the blood run as much as it
will," as if to proclaim that he was sufficiently disequilibrated to escalate
the briga to ultimate consequences. The police in São Luís seem to adopt
a similar stance. Their actions reinforce the popular perception of them as
a wild, disequilibrated force that does not so much enforce law as threaten
disorderly persons with irrational violence. Rather than quelling brigas
with tact or restraint, the police tend to escalate them by threatening the
participants with injury and death.

Genival provides insight into this popular perception of the police when he makes the following equation: "You're a little child, someone says to you, 'Don't do that, rapaz, stop that, child, because if you don't the Bicho-Papão will eat you,' and from there things continue: 'Look out, the policeman is coming this way.'" The Bicho-Papão is a formless, devouring monster, one of the imaginary terrors of a São Luís childhood. Dionísio remembers the way his father used the Bicho-Papão to impose respect:

> [When] a child [looks] within an adult he sees a monster, something that leaves him very terrified, and so he feels fear and respect toward the adult. There was a phase when I was a child, I had a certain respect and a certain fear [of my father], because at times I was very naughty, I played a lot, I fought a lot. He was a super-polite person [*uma pessoa super-educada*], but [at these times] he would put the politeness [*educação*] aside and use an aggressive side, except that he would not use aggression [itself]. He would just say that if I kept doing that he would come at me with a belt, you know how it is, and hit me. And then he would say that the Bicho. . . . He would terrify me [*me meteu assim um medo*], you know, [saying] that [the Bicho-Papão] would grab me, that he would eat me and everything else. Then I would become quite terrified [*meio assustado*], with that fear in my head. And then I would try not to do wrong things anymore. I would imagine that there was a beast like that, you know, super-aggressive, [that it would] come and grab me and kill me and other bad things. And then I would become terrified and try to stop [doing bad things].

Genival is saying that the police are society's Bicho-Papão: the blind, malevolent force that knows no bounds, that torments and kills when provoked by the disorderly actions of its victims. This is how it imposes silence, obedience, and "respect." Just as Dionísio's father intervened in his childhood brigas in the guise of the Bicho-Papão, so the police intervene in Pato's, terrifying him into an embrace with his enemy. Police intervention in a briga, in short, forces the briga to an exit by threatening to impose its own deadly climax on the event.[7]

[7]I think that in São Luís order is commonly enforced by an escalation of *disorder*, not only within homes and during brigas but also in situations of large-scale political conflict. Although a discussion would take us far afield, the evidence suggests that political authorities use what I have called wild force, incarnated in the police, to respond to what they portray as provocations of the populace. It may be that political interactions in São Luís (and in Brazil?) are conceived and (thus) behaviorally structured in a way heavily influenced by the cultural model of briga sketched here.

But everyone knows that pacification through terror sometimes fails and this lethal threat is realized. In April 1984, Cosme, an off-duty policeman, summarily ended a bar fight by shooting the student Sérgio through the head. Sérgio's and Cosme's actions raise questions of motivation that cannot be addressed solely through cultural analysis. In turning from briga-as-scenario to briga-as-event, the following chapter offers a psychocultural interpretation of Sérgio's murder.

Police in riot gear march on Independence Day, September 7, 1985, in a parade that also includes military vehicles and trained police dogs—a formal display of intimidation by the state.

Cover of a piece of *literatura de cordel*, a genre of popular poetry narrating the exploits of backlands bandits and folk figures. Brigas often play an important part in these stories. Portrayed is the legendary Lampião, a northeastern bandit of the 1920's and 1930's, in "The Arrival of Lampião in Hell." After being denied entry, Lampião breaks into hell and lays waste to it.

The leading headline of this São Luís daily announces, "Violent Carnival," a reference to the preceding night's murder of a *folião* by a military policeman. *Left*, a Carnival reveler. *Right*, the Casinha da Roça, a mock rural house that moves through the streets as women inside pass food through the windows. (*O Imparcial*, Feb. 11, 1986)

Front page of a sensational São Luís daily, featuring a grisly collection of violent deaths. Reported are two killings by police, a fatal car crash, a putrefying corpse found in the bush, and the capture of two thieves. (*Jornal Pequeno*, Apr. 14, 1984)

This newspaper headline reads, "Savage Murder: Merchant Is Attacked and Stabbed to Death with a Fishing Knife." Joaquim (*left*), the victim, and his killer, Valdecy, were drinking and got into a briga, which was broken up by a third party. Hours later the two began arguing again. Valdecy stabbed Joaquim, who ran for help. Valdecy pursued and killed him. Also pictured are Dona Alice, Joaquim's widow, and the crowd of local residents that gathered around the corpse. (*Jornal de Hoje*, Oct. 22, 1984)

10

THE MURDER OF SÉRGIO

Briga-as-Event

The previous chapters have presented a cultural model, or scenario, of briga, as abstracted from stories and commentary. Although I believe that the stories recount actual brigas, I chose to focus on the way são-luisenses construe such events rather than on the events themselves. Indeed, a real briga cannot be sensibly discussed without knowledge of the cultural constructions and cultural premises that make up its very essence, for a briga is fundamentally a cultural artifact.

Knowing a scenario enables one to interpret events. A naive interpretation, really a description, uses the cultural model to guide the narration of an event sequence: X provokes Y, Y connects, they become altered, the Quit-It Gang enters to separate them, and so on. But people sometimes attempt a more sophisticated interpretation. Such an interpretation assumes that the *participants* use the model—that they know the scenario and orient their expectations and actions around it. A sophisticated interpretation spells out why those particular actors, reading (or misreading) each other's actions by reference to this mutually understood code, did what they did. It provides an account of the behavior of those who share a model for interaction but whose perceptions and motives differ.

This chapter discusses a real event, the murder of Sérgio, a university student, by a policeman named Cosme. Sérgio's murder, which shocked a city accustomed to violence, was the culmination of a melee in a São Luís bar. For those at the scene, the briga resisted interpretation. The motives of the protagonists in the drama were unknown to the onlookers and impossible for them to divine. Moreover, eyewitnesses had trouble even grasping what had happened because the event did not conform in an obvious way to the briga scenario. The most baffling aspect of the murder was that Cosme and Sérgio had exchanged no provocations, insults, or blows before Cosme collared Sérgio and shot him through the head.

As noted above, a sophisticated interpretation of an event requires a double perspective. My discussion therefore examines how unique actors used a shared model. The briga scenario is a cultural phenomenon. But in any real-life situation, people with singular personalities and concerns bring this model to an interaction. Their behavior makes sense only if we take into account both cultural uniformities and personal idiosyncrasies. I argue that this briga fortuitously brought together two persons, Cosme and Sérgio, who were primed for disaster in complementary ways. At the time no one could have known this, but by reconstructing some of each man's personal history, we can render Sérgio's murder comprehensible as a consequence, like other deaths spawned by brigas, of an organized interaction that went systematically awry.

The Crime

By general consensus, the crime occurred as follows. Around midnight, sometime in the first minutes of Saturday, April 14, 1984, Cosme X, 29 years old, police officer (out of uniform at the time) and part-time bookkeeper, shot at point-blank range and killed Sérgio Y, 24, a fifth-year medical student at the Federal University of Maranhão.[1] This scene occurred just outside Vítor's Bar, one of three adjacent bars then popular as a meeting place for a young, predominantly middle-class clientele. The bars occupied the end of a narrow cobbled street in the Praia Grande, São Luís's colonial warehouse district, a stone's throw from the Beira-Mar, the curving avenue that runs along the margin of the Bay of São Marcos. The murder capped a briga featuring a battle between Sérgio and a waiter named Heitor, but

[1] Minor aspects of this account are fictional, including all names, some dates and locations, and certain other particulars. My intent is to avoid direct imputations of guilt and to preserve, insofar as possible, the anonymity of informants and of Sérgio's family. Because the policeman I call Cosme has never been tried—he ultimately fled from São Luís and had not resurfaced by the time I left the field in March 1986—*legally* he cannot be presumed guilty. However, every witness I interviewed emphatically stated that Cosme killed Sérgio and that there was not the slightest indication that his act was accidental. Except for Cosme and the two friends accompanying him at the time, who provided contradictory and apparently self-serving testimony, those who gave depositions likewise agreed that Cosme was the murderer. I find little reason to doubt that Cosme killed Sérgio deliberately. This at least is the assumption I make in this chapter.

it had also at one point or another involved various friends of Sérgio and some of Heitor's fellow waiters.

Aside from Cosme and Sérgio, the following individuals played key roles in this briga:

Félix, 14, son of Vítor
França, 27, policeman, friend of Cosme
Gaspar, 29, friend of Cosme, acquaintance of Sérgio
Heitor, 27, waiter at Vítor's, Sérgio's prime adversary
Ivan, 22, Sérgio's closest boyhood friend
Moacir, 22, waiter at Vítor's
Vítor, 50, the owner of Vítor's Bar
Wilson, 21, boyhood friend of Sérgio
Xavier, 21, boyhood friend of Sérgio
Zeca, 27, Sérgio's drinking companion, a recent friend

Let us begin by looking at this briga through the eyes of an involuntary witness with no ties to any of these principal actors.

Eyewitnesses

Ezequiel, a university professor, was conversing over beer with several colleagues at a table outside one of the bars adjacent to Vítor's.[2]

> It was [after midnight] and there must have been approximately, oh, 600 people, or a little less, students, people from the middle class, professors, artists, because it was at that time a place to meet. A briga began in one of the bars. Chairs had been placed out as far as the center of the street; there was enough room for a car to pass, but only on one side of the street. When the briga began, everybody became a little terrified. The beginnings of a stampede broke out, but just the beginnings. It was a briga between young guys, one of those buffooneries [*palhaçadas*] of young people.
>
> Then suddenly the briga began to get more serious, it went out of control, the Quit-It Gang that is always there in brigas couldn't stop it, and chairs began flying, iron chairs, [and] aluminum ones [too]. With this, things got worse: bottles began flying too. It's typical in these brigas that after bottles

[2]I interviewed Ezequiel, Léia, Xavier, Ivan, and Wilson ten months to a year after the murder. Despite the passage of time, the event remained etched in their memories.

start flying it's the signal for someone to break a bottle and make an instrument of aggression out of it, he can kill someone [with it], and so then things got serious. When bottles begin flying you start to see panic, the struggle generalizes.

I don't know where so many people came from, allied to the two groups or the two individuals. I still don't know how the briga started. I do know that suddenly it was as if it turned into two groups confronting each other, an incredible thing, at the beginning you had something like three, four, six people fighting at the maximum, suddenly you had practically the whole bar, 20, 30 people fighting, there were chairs flying, there were bottles, you saw the bottles falling, you saw the people with the bottles in their hands. At that moment I got frightened. I stood up. People were running all around me. All this must have taken, in my perception—by now it could be entirely mistaken—maybe some four or five minutes. At that moment came the first shot, and right afterward came the second, the two or three shots that sounded were cadenced and rhythmic. When the second shot sounded, I became terrified. In order to know where the shots were coming from, I moved closer. My reasoning was stupid. I wanted to see where the shots were coming from so I could get down, so I could hide.

Then the shots stopped and I saw a person [with] a weapon, a dark weapon, black, from a distance it resembled a pistol, a big one. The guy put the gun away. When he had started shooting, there was silence, no one moved. I had the impression that the guy put the weapon in his belt. [But then] he raises the weapon again. Everything had paralyzed, everything had calmed down, the tumult had ended, just at [that] moment he draws the gun again. He extends his arm. I didn't believe what I was seeing, I don't know if in this position he's going to shoot again. Only he didn't point the gun upward. He drew the gun slowly, his movement wasn't fast, it was a slow, studied motion. He pointed the gun at a person who was beside him. I saw Sérgio's head. So then he extends his arm fully, [with the gun] at point-blank range, the sensation I had was that it was in [Sérgio's] ear, and shot.

When he fired I thought, He killed a person, because there was no way [he could have missed], the target was as far away as [the end of] his arm. When he shot this last shot, which according to my calculations would have been the fourth, came the most tragic moment of all. There was a feeling of perplexity in the whole group that was there, nobody did anything. There were, without exaggeration, some five to eight seconds of nobody understanding anything. After maybe some five to eight seconds, the people near Sérgio leaned down and took hold of Sérgio. A young man, I don't know who he was, had an attack of hysteria. I stayed put, trying to see what had happened to Sérgio, if what I had seen was real or not, because I didn't believe that it had been real. It looked a lot like that scene in Vietnam, with that crazy colonel who shoots a guerrilla in the middle of a Saigon street, it was that scene that I reconstituted, I had never seen anything like that, and just then that young guy began to have an attack, "They killed Sérgio, they killed Sérgio."

When he did this came the most terrible moment. When the boy begins to shout, [Cosme] simply takes his gun and stands in a position like this, a military position, arm extended, and sweeps the whole group of people, pointing his gun, and he had in front of him at least 200 people spread out in groups in the direction of the sea. He simply sweeps all of us. This was a cold, calculated scene, the scene that most impressed me was this scene. He simply pointed [his gun]. I noticed that no one reacted and was certain that no one would react because he would have shot. And the boy shouting; I keep looking to see if Sérgio had been murdered or not. I was sure that Sérgio had been murdered and that [Cosme's behavior] was a move to terrify everyone. I thought, Sérgio was murdered, but I didn't want to believe it was true, and at this moment [Cosme] fled, I don't know how, I didn't see him disappear.

And the next moment is a very sad one, it's the moment when people take hold of Sérgio's body, two by the arms and two by the legs. Sérgio is in the air in the form of an arc, and they go to find a taxi and there are three or four taxis there but nobody offers to carry Sérgio's body to the hospital. This is typical of our concept of not getting involved in conflicts because in the end you're going to be a witness or you're the person accused, it's as if you were involved, in principle you're going to be a suspect, but this was a very terrible attitude, and so they carry the body of Sérgio, put him into a car [at last], and take him away. The people there went so far as to beat on the taxis [afterward]. It was the first time that I understood what this thing of collective hysteria is about. There were people who were laughing, but they were doing so not to laugh at what had happened but they were laughing in an uncontrolled manner. There were people who didn't have any expression at all left on their faces, people who began to speak without any sense, to ask senseless questions as if they hadn't seen [what had happened]. People stood there paralyzed.

Then began the various stories, to find out who it was, and we stayed there talking, who it was and who it wasn't, why the briga had happened, and meanwhile something happened that was one of the things that most struck me during the whole episode, a reason why I could never return to that place. The news of Sérgio's death had still not arrived, it arrived some 40 minutes later, more or less. The waiter in the bar where Sérgio had fallen grabbed a broom and went out with the broom, sweeping away all of that debris, and there was a pool of Sérgio's blood there, and then I saw him throwing water over it [to wash it away].

After some 30 or 40 minutes came the news of his death, someone brought it. We were very shocked, our reaction was very . . . It hurt a lot, nobody knew who he was. Most of the people there didn't know him. People began to disperse and the bar emptied quickly, after the news of his death. We stood around talking a little while [but] we didn't know what to do, so each one resolved it [in his or her own way]. Léia left, and had an attack of crying; later she told me that she was overcome with despair [*ficou desesperada*] [over at] her house. I had to take a tranquilizer to relax and be able to sleep, and Luís [another friend of Ezequiel's], it seems that he had some drinks [or] took a tranquilizer or something like that.

Through Ezequiel's eyes we experience the confusion of the briga: flying chairs and bottles, people running helter-skelter, the first shots.[3] These scenes are vivid but disjointed, like battle accounts from Euclides da Cunha.

[3] Ezequiel states that he heard four shots. Others counted two or three. Such disagreement appears repeatedly in the depositions, even when there is no clear motive for misrepresentation. Eyewitness accounts of crimes typically contradict each other.

With the first shots, the crowd scatters and then everyone freezes, motion-less and silent, "paralyzed." And then, incomprehensibly, illogically, Cosme approaches, seizes Sérgio, and shoots him. The brutal shock of this act is etched in Ezequiel's mind as a living reprise of the Saigon officer's famous execution of a Vietcong prisoner. And terrible scenes are yet to follow: Sérgio's friends carrying his body from taxi to taxi; Cosme sweeping the stunned crowd with his gun; the waiter cleansing the sidewalk of blood and broken glass. This is not so much briga according to any model I have presented heretofore as it is a set of surreal tableaux.

Upon hearing the first shots, Ezequiel moved closer, trying to penetrate the meaning of these events.

> I realize that in truth I moved closer in order to understand. When [Cosme] drew the gun and extended his arm, I realized his intention. I thought, He's going to blow Sérgio's brains out. Now that was something that was unbelievable to me, but on the other hand was inevitable. It was as if I was in a nightmare and I couldn't manage to prevent [what Cosme was going to do], I knew that it would happen. The idea of, for example, shouting "Stop!" or "Never that!" never passed through my head, no, my act at the time was an act of under-standing, an act of hallucination, an act of madness. I got very sick on account of [all this], I spent several days very terror-ized. I somatize all this a lot, all these problems of violence. Since I can't understand it, I somatize a lot.

Léia, who was accompanying Ezequiel at the time, had much the same difficulty in believing what her eyes were telling her:

> I was struck with terror, not believing that in that [middle-class] environment a gun would appear, and coming from someone who wasn't apparently involved in the briga. It was a very great surprise, because . . . as terrible as it was, what was going on there, I thought that it would get resolved right there . . . you know, like this, the person who's at risk will run away, will manage to escape, something like that. It's incred-ible, everything was so fast. Now, talking with you, I see that so many things happened, they were extremely rapid min-utes. [The gun was] the surprise, the thing that wasn't seen as a natural consequence [*uma decorrência*] of the briga. Maybe if a knife had appeared, it wouldn't have been as surprising as a firearm, because a firearm is something so, so irrevers-

ible, isn't it, especially like that at such a short distance, it
puts the victim into a completely impotent position. . . . But
even when the gun appeared, it didn't occur to me that . . . it
could . . . it could be used against a person. . . . I didn't see
the first shots, where they were aimed, people said that they
were aimed into the air, an alert, a form of intervening in a
briga, of calming down a briga, and really they calmed down
the briga, because the persons who were fighting stopped
instantly. [But] the shot that was aimed at Sérgio wasn't a
shot intended to interrupt something, it had already been
interrupted. That's why it was the most terrifying [*estarrecida*]
thing, because the briga had already stopped.

Everyone who witnessed the shooting had the same problem putting
the fragments together into a coherent whole. After Cosme had escaped,
Sérgio's body had been carried away to the hospital, and the subsequent moment of mass hysteria had passed, the crowd embarked on a fumbling search
for explanations, an attempt to piece together these events, to make sense
out of them by fitting them into a coherent scheme. The cultural model of
briga was pressed into service. Some speculated that Cosme and Sérgio had
had a rixa and that Cosme's act was prompted by vengeance, an idea that
might explain the shooting but could not clarify its relation to the briga
that preceded it. Some speculated that Cosme was a policeman because of
the way he handled himself and the gun. The idea that a policeman entered
the briga to pacify it and did so by killing made sense; some went further,
developing a political interpretation identifying Cosme as a depraved agent
of the violent state. Other speculations centered on the original cause of
the briga (it was said that Sérgio provoked it by leaving his table without
paying) and on the participation of disequilibrated persons, particularly the
waiter (Heitor) and Vítor's son (Félix).

Although, for example, it was not true that Sérgio and Cosme were enemies—by all indications they had never before set eyes on each other—
some of these speculations were correct. Sérgio *did* leave his table without
paying, and Cosme *was* a policeman. On the basis of the information available to most of those at the scene, who knew neither Sérgio nor Cosme,
the most acceptable story was probably that Sérgio had left without paying
and was accosted by certain truculent employees of the bar, giving rise to
the briga, which expanded when allies entered. The policeman Cosme then
intervened to end the briga by killing Sérgio.

But whereas people know that police intervention may be fatal for any
number of reasons, the problem with this plot, which does in a general
sense follow the briga model, is that it leaves too many loose ends to serve

as a satisfactory explanation of that specific incident. Not every policeman, certainly, would have shot someone in this situation (indeed, França, an off-duty policeman who was at Cosme's table, did not intervene), so why did Cosme do it? Why did he choose Sérgio as his victim? Sérgio's own behavior offers no-less-puzzling aspects: he acted almost as if he did not know, or did not care about, the probable serious consequences of his behavior, as predicted by the briga model. In short, those seeking a more sophisticated interpretation of the briga remained mystified.

One could argue, and most of the witnesses' conjectures imply, that Cosme was insane, or that he was evil, or that he was a "typically" and robotically violent cop. One could argue (but I did not hear this point of view expressed) that Sérgio, unlike other people, knew nothing of briga, or that alternatively he had lost his senses, perversely pursuing self-destruction. But that Sérgio did not know the briga scenario is not credible, and insanity, evil, automatism, or perversity do not explain behavior. My interpretation is thus based on two assumptions: (1) both Cosme's behavior and Sérgio's were explicable, and (2) both Cosme and Sérgio knew the briga scenario.

A Briga in Two Parts

Ezequiel and Léia became aware of the briga only after chairs and tables began to tumble and the uproar invaded their conversations. Like most of those present that evening, they had not noticed a previous, much less dramatic, confrontation in Vítor's Bar. There were in fact *two* brigas, or episodes, separated by approximately ten minutes, the second, deadly one a spin-off of the first.

To understand what happened, it is necessary to consult those who participated in the briga or observed it not as disinterested onlookers but as partisans. These include Sérgio's friends, who despite the emotional discomfort caused by recalling the events of that night consented to tell me about it, and others, such as the waiters and Cosme himself, who spoke through depositions given before the police in the days following the murder.

First Episode

Sometime around 11 P.M. Sérgio, his friend Zeca, and a third unidentified companion, probably Ivan, sat down at a table at Vítor's. They ordered a large bottle of beer, then another, and a soft drink from a waiter named Moacir. The Praia Grande lies close by Sérgio's old neighborhood, a mostly middle-class corner of central São Luís with tiled houses that spill down the slope from the cathedral to the sea. It happened that several of Sérgio's old boyhood friends were also visiting the bars of the Praia Grande that Friday night. In recent years the friends had drifted apart, though Sérgio had maintained a special relationship with Ivan, his confidant of many years.

Another old friend of Sérgio's, Xavier, was already in bed when he had a sudden urge to check out the scene at the Praia Grande. He ran into Sérgio; they drank a glass of beer together, and then Xavier left to talk with other friends. Not long thereafter a small briga broke out. Xavier ran over, thinking,

> It must be Sérgio, he's fighting over there. When I got there it really was him. So then I saw Vítor's son [Félix] coming after him with a machete. So then [someone] got hold of Vítor's son, and [someone] got hold of Sérgio, everything quieted down, and we started to calm down Sérgio. Wilson, a friend of ours, came over, asked what it was about, so we said such and such, that Sérgio had left [the table] and the waiter thought that he wasn't going to pay the check and everything. So then Wilson went up and paid the check.

Moacir, Sérgio's waiter, says in his deposition that after the young men had finished the drinks, they left without paying. Moacir followed them, politely soliciting payment from Sérgio, who looked into the air without responding. Félix, the bar owner's teenage son, who was accompanying Moacir, asked Sérgio to leave a document with him as a guarantee of future payment. The patrons of the adjoining bar, the Wharf, then began to shout, asking who the chiseler was; Moacir says that he and Félix then grabbed Sérgio by the shoulder, and a briga began because Sérgio refused to accompany them back to the bar. Suddenly another young man appeared, asking what was going on; Moacir responded that Sérgio had refused to pay the check, whereupon the man immediately settled the trivial bill. This ended the commotion.

There is not much difference between these accounts, and I think we can take as fact that Sérgio and his friends left the table after drinking, without paying the bill, followed anxiously by Moacir and Félix. That was natural enough, because the waiter is responsible for his patrons' debts, and Félix, a youth of fourteen, might well take it upon himself to assume a proprietary pose. But Moacir's statement lacks a sense of the tone of the encounter between Félix, Moacir, and Sérgio. Wilson, the friend who ultimately paid Sérgio's bill, recalls:

> Sérgio had felt very humiliated in that situation. The one who asked [Sérgio for the money] was [Vítor's] son, who said, "Ah! You left without paying, huh, it's something you always

do, you've got to pay," all kinds of things, in a loud, aggressive voice. [Sérgio] stayed quiet. [Then he said,] "What's all this, I'm going to pay, I'm coming back." [But] with the aggressive way the boy was making his demand, and holding on to Sérgio so he couldn't go away, Sérgio shoved back [*botou a mão*], [and] they started the briga.

This gives a convincing rationale for the events that followed. Félix's public accusation tinged with ridicule is exactly the kind of attack guaranteed to enrage the accused. The ensuing briga ended only when the Quit-It Gang entered and Wilson, tendering an apology on behalf of Sérgio, paid the bill.

But at that point a crucial incident occurred. The waiter Heitor, one of those who had ganged up against Sérgio, came up and tripped him from behind. Sérgio fell and struck his head on the ground. The interval between the two episodes of the briga therefore found Sérgio, his head bleeding profusely, angrily vowing revenge against Heitor.

Interlude

After Wilson paid the check, Sérgio and some of his friends retreated from the bar. When Heitor tripped him, Sérgio tried to go after the waiter, but Xavier and others restrained him and pushed Heitor away. They tried to calm Sérgio, but when he passed his hand over the back of his head and found blood, Sérgio was beside himself. At this point Wilson sought out Ivan, saying that Sérgio wanted to get Heitor and that Ivan must try to dissuade him.

Ivan was at that time recovering from a serious bout of hepatitis. Earlier that evening, Sérgio and Zeca, who had been drinking since early that morning, had stopped by at Ivan's house; the three of them sat for a while in a place Sérgio had always enjoyed, the small, breezy neighborhood park by the sea that commemorates the hanging of the maranhense hero Manuel Bequimão. Sérgio and Zeca then cajoled Ivan into accompanying them to the Praia Grande; it had been months since Ivan had gone out on the town. But Ivan could not drink because of his illness, and he left the other two at the table in Vítor's while he took a stroll around to check out the *movimento* (the "action"). When he returned, Sérgio and Zeca were gone: the uproar had already begun. Now, in response to Wilson's warning about Sérgio's intentions, Ivan approached his friend.

Since I was, let's say, his closest friend, he listened to [*obedeceu*] me when I spoke to him. He was leaning against a car. So then he put his hand to his head [and] showed [me] that he was bleeding, [saying,] "Hey, my head is bleeding!" So then I told him that he shouldn't fight anymore, that I couldn't even come to his aid because I was sick, I couldn't even run away from a commotion [*confusão*], imagine fighting, and I also said that all the waiters had gone into the bar and he could . . . get hurt, that all of them had gone to arm themselves, get knives and so on, since generally whenever there's a commotion here in São Luís all the waiters go to arm themselves with knives, it's normal here in a bar.

Ivan raises another dangerous possibility:

I told him he was drunk, that he wasn't in his normal [state], that he should leave it all for another day, another day he could go there and resolve things, just him and the waiter, and I even said to him that they had called the police, because he knew that if the police came there they wouldn't play around, they'd be slugging people from the moment they arrived [*eles chegam dando porrada*], they don't come to calm things down, they come in beating people up right away. I said, "Listen, those guys are armed and they called the police." So then he got terrified, because he knew what would happen if he started fighting. I said to him, "Rapaz, don't fight anymore, don't fight anymore because you might get stabbed and they might even kill you. [You could] get stabbed, go to the hospital and die," and I even emphasized to him, "Listen, they called the police, a guy in the other bar called the police, the police will be here any minute." Because this was a way to try to get to him, to get him to leave there and go home or somewhere else and forget what had happened. He went so far as to say to me that he wouldn't fight anymore: "No, I'm not going to fight anymore." It was this that put me at ease, because had he said to me, "I'm going to fight with that guy," I wouldn't have let him go. The only reason I didn't drag him away by force was because I couldn't make any physical effort. I always used to do that, I would grab hold of him, drag him away, he would grapple with me but I would take him, because we were very close friends.

Ivan's story was a lie: no one had summoned the police. But Ivan knew, and he knew that Sérgio also knew, that the police "wouldn't play around."

His invention of the call to the police was the best way he could think of to terrify Sérgio into putting his vengeful feelings toward Heitor on hold.

Ivan thinks he may have been the last person to speak with Sérgio. Five to ten minutes later, despite Sérgio's assurances that he was not going to fight anymore, a new and more serious briga erupted. According to Heitor, Sérgio and two unidentified friends attacked him, hitting him with a chair and punching him in the face. Zeca claims that this second episode of the briga began when Sérgio struck Heitor in the face. What is certain is that Sérgio was directly involved in this aggressive resumption of the briga. The fact that Heitor was the target implies that the aggression was Sérgio's act of revenge.

By now the initial cause of the briga had receded into irrelevance. The wheel of vengeance had begun to turn.

Second Episode

The details of the second, and fatal, episode of this briga are hazy—recall Ezequiel's jumbled description—but its outlines, as revealed in the combined testimony of witnesses, are clear. It began with an attack by Sérgio, perhaps assisted by Zeca, on Heitor, the waiter who had tripped Sérgio. From this point everyone agrees that things went very fast, and most can do little more than describe a confused and vicious brawl. Sérgio and Zeca, aided sporadically by other friends of Sérgio's, faced off against at least three waiters and Félix, who, according to several witnesses, were armed with chairs and bottles, perhaps even broken bottles. Sérgio's friends probably retaliated in kind, but by all indications the battle was unequal, with Zeca and especially Sérgio getting much the worst of it. Sérgio was unarmed when he died, and there is no hint that he ever brandished even a makeshift weapon.

Through all this confusion a central image remains in focus: Sérgio locked in a duel with Heitor, as Heitor's allies, when they can, rain down blows with chairs and bottles upon Sérgio. Sérgio, unshaven, drunk and dirty, bleeding and disheveled, never let go of Heitor despite the punishment he was receiving.

Ivan recalls:

> I saw [Zeca] coming out of the bar, guys hitting him with bottles, and [several of us] headed over there with the aim of calming down the commotion. When we got there, we saw Sérgio fighting on the sidewalk with the waiter who had cracked his skull, and then the briga got very ugly because it was two of them [i.e., Sérgio and Zeca] fighting against several waiters, and we started to shout for the briga to calm

down, and the briga was calming down and the only one left was Sérgio, who was furious with the guy because he had cracked his skull. He was hanging on to the guy.

That was when we heard [the first] shot into the air; everyone scattered, and only the two of them, hanging on to each other, were still fighting. That was when we saw the guy [Cosme] already on top of him. I was very close by. So then the guy comes up and pulls Sérgio by the shirt, and he didn't even resist, he didn't do anything, you understand? and right away [Cosme] stuck the firearm to his head, [right] to his head, and then we heard only the shot. Then he fell, he fell to the ground, and then Wilson came up behind the guy and said, "Rapaz, you shot the guy, you killed the guy." So then [Cosme] moved off in front of me and in front of Xavier, so then Xavier tried to move toward him to grab him, so then he cocked the gun again and said: "Look, nobody move [*não entra ninguém*]." With a gun pointed toward me and Xavier and the other people there, like a bang-bang Western movie. Because if anyone moved toward him it would be one more who would get shot.

The guy got on his motorcycle and went away. We tried to help our friend. A guy there [with a car] helped out. We took him to the hospital, he even got to the hospital alive, and he was tended to by his own medical colleagues who were on duty there. They took an x-ray and it was determined that if he managed to live, he would be paralyzed from the neck to the feet, he would be a little . . . confused [*perturbado*]. So we went to look for the neurologist. We explained that the bullet had gone in here and exited on the other side, and then he said, "Rapaz, then you'd better go back and calm his family, because . . . he's going to die, it's [just] a question of minutes or hours [but] he's going to die." We went back to the hospital. When we got there, he had gone up for an operation. It took five or ten minutes up there for him to die. That's what happened.

Xavier's story is as follows:

After everything had calmed down [and] nobody else was fighting, I turned to Sérgio. Sérgio was in a clinch with

Heitor, Sérgio against the wall and Heitor in front of him.
And the two of them throwing punches, right. And I took off
toward them, running, a distance of more or less ten meters,
and *he* [Xavier's emphasis], Cosme, who had already got up,
fired a shot into the air and everyone ran off, right. . . . What
happened. I shouted to Cosme, "Rapaz, help me calm this
thing down. Help me calm it down, let's separate them." I
was a little reluctant because he had a weapon in his hand
and any minute it could go off, right. And I headed over
there walking fast. He was faster than me, since he was closer,
he must have been some three meters from Sérgio then. He
grabbed Sérgio by the collar, on his left side, took the revolver
and gave him a blow to the chest, more or less to the chest,
with the revolver. Next he placed the revolver to the head of,
of . . . of Sérgio, and fired. At that moment I was very close
and Sérgio fell at my feet.

With this I lost [it], I became uncontrolled, I didn't know
what to do, and wanted to approach him, that was my reaction, to approach him, me and Ivan. When we tried to
approach, Cosme cocked the gun again and threatened us,
saying if we approached him he would shoot. My first reaction [was that] he had not fired really to, that he had shot to
graze him, just so he would become dizzy [*tonto*] [and] fall. I
think nobody imagined [what had really happened].

Accounts of the end of the briga show remarkable consistency. (1) The
briga begins to break up as Sérgio's friends (and possibly others) call for
things to calm down; (2) Cosme fires into the air, probably twice, and
everyone scatters from the vicinity where the fighting has been going on;
(3) Sérgio and Heitor remain in a clinch; and (4) Cosme goes up to Sérgio,
seizes him by the collar, and shoots him at point-blank range in the head.

The only significant dissent comes from Cosme himself, who in his
deposition places the blame on his police colleague and tablemate, França.
Cosme claims that in the early stages of the briga he disarmed both Félix
(of a machete) and a waiter (of a wooden club). He was otherwise reluctant
to intervene until chided by some of the bar patrons who recognized him
as a policeman: "Don't you see what's going on here?" With this, França
urged, "Cosme, let's end this thing." The two men drew their revolvers.
Cosme fired a shot into the air; another shot, probably from França's gun,
followed immediately. The crowd dispersed, but some of the waiters continued fighting with a young man (whose name he knew was Sérgio) and

some of the young man's friends. Cosme grabbed hold of Sérgio so as to pull him free of the briga, firing once again into the air; just then another shot sounded and Sérgio fell to the ground. Cosme said to Sérgio, "Get up, cara, quit faking it!" (*Vamos, cara, deixa de sujesta!* [sic]); França exhorted him, "Hey, rapaz, the guy is dead; take off, because I'm going to take off too." Cosme says he does not know if the shot that killed Sérgio was fired from his weapon; his intention was to pull Sérgio away from the fight, not to kill him. Someone shouted, "Grab that guy!" and Cosme, fearing lynching or arrest, fled on his motorcycle. He never, as some had maintained, threatened the crowd with gun in hand. (He claims, by the way, that he lost his gun right after this incident.)

Cosme's story lacks credibility, differing radically in important respects from the consensus of eyewitness accounts. No one else, for example, saw França with a gun. Everyone agrees that the briga had petered out by the time Cosme approached Sérgio; only Sérgio and Heitor were still fighting. Everyone saw Cosme put his gun to Sérgio's head after seizing Sérgio by the collar. And of course the threat to the crowd after the murder created an indelible impression on the many who witnessed it.

Moreover, much of Cosme's story obviously seeks to put his actions in the best light. He disarms Félix and the waiter. He responds to an appeal to him, as a policeman, to end the fight. His aim in grabbing Sérgio's collar is to whisk him out of danger: indeed, Cosme complained to the police, after his imprisonment, that he had only been trying to help the victim and ended up getting blamed for something he did not do. This is not to dismiss entirely the notion that Cosme may have seen himself as a savior (I will have more to say about this later on), but in this official statement he is trying above all to evade responsibility for Sérgio's death, portraying himself as the good policeman, the devoted public servant who keeps the peace and goes to the aid of the helpless. Finally, Cosme makes a none-too-subtle attempt to pin the blame on França, who in Cosme's account is the only other person with a gun at the time of the murder.[4]

I do not see how this account can be taken seriously as a representation

[4]França's story accords with Cosme's until the moment of intervention. He denies ever pulling his gun: instead, when Cosme fires into the air he goes off to investigate some other gunshot, the source of which he never determines. When he returns, Cosme is holding Sérgio's shirt, with his gun in his fist, urging the bloody Sérgio to get up. Gaspar, Cosme's other table companion, offers yet another ending. There is a shot, then França (minus his gun) gets up to see who is shooting, then Cosme fires into the air. This does not end the fighting between Heitor and Sérgio, so Cosme forces his way between them, his pistol drawn, and an arm hits Cosme's hand, causing the gun to discharge accidentally. One gets the impression that the three tried to cook up a consistent story, managing somewhat of a consensus on the early details but failing to agree on a finale. Cosme implicates França, Gaspar tries to give Cosme an out via an accidental bump that escapes everyone else's attention, and França, although he sees the smoking gun, nevertheless does not witness the actual shooting.

of what actually happened. It is a story told by a killer trying to confuse the issue.

Why did Sérgio keep fighting? Why did Cosme shoot him? Answering these baffling questions requires shifting attention directly to victim and killer.[5]

The Victim

Descent into Briga

Sérgio's behavior in this briga raises many questions. I start with the assumption that Sérgio knew the briga model.

The preliminaries to this briga commenced when Sérgio and Zeca left the table. This act may or may not have been innocent. That Sérgio intended to dodge the check is a real possibility: friends report that he had done so before. But in São Luís unpaid bills traditionally come out of a waiter's pay; Moacir was unlikely to allow Sérgio and Zeca to leave unchallenged, especially since both were drunk and Sérgio at least was unshaven and disheveled in appearance—"like a vagabond," in a friend's words. Sérgio and Zeca's departure had, from the waiter's standpoint, all the earmarks of a provocation, a kind of sacanagem, and Sérgio must have known this. By this reading, Moacir and Félix connected by stopping the pair who had left the table. They wanted an apology in the form of a payment, but Sérgio refused, and Félix took hold of him to drag him back to the bar.

Wilson offers a conjecture about how Félix's interference affected Sérgio:

> He felt really humiliated because his family was well off, all those people who had been to school with him were there, it was a very popular place, and he was placed in the situation of a marginal, right, he was in the situation of someone who walked away without paying, he was very drunk, he was dirty, so he really felt like, like. . . . Poxa! . . . a marginal, something like that. He didn't say that, but I felt his anger [revolta] at the situation in which he had been placed, the boy saying that he hadn't paid, that he wanted to leave without paying and so on.

---

[5]The following discussion relies heavily on speculative psychological analysis. Reliable psychological profiles of Sérgio or Cosme would demand clinical data impossible to obtain. Nevertheless, I believe that events such as this one cannot be understood without reference to psychological factors. Because I suggest that Sérgio's personal problems led him to seek out a dangerous situation, some may feel that I have shifted attention away from Cosme's actions. I wish to state clearly that I regard Sérgio as the innocent victim of an inexcusable crime.

A similarity gradually emerges between this confrontation and the bus conductor's challenge to Tito, who was trying to board with a phony student card. The conductor's behavior was an "in-my-face" unmasking. Worse, it took place before an assembly of acquaintances: it was profoundly shaming. Félix's restraint of Sérgio, an analog of the conductor's obstruction of Tito, was likewise a public, "in-my-face" unmasking. The effect it had on Sérgio suggests two possibilities, not by any means mutually exclusive. Sérgio was in fact chiseling the drinks, or he felt the sting of the implicit accusation ("Marginal!") in the same way, say, that Tito suffered the pain of being called a maconheiro—a deforming caricature that frightened and infuriated him because he suspected it to have a germ of truth. Being openly accused just around the corner from his childhood home in a place frequented by people he knew must have made Sérgio's mortification a thousand times more excruciating.

Tito's confrontation with the conductor never came to blows, but in Sérgio's case several destabilizing factors were at work. First, Félix was certainly (from Sérgio's point-of view) a moleque, a punk, a boy playing at being a man, and to be challenged by a pretentious fourteen-year-old had to be infuriating. Second, Sérgio was drunk, and this probably weakened his sense of self-control. Third, Sérgio showed signs of a deeper disequilibrium than the temporary imbalance induced by alcohol, as we shall see.

For all these reasons, Sérgio's provocative act of leaving the table escalated into a briga. Sérgio did not take advantage of any of the exits available to him. He provoked the waiter and Félix by abandoning the table. When his adversaries connected, Sérgio had a chance to apologize by paying for the drinks, but he did not. Félix then called him a chiseler; this public accusation was humiliating, and Sérgio passed up a last-ditch try for an exit. Instead of paying the bill, leaving a document with the bar owner, or soliciting a loan from one of his friends, he responded to Félix's verbal and then physical aggressions, and the briga was on.

Throughout this first episode, then, Sérgio persistently cleaved to a risky path through the briga, not so much by virtue of any extraordinarily aggressive actions on his part as by a refusal to seek exits. It is as if he allowed himself to be swept downward into the danger zone of briga. He was rescued from a catastrophe by Wilson and the Quit-It Gang, but he resumed the pattern, which (knowing the briga scenario) he must have recognized as potentially disastrous, almost immediately.

Toward the end of the first episode of the briga, Heitor tripped Sérgio. Sérgio, incensed, his head bleeding, wanted revenge. He must have known this was a very dangerous proposition. Resuming a briga at the level of physical violence leaves one with an unpalatable selection of exits and the promise of new rounds of violence in the future, even if one escapes unscathed from the present briga. Moreover, Ivan had told him that the waiters had armed themselves with knives and that someone had called the police. This shifted the probabilities radically in the direction of catastrophic consequences and further reduced the chance of finding a safe exit. Yet whatever Sérgio was thinking and feeling impelled him to ignore, or accept, the risk. He sought out and struck Heitor, and the briga picked up again, wilder and more violent than before.

In the final scenes of this briga, Sérgio determinedly tried to slug it out with Heitor, while Heitor's allies beat him with chairs and bottles. Sérgio neither armed himself nor fled. He rode the flow of the briga toward disaster. The Quit-It Gang scaled down the briga, but Sérgio remained clinched with Heitor, "as if embracing," in Heitor's words. Even Cosme's shots into the air did not dissuade Sérgio from pursuing his obsession. The exits shut down one by one.

Sérgio acted so as to place himself in a potentially catastrophic situation. In essence, he painted himself a victim. This is not to say that his behavior was necessarily suicidal, since death was not the only possible exit from this briga. What Sérgio did resembled more a spin of the cartridge cylinder of a gun in a weird variant of Russian roulette. His actions have a sense of finality, of surrender to some unknown fate.[6]

Sérgio's behavior bespeaks desperation. It is the behavior of someone who, using the term usually applied to those in the final throes of alcoholism, is hitting bottom, seeking death or salvation. Indeed, Sérgio's actions in the preceding months and days tend to confirm this tragic conclusion.

Sérgio: Biographical Notes

Sérgio Y, 24 at the time of his death, would have graduated from the Federal University of Maranhão with a degree in medicine in December 1984. Like his seven siblings, Sérgio was following a family occupational tradition inspired, it was said, by the death of his father in 1968 as a result of a botched surgical procedure.[7]

Sérgio's father had been a prosperous merchant, and in the middle-class neighborhood where Sérgio grew up the family was regarded as comfortably well off. But according to his friends, Sérgio was not one to put on airs. They described him as generous, unpretentious, even "humble," caring

---

[6]At least one of the brigas presented earlier had much the same feel: Gato's disequilibrated performance at the terreiro of Salomão ("Gato's Briga"). Gato's escalating aggressions guaranteed that he would eventually suffer serious consequences: in the end, the crowd that came to Salomão's defense beat him unconscious. Gato's actions were unprovoked, however, and undeniably more violent than those of Sérgio.

[7]One of these siblings may have been a lawyer rather than a doctor. My field notes are inconsistent on this point.

little about clothes and "artificial things." A defender of the underdog, he hated to see a father strike a child or the weak humiliated by the strong. Nor could he bear humiliation himself: he had a short fuse. Undoubtedly Sérgio had a tendency to get involved in brigas from time to time.[8]

Ivan, Xavier, and Wilson, all of whom grew up with Sérgio from the days when they made kites together, fished in the estuary, and played soccer in the street, share an appreciation of his sensitivity and feistiness. His other salient qualities seem to have been intelligence, presence, and a brooding quiet. The friendship among the boys had been intense during their early and middle teens but had weakened in recent years. In part this was because Sérgio's family had moved to an affluent suburb, but some less palpable barrier had also begun to form. Although Sérgio continued to visit his old neighborhood in the center of town, he and his former companions gradually drifted apart, a development the latter regard with regret and diffuse feelings of guilt. Wilson conveys the sense that Sérgio had adopted an unhealthy way of life and that his old friends may have shunned him because of it:

> He was an athlete, he was the swimming champion of Maranhão, he was a person in demand, he was a person who was an attraction. In his youth he never suffered the kind of disappointment of not being anybody, of not having a goal to reach. This came later. I put a lot of this on the pressure of his course of study. I think that he, as a guy who was withdrawn, never was much for making friends. [He was] a very quiet guy, he always was drawn into himself [*calado na dele*]. What he had was us, his friends, and we drifted away from him. We'd had our childhood and started to get to a new phase, where we were discovering ourselves, we were being born into life, really.
>
> Along with this, the [new] people he was relating to, he being someone with education [and] knowledge, didn't have a level of conversation to be with him. I couldn't believe these were really new friends. They were people he sought out so as not to be alone, it's because maybe the only one of his real friends who really continued having contact with him was

---

[8]Two people told me stories they had heard of Sérgio seeking refuge from pursuers as a result of brigas. Both stories had him bleeding and in great danger. In one case, his protector reportedly told the pursuers he was not there; in the other, the protector had to prevent him from leaving her house, where she had treated his wound.

Ivan, but not in the way [that we had before]. We were very
united, very united, we would always go around together, we
did everything, it was our turma against the turma of others,
understand, and all of a sudden this was completely undone.
   [This happened when I was] eighteen. That was when we
began to sense in Sérgio that change. I myself sometimes
passed by [the neighborhood quitanda], he was always drinking there, I didn't like being in that place, drinking with those
people, and he [would be] there, he would call me, I would
say, "No, I have to study" and so on, and I would feel bad.

Wilson was not the only one of Sérgio's old friends to worry about his
new companions. Ivan tried to discourage him from continuing these new
friendships, to no avail:

I would say to him that those guys who were always going
around with him were just good-time buddies [colegas de lance],
to get drunk with and go to bars with, because if anything
really happened to him, they would leave him there and
scram [tirar o time]. I got tired of telling him this, but he wasn't
paying much attention to what was going to happen to him.

Progressively isolated from his closest friends, Sérgio simultaneously
went through the disintegration of a long and intense relationship with
Irene, a young woman who also lived in his old neighborhood. By the time
they finally broke up in January 1984, Sérgio and Irene had been together
for four or five years, but the relationship had passed through periods of
anguish. They had separated for a time in 1983, and Sérgio had found a
new girlfriend. But he always said that he still loved Irene, and the breakup
seems to have profoundly depressed him. In early 1983, he began to have
problems in school, and by the second semester he had lost interest and
failed his courses. Sérgio and Irene did get together again, in October or
so, but by then it was too late for him to salvage the semester. The conflicts
between Sérgio and Irene continued. Although, says Ivan, "he was very
tender with her, very considerate, every night he went over there," there
was a problem: sometimes Sérgio "would arrive smelling of cachaça." Irene
did not like Sérgio's heavy drinking: "She said that she'd broken up with
Sérgio because he was drinking, she wanted him to change, to quit drinking
and he could return."
   Problems between the two came to a head at a New Year's party on January 1, 1984, when Sérgio became jealous over Irene's attentions to another

man. They broke up two days later; after the split, Sérgio began drinking even more heavily—drinking, says Ivan, "just to get drunk so as to go home, lie down and sleep and only get up the next day."

When Sérgio drank, he typically became more quiet and withdrawn than he usually was. Ivan says,

> Sometimes he would spend the whole night just drinking, but he wouldn't talk to anyone, he would just sit there motionless [*parado*]. Sometimes we would touch him, to wake him up. He would turn around and say, "Let go of me," and turn around again. He thought a lot, mainly when he was drinking, he would spend a lot of time without talking to his friends who were around him, as if he wasn't there, as if he was very far away.

To make matters worse, relations between Sérgio and his family were, by all appearances, also unsettled.[9] The father's early and tragic death was obviously a central emotional event for the family members, memorialized through what others perceived as pressure on the children to study medicine, as though this would compensate for the surgeon's fatal error. Sérgio never spoke to his friends of his father's death, although he was seven at the time, the second youngest of the children, and it surely affected him profoundly. There are hints in Sérgio's biography of unresolved grief and attendant guilt. We can never know for sure, but his intense response to the loss of Irene and to what he perhaps saw as desertion by his old friends may well tie up with the lingering grief of this early trauma.

Sérgio's behavior just prior to his death was causing understandable concern—he was drinking heavily, he had wrecked the car after a string of accidents, and he often left the house without word of his destination—but the form his family's concern took annoyed him. When Sérgio would vanish from the house, his mother would telephone his old friends, sometimes three or four times during a weekend, trying to get in touch with him, because she knew that he often hung out at the quitanda in his former neighborhood. Sérgio would usually then send word back that he was all

[9]My information here is secondhand: I felt that the interviewing required to clarify Sérgio's family situation would have been too delicate under the circumstances, and I was reluctant to cause members of the family more pain than they were already experiencing. In any case, the key individual, Sérgio himself, would always be inaccessible. I met Sérgio's family once, however, at a mass recited on the first anniversary of his death, a dolorous occasion. Sérgio's mother presented me with two small leaflets containing words "psychographed" by the famous medium Francisco Cândido Xavier. These were messages from the other world. Sérgio sent greetings to family members and said that he had begun new studies in order to help those whom drugs had carried off "to suicide and to premature death."

right and she was not to worry. But Sérgio chafed at these efforts to monitor his actions. His irritation seemed related to his distaste for the study of medicine: several of those who knew him thought that his heart was not in it, that had there been no family pressure he would have preferred a different field, such as engineering.

On the day before he died, Sérgio, who had just returned to school, visited Ivan. He spoke of doing his residency in Rio, buying a motorcycle there, and having a great time with all the "beautiful *cariocas* [women of Rio de Janeiro]." Sérgio may have been spinning dreams of Rio, but he was in trouble. The evidence indicates that he was an alcoholic whose drinking had disrupted his relationships with friends, lover, and family. Breakdowns in these relationships probably drove him to drink more. His work at the university had suffered for a full year. He gave every sign of withdrawing into isolation at the same time that he resisted making the passage into adulthood. He remained where he was, locked into patterns of behavior no longer compatible with the adult and professional statuses he was called on to assume. Wilson observes:

> We used to do kids' things, we'd go to the movies and sneak in, [we'd] hop off the bus at the back [i.e., without paying the fare], you know, the irresponsibility [of] youth. When we were young we [left bars without paying] several times, but he continued this. . . . I mean, Sérgio died at 23, 24, [he kept it up] until his death, you know. [He continued with this same] behavior, only that when you are children, people look at it in a different way. He was already a man, I mean, the consequences are different, aren't they. People already were beating him up, and he would fight, and other things would happen. I think that Sérgio didn't have enough support. I blame myself a lot, but it's the kind of thing where you are thinking about yourself a lot, too. So support for Sérgio was lacking, somebody who could orient [him], could listen [to him], I think this was really lacking, I think that he felt himself to be a guy who was really alone, abandoned [*desamparado*].

Schismogenesis

Sérgio had arrived at a desperate impasse. His excessive, destructive drinking and his seeming inability to make the transition from adolescent to adult, despite the increasing cost of failing to do so, are signs of what

Bateson called schismogenesis. On the day Sérgio died, his behavior was unequivocally and intensely schismogenic.

According to Bateson, schismogenesis refers to a state of positive feedback, when an interaction becomes a vicious circle such that A's acts stimulate B's, which then stimulate A's even further, and so on. Schismogenesis can be either symmetrical, in which case A's and B's actions are essentially alike (interactions involving competition or rivalry, for example), or complementary, such that the actions of A and B differ but fit together (interactions involving, say, dominance and submission, or succoring and dependence) (Bateson 1958 [1936], 1972a [1949]: 109).

Bateson later tried to apply these concepts to the alcoholic's dilemma. He suggested that an organism in a stalemate, unable to change a painful behavior pattern, may enter into a schismogenic loop, repeatedly intensifying the unpleasant behavior. This drives home the bankruptcy of the pattern, enabling a behavioral sea change—if a threshold is reached before death occurs. Alcoholics know this as "hitting bottom." "The tendency to verify the unpleasant by seeking repeated experience," wrote Bateson, "is a common human trait. It is perhaps what Freud called the 'death instinct'" (1972c [1971]: 328).

Sérgio must have been aware that something was wrong. He may not have known exactly what, but he probably sensed that it had to do with his drinking, his cracking up cars, his fighting, his impaired relationships with others, and his generally self-destructive behavior. On that Friday he engaged in an orgy of schismogenesis. He had been drinking since early morning. The alcoholic's drinking, argues Bateson, is often a symmetrically schismogenic act. This symmetry can take the form of rivalry with a drinking partner (matching drink for drink). It may also match the drinker against the bottle: the alcoholic "must now prove that the bottle cannot kill him" (p. 326). Sérgio was with Zeca all day, and they were drinking buddies. In São Luís, drinking does tend to be symmetrical; Sérgio's drinking that day probably had the first characteristic of matching drink for drink. Whether Sérgio was engaged in the second and more serious form of symmetrical drinking, the drink to the death (or, perhaps, to miraculous salvation), is uncertain, but the possibility cannot be discounted. Sérgio's drinking that day may have had the unconscious intent of raising the discomfort level to such a screaming pitch that change might become feasible, or, alternatively, that out of the seemingly rejecting universe Sérgio inhabited someone might materialize to save him.

This hypothesis gains credibility in light of Sérgio's actions at Vítor's. From the time he got up and walked away from the table with its empty beer bottles, he had cast himself into that most schismogenic of events, briga. He never struggled against the current; he rode it all the way down. It was as if he were staking everything on discovering what was at the end of all that he was suffering: his old friends? Irene? his father? a new Sérgio?—death? We can never know, and I think probably he did not know, and he certainly did not imagine the possibility of encountering Cosme in the very depths of that briga.

The Killer
Who Was Cosme?

Cosme must remain something of a riddle. Getting information about Cosme was a delicate matter, for Cosme was a policeman. Probing into the affairs of the police in São Luís is both difficult and risky. I had no desire to receive threats that I would be found "with my mouth full of ants" (*com a boca cheia de formigas*), as did a prominent são-luisense broadcaster, an eyewitness who described Cosme's murderous actions on television. Hence my inquiries were discreet and indirect. I did not feel comfortable approaching persons who were intimately acquainted with Cosme, as I had done in the case of Sérgio.

Given this constraint, which forces us to look at Cosme as through the wrong end of a telescope, what can we say about him? Cosme was 29, married, with two young children. He was a police commissioner (*comissário*: a rank higher than that of an ordinary policeman) who worked out of the fraud department. By all appearances he led a life that in its gross features was organized and stable: he had a reasonable income, lived with his family in a house in a decent neighborhood, and moonlighted as a bookkeeper. Unlike most police, he had attended university. His principal recreation was riding his motorcycle. A neighbor described him as an unremarkable, regular person, much as those who noticed him at Vítor's on that Friday night would comment, "He was sitting there drinking, just like everyone else."

Cosme, however, had a serious blot on his record that suggests he was not "just like everyone else." On March 6, 1983, following a dispute at a festa sponsored by the Residents' Union of an outlying bairro, Cosme shot a 21-year-old taxi driver named Joel through the chest. Joel did not die, but he remains paralyzed from the effects of the bullet.

The depositions given by Lúcio, Cosme, and Joel conflict in certain respects, but some things seem clear.

1. The doorman Lúcio challenged Cosme at the club entrance because he was wearing shorts, improper attire for a club event. When Cosme identified himself as a policeman and demanded admission, however, Lúcio reluctantly acceded, permitting Cosme, along with a policewoman named Laura, to enter.

2. There was a disturbance in the bar that involved Cosme, who tried to make an arrest. Lúcio and Joel, who was also working that evening as a doorman, intervened, asserting their right to keep the peace inside the club. During the commotion, someone, probably one of the club's security guards, insulted Cosme and Laura, adding, "You're police out in the street, not here inside."

3. Cosme was evicted as a result of the uproar, but the confrontation between him and the club workers spilled into the street. There was an exchange of blows and Cosme was knocked to the ground by Joel, at which point Cosme drew his gun and fired.

Essentially, the matter had to do with domains of authority. The doormen and guards claimed the club as their turf. From their perspective, Cosme's entry, in defiance of the rules, resembled an invasion. Cosme added fuel to the fire by attempting to exert his authority *within* the club. By challenging this pretension and forcing Cosme's retreat, the guards reasserted their sway. What happened next, at the doorway, is confused; for this we turn to a first-person account by Tiago, who was in the club that night, accompanied by his friend Chiquinho:

> Seu Cosme [a respectful form of reference] was saying some stupid, obnoxious things [*besteiras*] owing to the alcohol but was now outside the club, so this taxi driver [Joel], it seems he was offended by the stupid things Cosme was saying, and so he decided to give Cosme a few punches. [Cosme] was insulting [*xingando*] him, saying some "porras," some "shits," some "son-of-a-bitches," things like that, and then, cara, the taxi driver began a slugging session [*uma sessão de porrada*] on Cosme. So then Cosme went to give the guy a punch, a sock, after he had gotten several punches himself. He missed the guy but the guy gave him a punch and he fell to the ground. He had a shoulder holster; he put his hand to the holster as he was falling, and when the taxi driver came up to him, he shot him, it hit him in the middle of the chest and came out his back, there's still a mark on the wall there.
>
> So then at the same moment Cosme got on his motorcycle and started it up, while the guy was running like a madman. I don't know, I'm not going to tell you what it felt like, what he was feeling, because I've never been shot, I can't give a comparison, but somebody who was shot once told me that it *burns* [his emphasis], so for sure the guy was feeling a lot of heat and was running.

So then when the guy, Cosme, when he got on his motorcycle, [my friend] Chiquinho said to me to give him a kick,
[but] I didn't give him one because the briga had nothing to
do with me, it had only been a week since I arrived here in
São Luís and I didn't even know what the briga was about.
[Chiquinho didn't kick Cosme] because he was afraid of getting shot, too, because let's say that I gave a kick to the guy,
and he fell down, he's going to do the same thing [to me] that
he did to the other guy, right?

From my point of view, the taxi driver deserved even more,
because he wasn't a security guard, he was just a member who
was enjoying himself like anybody else, right, and even if he
was a security guard, his duty is to maintain order within the
club, outside the club it's no longer his business, it sure isn't,
compadre, because on the street the ones who should command are the police, they're the ones who are paid for just
that, a club security guard doesn't have anything to do with
what's going on on the street.

Cosme's forced entry into the club evidently rankled the security personnel. Eviction by the security guards (and Joel) must have similarly stung
Cosme, but this action restored the status quo ante: policeman in the street,
security guard in the club, domains intact. Cosme's invasion had been re-
pelled. But with Joel's aggressive entry into the street—Cosme's turf—the
tables turned, and now Cosme had the right to repel the invasion, which he
did, violently and drastically.

What does this briga tell us about Cosme? First, it reveals a streak of
arrogance. Dress rules are common in São Luís; Cosme claimed a special
privilege. There is no indication that Cosme was treated less than respect-
fully by Lúcio at the door. São-luisenses are not surprised when police
behave in an authoritarian manner, but not all police do, and it is behavior that other people always resent. Cosme's attempt to arrest someone
inside the club gives further evidence of the same tendency: he was trying
to enforce order in a zone outside his authority. Second, Cosme showed a
propensity to use unwarranted, extreme violence. Cosme claimed to have
seen Joel pull a weapon out of his belt (although he could not say what
kind of weapon it might have been), and Laura, in her deposition, went even
further, arguing that both within the club and without, Cosme was pursued
by people (not just one person) with clubs and knives, but no one corroborated these allegations. That Cosme was threatened with a weapon seems
unlikely. The alternative interpretation of the testimony of the two police

agents is straightforward: an attempt to justify the shooting on the basis of self-defense.

I have resurrected this case not simply to suggest that Cosme was an overbearing and violent police officer. The shooting of Joel was under active investigation at the time Sérgio died. Although it would have been remarkable if Cosme were brought to trial and convicted of attempted murder—police are almost never found guilty of crimes in São Luís—conceivably Cosme might have been dismissed from the police force. In addition, this ugly incident was staying alive in the newspapers, and no matter how arrogant or vicious Cosme may have been, the event, with its public humiliation, its potential for inducing guilt, and its possible penalties, must have been painful.

It thus seems more than coincidental that on the morning of the day on which Cosme shot and killed Sérgio he had been summoned before a judge to testify once more on the shooting of Joel. We now turn to consider how these two violent events may have resonated with each other in the mind of Cosme.

Savior and Executioner

What might have gone through Cosme's mind on this fatal night? When he walked into the bar that evening, Cosme may have recalled the briga of a year earlier that had resulted in Joel's paralysis, a briga he had been forced to replay in his testimony that morning. The incident in the Residents' Union must have been traumatic for Cosme. He had been barred entry; then, although he finally got through the door, he had been unable to exercise his authority within the club and had been insulted and ejected by the security personnel. Once outside, he was attacked and beaten by a young man who was not even a real security guard and knocked to the ground. The club authorities had humiliated Cosme as a policeman and as a man, and he did not, by all indications, easily suffer humiliation. And then came the shooting, the inevitable gossip, questions about his fitness to continue in the police force, and the drawn-out investigation.

When a briga erupted in Vítor's, Cosme did not interfere either to break it up or to make arrests, perhaps out of a reluctance to get involved in another unpredictable situation like the one that blew up on him, and in which he blew up, at the Residents' Union. He became aware of this briga early, during the first episode. The briga must have been a topic of conversation between Cosme and his tablemates, Gaspar and França. Gaspar once lived in Sérgio's old neighborhood; he was acquainted with Sérgio and probably knew of his reputation for getting in trouble, for heavy drinking, and for occasionally walking away from checks. Hence even though Cosme did not know Sérgio, by the time the briga resumed there is every reason to believe he knew a lot *about* Sérgio. And Sérgio's behavior showed that he was ignoring the dangers of briga; he seemed determined to reject exits, as if to force a drastic intervention.

What could have been Cosme's reaction to this scene? In the briga at the Residents' Union he had been beaten by a band of "bar police" like Heitor, the other waiters, and Félix. Sérgio, like Cosme at the Residents' Union, was under attack: he deserved to be defended, to be saved. Yet wasn't Sérgio asking for trouble? Sérgio had provoked the briga by leaving the check unpaid, and he would not stop fighting. Sérgio was the criminal, the marginal, the disequilibrated person in this transaction. Sérgio should be stopped. The briga was going too far, and it was out on the street, beyond the doorway of the bar, on Cosme's turf. This was *his* job, a policeman's job, not Heitor's, not Félix's. We can imagine the state of confused but powerful emotional excitation that these intersecting lines of thought might have induced in Cosme, a proud and rash man, but on this night, recalling that *other* briga, reluctant to act. Yet the briga was not going to wind down on its own; he had to stop/save Sérgio. And so Cosme rose from his chair and fired into the air: *this* would end the briga, he was doing his duty, he was saving Sérgio and restoring order.

The crowd scattered. But Sérgio did not heed the warning shots: he clung determinedly to Heitor. Sérgio refused salvation, defied a policeman, rejected Cosme's help. Cosme rushed to Sérgio, to stop/save/punish him. He seized Sérgio by the collar, pulled him away from Heitor—and shot him in the head. In the blink of an eye, savior became executioner. Incredibly, the bloody Sérgio sank to the ground; uncomprehending, Cosme urged, "Get up!"

Once again, Bateson points out a psychological rationale for apparently bizarre behavior. Although the usual relationship between adversaries in a briga is one of symmetrical schismogenesis, I would argue that Cosme's relationship with Sérgio was one of *complementary* schismogenesis. Cosme was poised as either Sérgio's savior or his destroyer. On the one hand, the deeper into the briga Sérgio went, the more desperate was his plight; Cosme, as both (in a sense) his alter ego and someone officially charged with protecting the helpless, became more and more drawn into the role of savior. On the other hand, the more Sérgio revealed his determination to reject exits, the more he accrued blame for the disgraceful event, consequently the greater became Cosme's responsibility, as a proud and aggressive police officer charged with preserving order, to step in and eliminate what he saw as the root cause of the disturbance. As Sérgio descended more and more deeply into the briga, assuming the double role of victim and marginal, Cosme became increasingly, and complementarily, positioned in the contradictory roles of savior and executioner.[10]

Complementary schismogenesis, in Bateson's view, tends to produce a kind of orgasmic climax. The rising curves of intensity, he writes, will be "bounded by phenomena comparable to orgasm," that is, the "achievement of a certain degree of bodily or neural involvement or intensity may be followed by a release of schismogenic tension" (1972a [1949]: 111). I am suggesting that Cosme's sudden and otherwise inexplicable act was a climax of this kind, a rush to discharge the mounting tension that the briga had produced in him. Because he found himself conscripted into two contradictory schismogenic processes at the same time, Cosme passed instantaneously from one resolution to the other, its diametrical opposite. The tragic irony for Sérgio was that in finding in the deepest recesses of this briga an unlikely savior, he should simultaneously have encountered a most likely executioner.[11]

Postscript

Several days after Sérgio's death, his friends and classmates organized a march demanding that Cosme not get off scot-free, as had happened, for example, in the case of Zacarias, a policeman who had murdered his former girlfriend inside a Praça Deodoro police box in January of the same year. Local newspapers reported that the police had made no effort to locate or arrest Cosme.

On April 23, Cosme, with his attorney, appeared at the First District Police Station to give his version of the events of April 13–14. Cosme denied having committed the crime, lamenting that "all of this happened because I went to help the victim and ended up being blamed for something I didn't do." He was then lodged in a special cell to serve twenty days of dis-

---

[10] A few days after the killing, Cosme visited his police colleagues, reportedly telling them that his gun went off as he was trying to pull Sérgio from the waiters who were beating him unmercifully. At one point he burst into tears; it was unclear whether he was crying "out of remorse or because he was being unjustly accused" (*JP*, April 18, 1984).

[11] A woman in São Luís once told me a story of a similar incident that had a different ending. The protagonist was a friend of hers, a black man, probably, like Sérgio, in his twenties. The person, literally thrown in the garbage at the moment of his birth, was eventually raised by a white middle-class family. He had a reputation for drinking heavily and then provoking fights. One day he left a bar in the Praça João Lisboa, in the heart of the city, without paying for what he had drunk. When the bar owner accosted him and asked for the money, the *brigão* punched him; the bar owner then shot him in the lung. He did not die. When he recovered, he began going to the bar to help out the bar owner, without pay. He also, according to the woman, gave up fighting. Like Sérgio, this man seems to have pushed events to the point of death or salvation. Unlike Sérgio, he may have found salvation.

ciplinary imprisonment, a normal procedure in cases of serious infraction by police personnel. He was neither dismissed from the police force nor held under the law of preventive detention, which would have permitted his incarceration for a longer period.

A judge issued an order for Cosme's preventive detention the day after he was released. The police claimed they could not locate Cosme; there were speculations that he had fled the state or even the country. In August, however, he surfaced in São Luís. His lawyer explained that Cosme had come to try to get the decree of preventive detention revoked. Again he was housed in a special cell, where he would, if the decree were maintained, complete at least three months of imprisonment.[12]

In early October, the governor of Maranhão signed an order dismissing Cosme from the police force. No longer a public employee, Cosme lost his privilege of occupying a special cell on friendly territory, away from the other prisoners. But on October 23, when he found he was to be transferred to the common jail, Cosme "escaped." According to the police, he had asked to take a shower. Upon leaving his cell, so it was said, he overpowered the single guard on duty, locked him in the cell, and fled.

The following morning, Cosme's wife called a police officer to ask that someone come to her house to retrieve the guard's gun and keys.

All three bars closed their doors for good within weeks of the shooting. Up to the time I left São Luís in mid-March 1986, Cosme had not reappeared, except in rumors: from time to time someone claimed to have spotted him on his motorcycle speeding through the streets of the city.[13]

[12]It was widely reported, however, that he had the run of the station where he was lodged.

[13]This image of the killer riding through the streets of São Luís resonates with the famous legend of the city concerning Ana Jansen, a long-dead aristocrat said to have been a sadistic torturer of her slaves. According to the legend, late every Friday night her carriage, pulled by headless mules (or headless horses), clatters madly over the cobblestones on its circumvolution of São Luís, a "journey of expiation" that lasts until dawn (Serra 1941: 154).

PART IV

CONCLUSION

How hard it is to wake up silenced
If in the hush of the night I go mad
I want to hurl an inhuman cry
Which is a way to make myself heard
All this silence makes my head reel
Reeling, I stay alert
Up in the grandstand, so at any moment
I can watch the monster of the lake emerge

The world may not be small—SHUT UP!
Nor life a consummated fact—SHUT UP!
I want to invent my own sin—SHUT UP!
I want to die of my own poison—SHUT UP!
I want to lose your head once and for all—SHUT UP!
My head to lose your judgment—SHUT UP!
I want to breathe the smoke of diesel oil—SHUT UP!
And get drunk on it till someone forgets me—SHUT UP!

—From the song "Cálice" (Chalice / Shut Up!),
by Gilberto Gil and Chico Buarque

11

THE CULTURAL CYBERNETICS
OF VIOLENCE

Cultural Integrations

Culture, argues Clifford Geertz in a famous, striking passage, is something like an octopus, an "ungainly entity" composed of "partial integrations, partial incongruities, and partial independencies" (1973c [1966]: 407). We cannot assume cultural coherence: searching for patterns in culture is an empirical enterprise, an effort to distinguish the "clusters of significant symbols" that together make up the disjointed system that is a particular culture.

Carnival, briga, and desabafo compose a tightly integrated cultural cluster. Its outstanding feature is that Carnival and briga signify, respectively, "good" desabafo and "bad" desabafo. Since são-luisenses see desabafo as the means for bringing psychological and social systems into equilibrium, Carnival represents self and society *under control*, whereas briga signals the reverse, self and society *out of control*.

The Carnival-briga-desabafo cluster is, I claim, cultural in a specific sense: it is, in its broad outlines, a shared cognitive phenomenon. That is, the configuration is both *psychological* (present or available in individual minds) and, because são-luisenses generally seem to know and understand this same configuration, *cultural* in nature. It is an assemblage of what cognitively oriented anthropologists have recently termed cultural (or "folk") models (Holland and Quinn 1987).

Cultural Models
Knowledge Structures

A cultural model is a complex, shared knowledge structure. I use the word "structure" to emphasize that a cultural model has interrelated parts, which are themselves structured. Hence cultural models compress within themselves enormous amounts of organized shared knowledge. To date, no consensus has evolved about what degree of complexity qualifies a knowledge structure to be a cultural "model," and researchers have called all kinds of things cultural models. Dorothy Holland and Naomi Quinn's (1987) edited volume includes as examples everything from the Western model of the mind to theories of home heating control. The term "cultural model" is thus more suggestive than precise.

A simple cultural model might be the model for FACE, described by Donald Rumelhart (1980: 39–40), which shows clearly how knowledge structures (often called schemas)[1] pyramid into larger knowledge structures, or, to take a top-down view, embed one within another. The FACE schema is a configuration of subschemas representing its constituent parts: MOUTH, NOSE, EAR, EYE, and so on. These subschemas are likewise configurations of sub-subschemas: an EYE consists of an IRIS, EYELASHES, an EYEBROW. Possibly we could, were we so inclined, follow the tree (or network) of schemas downward to an elementary level of basic schematic components.[2]

For sociocultural anthropologists, the models of prime interest are those that pattern and motivate social relations. The cognitive science literature is multidisciplinary, however; its contributors include linguists, psychologists, and artificial-intelligence researchers, as well as sociologists and anthropologists. Accordingly, researchers do not necessarily concern themselves with the social relevance of cognition. One of my major objectives here has been to isolate a shared cognitive complex of undeniable *social* consequence.

---

[1] Schema theory is one of the foundations of the field of cognitive science; see Rumelhart's 1980 paper for an introduction. For a useful current overview of cognitive semantics, see Lakoff (1988); he presents his general position at length in his 1987 book. Dougherty (1985) and D'Andrade (1990) give historical overviews of the field of cognitive anthropology. Those interested in cultural models will find Quinn and Holland (1987) and D'Andrade (1984, 1987) especially illuminating.

[2] The linguist Mark Johnson (1987) writes of "image schemas" rooted in bodily experience. An example is the CONTAINER schema, composed of the elements INTERIOR, BOUNDARY, and EXTERIOR, which, argues Johnson, arises in (precultural) sensations such as inhaling and exhaling, eating and excreting. Johnson points out that we extend these primary schemas to other domains, using them to build more complicated cognitive structures. São-luisense folk psychology, with its emphasis on the notion of desabafo—the venting or expulsion of bad stuff from the inner world—draws on the CONTAINER schema.

Briga and Carnival, models of social interaction, are many-layered cognitive constructs. This study has excavated only the upper strata of these cultural models. Cultural fabrications such as provocation and desabafo have no self-evident meaning; they are themselves complicated knowledge structures.

Intersubjective Sharing

Knowledge structures can be idiosyncratic, the property of a single individual, but *cultural* models consist of structures that are intersubjectively shared.[3] This means that

> interpretations made about the world on the basis of the folk [i.e., cultural] model are treated as if they were obvious facts of the world. . . . A second consequence of the intersubjective nature of folk models is that a great deal of information related to the folk model need not be made explicit. (D'Andrade 1987: 113)

Intersubjective sharing, in other words, lends to cultural models a matter-of-factness; hence communication involving folk models is a shorthand that leaves a great deal tacit. Briga stories, for example, select certain aspects of the event they describe, letting the listener fill in the gaps by making inferences drawn from knowledge of the entire model.

Intersubjectivity permits individuals to collaborate in the performance of an intelligible event. In the preceding chapter I suggested that Sérgio, Cosme, and the others at Vítor's Bar oriented their behavior around the shared perception that what was going on was a briga, an event entailing a multitude of circumstances and possibilities. No one publicly spelled out all these entailments—indeed, no one officially declared the event a briga— because no one had to. People assumed appropriate roles: antagonist, ally, peacemaker, witness, "wild force." They interpreted the actions of others, imagined various possible interactional sequences, and inferred the internal states of the combatants in a manner consistent with the briga scenario. They geared their own actions to these calculations so as to generate a recognizable, if in some respects puzzling, interaction. They could do all this because they shared a set of detailed ideas about briga—because briga is a são-luisense cultural model.

[3]Roy D'Andrade (1987: 113) explains intersubjective sharing in this way: "A schema is *intersubjectively shared* when everybody in the group knows the schema, and everybody knows that everyone else knows the schema, and everybody knows that everyone knows that everyone knows the schema."

I call the Carnival-briga-desabafo complex a cultural cluster to differentiate it from its elements, three cultural models (of which two are scenarios and one a folk theory). The terms "cluster" and "model" simply indicate different levels of cultural integration, a cluster being an array of models. The distinction is heuristic. A scenario is a cultural model of an event; a folk theory is a widely shared set of propositions about how something works, a popular rather than expert or scientific theory. The Carnival-briga-desabafo cluster, then, encompasses the Carnival and briga scenarios and their common foundation, a folk theory of the mind oriented around the notion of desabafo.

Preceding chapters have discussed these three cultural models at length. I summarize and comment on them briefly below. My main objective is to give a bird's-eye view of a singularly important, high-level cultural structure.

The Carnival-Briga-Desabafo Cultural Cluster
A Cultural Model of Carnival

Carnival and briga are social interactions. Considered as scenarios, they are little worlds of the collective imagination, nice examples of what Roy G. D'Andrade (1984) calls "culturally created entities."[4] Games like baseball or chess, set outside "real life" and governed by arbitrary rules, exhibit clearly the main features of such cultural creations (D'Andrade 1984: 91). A day at the ball park will easily convince most people in the world that baseball is both arcane and artificial—that understanding the strange movements on the field, or why those around you erupt into cheers or curses when nothing seems to have happened, requires special, complicated instruction. The baseball fan, too, can probably be persuaded that "balls," "strikes," and "the infield fly rule" are cultural constructs within a still larger construct, baseball. It is not only games, of course, that are culturally created. As David Schneider has long insisted (1968), even the notion of kinship, something both natives and anthropologists tend to view as "natural," rests on assumptions that are fundamentally cultural inventions.

There are some advantages in looking at Carnival and briga as games.[5] Games are engineered events: they must specify explicitly who is to partici-

---

[4]My discussion in this paragraph draws heavily on D'Andrade (1984: 89–96).

[5]There are, of course, alternatives. A dramaturgic perspective on social interactions can be revealing, as Erving Goffman and Victor Turner, among others, have amply demonstrated. The idea of a dramatic "script," however, seems best suited to the study of ritual, which tends to be formalized and hence invariant (Rappaport 1979). To speak of Brazilian Carnival, for example, as having a "script" is perhaps to stretch an analogy to the breaking point. But I think briga can be profitably analyzed as either a game or a drama.

pate, what counts as what, what is at stake, and what actions are called for. By laying out exactly what one needs to know to bring off an event that is obviously a cultural construct, they suggest the instructions a scenario can be expected to include. Like the official rule book for baseball or chess, a scenario contains directions that if followed enable people, acting jointly, to produce a given event.

Games devise or use cultural constructions for a variety of purposes. The chess player is, of course, a cultural product, as are pawns and knights. But the players' actions are no less culturally constituted. Castling in chess, striking out in baseball, and connecting in briga are constructed acts peculiar to those events. Cultural constructions may be unique to the particular game being played (the Quit-It Gang, blocos, rooks, squeeze plays), or they may be more generalized entities (police, parades, winning) used by and given a special meaning in the context of that game. A scenario therefore does two things simultaneously. It stipulates the behavior that permits a successful performance of the event while at the same time specifying the repertoire of participants, objects, and actions that make it possible to bring the event to life.[6] Through this repertoire we can trace the cultural roots of the scenario—the understandings piled upon understandings from which the scenario is constructed.

One plays Carnival, for example, within a certain physical and temporal space. Carnival is an annual event that peaks during the days immediately preceding Lent, ending on the morning of Ash Wednesday. Although "Carnival is everywhere," its privileged locations are the streets and the clubs. Playing Carnival means following a set of guidelines that transform or invert certain everyday injunctions. Underlying these various transformations is the global prescription to desabafar. Desabafo manifests itself publicly in expansive behavior. People expel anguish over their existential plight and resentment over daily humiliations. They become foliões: they dance without stopping, display sexuality, drink enormous quantities of cachaça, sing and shout. They treat one another in an egalitarian manner, show tolerance, refuse to take offense, and abstain from (overt) aggression for if desabafo goes beyond the line that separates it from provocation, Carnival dissolves into briga.

Carnival's guidelines draw upon innumerable cultural constructions. Some of these (folião, entrudo) are specific to Carnival, whereas others

[6]D'Andrade (1984: 93) contrasts "constitutive rules" ("ideas that create realities") with "regulatory rules" ("ideas that order or constrain action"), following John R. Searle (1969) and David Schneider (1976). The analytic categories distinguish "stuff out of which a performance is made" from "rules for generating that performance." But the "rules" of Carnival, unlike those of formal games, are flexible rather than fixed. This is an important reason why the game model, useful as it is, should be applied with care to informal interaction scenarios.

(cachaça, desabafo) are not, although within the bounds of the festival they take on special meaning.

São-luisenses' knowledge of Carnival goes far beyond what this summary statement suggests. In one way or another, for example, the Carnival model is linked to understandings about the Catholic religion, about the relation between music and emotion, about the meanings encoded in Brazilian urban geography (DaMatta 1978, 1985), and (crucially) about the nature of human experience and the workings of human psychology. Where Carnival leaves off and other models begin is a matter of the "partial integrations, partial incongruities, and partial independencies" of this region of cognitive and cultural space. In my judgment, the cultural model of Carnival sketched here is a cohesive, well-defined, and widely shared entity that bumps up against another tightly integrated cultural entity, briga. Both of these, moreover, rest essentially upon yet a third model, namely, são-luisense ethnopsychology.

A Cultural Model of Briga

Like Carnival, briga is culturally constituted, but the two scenarios differ significantly in certain respects. In the first place, briga has a much more definite temporal structure than does Carnival.

As Roberto DaMatta has observed, Brazilian Carnival has no climax equivalent to the New Orleans Mardi Gras parade of the krewes down Canal Street on Shrove Tuesday (DaMatta 1978, 1983). It is true that the samba school competition bears a superficial resemblance to the parade of the krewes. But in São Luís, for example, the main contest occurs on Sunday night, smack in the middle of Carnival, an unlikely moment for a climax, and indeed there is no sign that Carnival winds down after this parade. A major difference, I think, is that New Orleans Mardi Gras is more spectacle than festival and Brazilian Carnival the reverse. A spectacle is something for the eyes, for an audience; a festival is something for the whole person, in which there is no distinction between audience and participants. The Canal Street parade is the grandiose apex of an event designed essentially for spectators; the parade of samba schools is a spectacle set amid an essentially spontaneous festival lacking any participatory climax.

Briga has, in contrast, a scripted quality, although in important respects its "plot" differs from the classic cognitive scripts described and elaborated by Roger C. Schank and Robert P. Abelson (1977). Abelson defines a script straightforwardly as "a coherent sequence of events expected by the individual, involving him either as a participant or as an observer" (1976: 33). Individuals may learn different scripts, he continues, but many scripts are "culturally overlearned"—in the terminology used here, intersubjectively shared. It would seem that briga, with its provocations, connections, escalations, and explosive conclusions, is, according to these broad specifications, a cultural script.

Schank and Abelson have devoted most attention to relatively simple scripts like the "restaurant script," in which a hungry customer enters a restaurant, orders a meal, is served, eats, pays, and leaves. But briga is a more volatile enterprise than downing the blue-plate special. Schank and Abelson focus on situations in which actors collaborate to complete the script as smoothly as possible. The diner wants to eat; the waiter wants a nice tip; the cook wants a paycheck. Everyone tries to get through the script gracefully, avoiding obstacles and errors, such as the waiter's failure to give the prospective diner a menu. Such snafus require subroutines (catching the waiter's eye and requesting the menu) to get things back on track. Although things may go wrong, there is no motivation for subversion.

Briga violates the presuppositions of the restaurant script. Briga's dramatic climax is disastrous, a killing and a death. Rarely can someone be said to want this outcome. Rather, the outcome is a sign of something having gone wrong, not with the script but with the actors. Participants and even spectators usually try to force an exit. A briga remains "a coherent sequence of events expected by the individual, involving him either as a participant or as an observer," but the actors do not necessarily cooperate to move smoothly through the script. If briga is a script, it is a different kind of script from the one followed by diner, waiter, cook, restaurant owner, and cashier.

From a cognitive point of view, although it has one especially meaningful sequence, the briga script has many potential sequences and hence a high degree of unpredictability within a certain understood range of possibilities. Unlike the restaurant script, it is much elaborated in the direction of exits. In other words, the briga script clearly and precisely specifies how to generate "obstacles" and "errors" as well as how to follow the main line of the script. The briga script is not a collaborative effort by actors striving to complete a performance, but rather a meaningful cognitive model elaborated around the disturbing question, Will someone die (kill) here?

This unpredictable, manifold aspect of the briga script grows out of the intense emotional contradictions embedded within the sequence. Briga arouses emotions of fear, vengefulness, and humiliation, impelling the actors simultaneously toward disaster and toward exits. Schank and Abelson have tended to deal with situations, such as interactions in restaurants, in which affect plays a minimal role. But a briga is driven less by the achievement of some identifiable, preestablished goal than by the strong emotions aroused by the briga itself. Although calculation plays a large part in briga, this calculation is very largely self-referential. It refers to the briga situation itself; its aim is to penetrate the swirling fog of emotions sufficiently well to find an acceptable way out.

Briga's emotional charge is unusually strong, but I think all except the most routine of interactions, such as eating in a restaurant, generate emotions that make collaboration, and hence outcomes, problematic. These typical emotions and the problems they may introduce to the interaction are as much a part of the cultural model as the possible sequences themselves. An American who thinks, say, of what might happen when asking a friend for a favor will have little difficulty constructing several conceivable interactional sequences and anticipating the emotions that might arise and perhaps complicate such a transaction. The most interesting scenarios are likely to be those, like briga, in which collaboration cannot be assumed, outcomes are variable, the interaction comes to generate its own goals, and emotional responses are essential elements.

Briga may have a more precisely defined temporal structure than Carnival, but it lacks Carnival's precise temporal coordinates. Briga has no special hour. The cues for the erection of briga's frame are interactional. A briga comes into existence through the conclusion of a compact between two individuals by means of which they agree to become antagonists, that is, participants in a briga. Even a rixa, or feud, has its roots in a compact that was concluded at some time in the past. A briga's beginnings are simple: the event requires a provocation and a connection. It originates in culturally constructed interactions, mini-scenarios. To provoke someone, you say or do something that your adversary will experience as a violation or invasion, as a negation or diminution of his or her personal worth—as a humiliation. To connect, you send a signal, through word or gesture, that you have taken notice of the provocation. Barring an apology on the part of the provoker, the "game" can begin.

The antagonists may now move to an exchange of verbal and physical aggression, which threatens to escalate to a bloody climax if one or both of them become altered, such that the desire (or, as Tito puts it, the "need") for vengeance overwhelms considerations of personal safety and the restraints of conscience. Vengeance, in Léia's words the *moto perpetuo* of a briga, is repayment, often with interest, of a felt injury. The injury, perhaps even at physically violent stages of briga, is more an injury to honor than to the body—a pronounced sense of violation or of humiliation. Whether vengeance drives the briga toward disaster or self-control guides it toward an exit depends on an internal system state, the situation addressed by são-luisense folk psychology. It is perhaps not stretching a point to argue that a briga has as much to do with this internal psychological drama, a familiar and highly significant one for são-luisenses, as with any observable confrontation. In other words, using the x-ray vision that comes with knowing the briga model, one sees in a briga both a potentially mortal conflict between two persons and an interior confrontation between emotion and structure. Briga puts a life-and-death inner drama out on the street.

A briga ends with the physical separation of the antagonists or with the serious injury or death of a fighter or other person present at the scene. Physical separation may be voluntary, as when a person runs away. More commonly, the Quit-It Gang or in some cases the police intervene to pull the opponents apart. Separating the antagonists can be dangerous for the members of the Quit-It Gang, who may themselves be injured or killed. When the police enter a briga, however, they typically do so in a terrifying, violent fashion, clubbing people and hauling them away to an unknown fate at the police station.

Hence to "play" briga, you must know how to provoke, connect, insult, and physically attack an opponent. You must also know how to find a way out of the interaction, through apology or other means. Furthermore, you need to know about rixas, alteration, the Quit-It Gang, vengeance, and the police. Finally, you must understand how various contingencies string together into typical sequences, since the "game" has many possible endings. In short, the rules of play tell how the interaction can develop and how to maneuver among the various possible routes through the event.

Again, some of the cultural constructs implicated (provocation, the Quit-It Gang, rixa) are specific to briga, and some (police, humiliation, apology) are integrated into a wide range of cultural models. Understanding briga means understanding a host of other cultural creations, among which figures prominently são-luisense folk psychology.

A Folk Psychology

Both the Carnival and briga models rest on myriad subsidiary understandings. One set of such understandings, however, stands out as a critical component of both models. This is the body of propositions that constitute são-luisense folk psychology, an indigenous, sophisticated theory of emotion and inner conflict. São-luisense folk psychology tells what it is to be a self-controlled, vital, moral person; in doing so, it indicates how chaotic individual desires can be reconciled with social harmony. The key element in this reconciliation is desabafo, the periodic venting of psychological pressure. In the ideal Carnival, revelers manage desabafo successfully, fashioning an illusory social utopia. In briga, desabafo goes awry, and blood flows. Carnival and briga represent two disparate outcomes of desabafo; this is a major reason why this book has given these two events joint consideration.

São-luisense folk psychology posits an internal generator of impulses and desires that are predominantly sexual and aggressive in nature. To some degree, this internal generator operates independently of external conditions. But it can also be stimulated by others' provocations and aggressions. One cannot always act upon internally generated impulses and desires, for they may be disruptive or destructive, harmful to relationships with others or to oneself. Hence one needs a structure, or set of structures, to impede the dangerous eruption of impulse into behavior. This structure acts as a gatekeeper, permitting or forbidding the public expression of private urges, depending on the external situation. São-luisenses describe the gatekeeper as some compound of rational calculation, religious strictures, and moral imperatives. They seem to have a vivid sense of the disjunction between an unconstrained, sometimes perverse interior world and an exacting world of everyday social interaction.

Because structure checks the manifestation of certain impulses in behavior, one experiences frustration. Over time these frustrations accumulate, becoming a burden or, alternatively, festering. Sooner or later frustrations and resentments will seek expression, if not through a controlled expulsion of some kind, then through a chaotic eruption dangerous both to the person and to others nearby.

The unpleasant, perilous consequences of warehousing bad emotions can be avoided by means of desabafo, which is, ideally, a controlled, rather than uninhibited, release of inner pressures. Controlled desabafo can be realized in many ways—by a drinking binge, a verbal outpouring of complaints, a night of ritual dancing at a terreiro, or, of course, by playing Carnival. The raison d'être of Carnival is desabafo. Drinking, dancing, singing, shouting, and a relatively open display and indulgence of aggressive and sexual impulses constitute the healthful, equilibrating desabafo of Carnival.

But there are limits to carnivalesque desabafo. This study has focused on the problem of aggression. Carnival permits certain stylized aggressions (e.g., entrudo), but forbids provocations, actions that inflame the emotions and initiate the briga sequence. It is here that we discover the link between Carnival, briga, and desabafo.

São-luisenses conceive provocations, and sometimes aggressive connections, as *uncontrolled* desabafos, the products of temporarily or inherently "disequilibrated" individuals. Here, people do not vent aggression "into the air," as they should, but rather direct it at a human target. The desabafo therefore ceases to function as a harmless and salutary psychological stabilizer, becoming instead a malignant symptom of disequilibrium that threatens life, limb, and social peace by drawing people into violent conflicts.

Carnivals and brigas put on public display an interior drama—the way individuals resolve, or fail to resolve, the inevitable tension between impulse and structure. São-luisenses conceive this tension in cybernetic terms, although of course they do not use words like "system," "governor," or "feedback." Nevertheless, they clearly recognize that desabafo is essential for social and psychological well-being. Persons are deemed equilibrated not because, according to a crude version of self-control, their psychological structures always smother dangerous emotions, but because they are adept at containing the necessary periodic breaches in these structures.[7] But equilibrium cannot be taken for granted, and failure invites catastrophe. Hence the mental world depicted by Tito and others resembles a boiler with a questionable servomechanism.

In indigenous terms, a good Carnival, like restorative ritual, at once signals a problem and resolves it. Such a Carnival reassures são-luisenses that the control mechanism is working right, that things cannot get out of hand. Not so briga. A violent briga tells são-luisenses that things are wrong, and worse, that because the control device has malfunctioned, they cannot be rectified.

[7]Neither English nor Portuguese distinguishes lexically between the two types of self-control contrasted here. What we might call Control 1 is the everyday containment of dangerous emotions by moral, religious, and rational structures. Control 2 is the modulation of desabafo, the special skill of equilibrated persons (Linger 1990: 75, note 19).

12

BRAZILIANS AND THEIR DISCONTENTS

Quero provar a mim mesmo que eu não sou assim
[I want to prove to myself that I'm not like that].
—Wall graffito, São Luís

Brazilian Civilization Revisited

Civilization (*Kultur*), Freud tells us (1961 [1930]), has its discontents. The price of living together is frustration and guilt: to escape the terrors of barbarism we must curb our innate sexuality and destructiveness. Civilization therefore reduces the instincts to a "conquered city," whose menacing, punitive "garrison" is the superego (p. 71). The measure of a civilization is the balance it strikes among the evils of anarchy, the pleasures of instinct, and the sufferings of conscience.[1]

In the Brazilian origin myths of Gilberto Freyre and Euclides da Cunha, guilt restrains neither the master's lust nor the soldier's fury. The Big House and Canudos, uncivilized crucibles of the nation, are freighted instead with the vices of savagery: insecurity, arbitrariness, and violence. Freyre is sanguine: the Brazilian solution is a lucky invention, an inadvertent but happy synthesis of the contradictions embedded within the pliant Portuguese version of slavery. Masters and slaves, bedmates by virtue of circumstance or coercion, become the progenitors of a hybrid civilization that is concil-

[1] I use Freud's familiar terminology as a convenient way of phrasing this quandary, but I find it difficult to think of sexuality or aggression as instincts, independent of social experience. The *capacity* for expression of sexuality or aggression has a biological base, but the expression itself takes place within, and is crucially shaped by, a determinate sociocultural milieu. Although the issues are profound and complex, I think the inescapable dilemma is that social experience produces strong and ambivalent emotions, not all of which can be expressed in behavior without causing serious interpersonal disruptions. Society, the source of dangerous emotions, must therefore fence them in—giving rise to civilization's discontents.

iatory, generous in spirit, relatively guilt-free, a civilization tolerant and forgiving of erotic satisfactions and unmenaced by forces of destruction. But Cunha sees things in a radically different light. In the spiny Bahian backlands, Eros is absent and Thanatos everywhere. Cunha accuses: the annihilation of Canudos was a crime perpetrated by the wolf in sheep's clothing that passes for civilization in Brazil. He would give the nation a conscience, paying the penalty of guilt rather than accepting or ignoring the horrors of genocide, but he concludes pessimistically that Canudos was just "the first assault" in a mad, atrocious, but historically inevitable process of extermination, a final solution carried out by a sham civilization (1944 [1902]: xxix). The pressing issue here is whether Brazilians can forge a tolerable civilized society from the savage and fateful encounter of Portuguese, Indian, and African.

My concern in São Luís was not with historic encounters between peoples, but with commonplace encounters between persons, their ordinary but extraordinarily difficult work of, in Freud's words, seeking some sort of "expedient accommodation" between the exigencies of instinct and society (1961 [1930]: 43). São-luisenses understand the problems of living in society and fashioning a good civilization in much the same terms as Freud does—albeit with a considerably greater tolerance, not to say gusto, for illusion; in this they are perhaps more realistic than he is—but they fear that the problem remains fundamentally unresolved. São-luisenses recognize that their face-to-face encounters are often volatile, sometimes mortifying, and occasionally disastrous.

I have examined two kinds of encounters familiar to everyone in São Luís. Carnival proposes that the reconciliation of instinctual and societal imperatives is possible. Briga, by contrast, is a calamity that forces one's attention to the discontents and dangers of living among others. Typically thoughtful são-luisenses do not need Freud to point out to them that social life—which is to say human life—is inherently problematic. They have made of this universal and unavoidable human dilemma, a dilemma locally exacerbated by ubiquitous and much-resented impositions of "superiors" on "inferiors," a cultural centerpiece, and no one is more keenly aware than they are that although they often extemporize brilliantly, too often things go woefully wrong. A "coded message written in blood" (Linger 1990), a briga signals the vulnerability of self and society to the arbitrary ragings of brute force that Freud saw, and são-luisenses see, as the signature of barbarism.

For são-luisenses and, I believe, for other Brazilians as well, briga's exact meaning may be elusive, but its disturbing message of vulnerability seems unmistakable. If briga is for Brazilians an autocommunicative alarm bell, a clamorous symptom of their discontents and their endangered civilization, it is for me, someone with the peculiar perspective and training of an American anthropologist, an index of linked, culturally mediated social and psychological predicaments.[2] Social arrangements always have psychological implications, but both interpersonal relations and private experience are embedded within a specific cultural context. Given the cultural context I have outlined, I argue that Brazilian social arrangements generate characteristic intrapsychic quandaries revolving around issues of self-respect and aggression. These quandaries render briga a compelling event replete with meaning, but for most people that meaning, however urgent, seems partially obscure. Whether briga's alarm bell will motivate changes in social arrangements depends fundamentally on cultural innovation, that is, on how the problem of briga gets interpreted within Brazilian society.[3] This book is meant as a contribution to that discussion.

In presenting the following conjectures my intent is not to pass judgment on Brazil or Brazilians—surely no American, given our own violent past and present, and our own social injustices, is in any position to do so—but to examine from one more angle our common dilemma as human beings: the intrinsically difficult task of living decent, satisfying lives together.

The Social Predicament

Comparing briga with Geertz's Balinese cockfight (1973a [1972]), I have argued elsewhere (Linger 1990) that the extraordinary salience of briga for são-luisenses stems not so much from the fact that, as in Geertz's Bali, the bloody confrontation metaphorically expresses (and therefore, by an extension of Geertz's reasoning, in some measure dissipates) violent subterranean emotions as that it demonstrates, graphically and unforgettably, that hostility can erupt with devastating effect into actual social interactions. A briga "says" that the problem of aggression is acute and pressing. For Balinese, the cockfight is a piece of cultural improvisation that patches over a

---

[2]This is not to say that people without specialized training are incapable of making essentially the same analysis as the anthropologist. São-luisenses' explanations of human behavior often suggest that our "etic," "scientific" theories are not much more than somewhat systematized and elaborated versions of folk theories. Certainly my own analysis has been substantially informed by those of friends and acquaintances in Brazil; at times it is hard to know where their reflections end and mine begin.

[3]There is no good reason to think that the Carnival-briga-desabafo cultural cluster is restricted to São Luís. I have done no systematic research elsewhere in Brazil, but Brazilian "culture-at-a-distance" materials (Mead and Métraux 1953), such as the popular songs I have quoted, show essentially the same preoccupations expressed herein by são-luisenses. Certainly Carnival and briga are nationwide phenomena, and urban violence is, if anything, more pronounced in the great industrialized cities of the South. Nevertheless, there may be regional variations in cultural models; I cannot say for sure how great such variations might be. São Luís is exceptional in certain respects: it is probably more hierarchical, more patriarchal, in general more "traditional" than many other Brazilian cities.

point of sociocultural frangibility; for Brazilians, briga marks a rent in the universe, a locus of disastrous failure.

If briga is not a performed metaphor of the hidden emotional correlates of everyday social relations, it nevertheless, like the cockfight, has social roots. For Geertz, the cockfight's cruelty displays resentments generated within the intricate, strongly ascriptive Balinese social hierarchy; hence he describes the cockfight, borrowing a term from Goffman, as a "status bloodbath"[4] (1973a [1972]: 436) contrasting radically with the subdued, peaceful tenor of everyday interactions. In Brazil, as in Geertz's Bali, self-esteem derives crucially from one's position on the social ladder, however differently those ladders have been built. Like the cockfight, briga is fueled by the usually suppressed bitter emotional residues of hierarchy, the resentments that accumulate more heavily as one descends into society's lower reaches. These specifically Brazilian resentments originate in the indignities of living as a socially and politically incapacitated individual in a system strongly characterized by the arbitrary exercise of personal power and influence. What becomes valued when living within such a system, not as something necessarily "good" but as a premoral affirmation of the self, is the ability to withstand impositions by others and, conversely, to impose one's own will upon them. That defense and assertion of the self sometimes become violent depends, to be sure, on personal and situational idiosyncrasies, but this culturally infused social system, with its destructive emotional fallout, has the status of a force majeure.

There is much circumstantial evidence in support of this analysis. For example, provocations frequently take the form of symbolic nullification of the person provoked—her or his consignment, through word or action, to a category designating social refuse (maconheiro, ladrão, marginal, fuleiro, palhaço, and so on). These are types who simply do not count in the scheme of things. Such an accusation simultaneously elevates the accuser and demotes the accused in two ways: first, by implying that the accused is a nonentity with, as Tito's brother put it, "no right to speak"; and second, by virtue of the act of accusation itself, an act that (if not answered) provides de facto evidence of the accuser's domination of, and therefore superiority to, the accused.

Another technique, frequently used in combination with the erasing type of verbal accusation, is (following DaMatta's [1978] illuminating distinction) the figurative demotion of the target from a person (i.e., someone with a discrete identity and some set of determinate relationships with others,

---

[4]Goffman's use of "status bloodbath" (with reference to social gatherings like parties: see Goffman 1961: 78) indicates to me that he is referring to a *leveling* of statuses rather than, as occurs in both the cockfight and the briga, hot contention over relative status. The phrase so vividly suggests the latter, however, that I will follow Geertz's apparent reinterpretation.

someone who counts) to an individual (one of the mass, and therefore, again, a social cipher, a degraded and defenseless human being). This is what happened to Tito, for example, when he was stopped like "an animal" by the upraised leg of the bus conductor, who invoked an impersonal regulation against him, and to Sérgio, when accosted by the waiters as he was leaving the bar.[5] As DaMatta observes, impersonal laws in Brazil are seen (and to a great extent function) as devilish tools of the powerful and privileged rather than as egalitarian guarantees: disguised as universalistic regulations, they are in reality arbitrarily wielded weapons of privilege. The invocation of such laws can kindle revolt (DaMatta 1982) as the victim tries to force an acknowledgment of his or her concrete existence as a person deserving proper consideration.[6] Tito's aggressive response to the conductor's obstruction of the turnstile and Sérgio's striking out at Félix and the waiters exemplify such revolt. Hence a provocation typically involves a symbolic subjection or debasement, and a connection, a refusal to accept consignment to the scrap heap of the hierarchy.

To understand better the motivation for these provocations and connections, it is important to recognize that brigas occur mainly (though not exclusively) within the lower socioeconomic strata. In Gilberto Gil's song "Domingo no parque" (Sunday in the park), José is taking his usual Sabbath stroll when he discovers his lover Juliana riding the Ferris wheel with his best friend João. As the Ferris wheel spins, José becomes disoriented—disequilibrated—and before we know it José's hands are covered in blood and Juliana and João lie dead on the ground. José's knife slashes the two who have betrayed him, at the same time ripping through the civilized facade of Sunday in the park. As Gil tells the story, José works in the market, João in construction; these are workingmen, well down in the Brazilian social hierarchy. São-luisenses' perception that the person who provokes or attacks another projects resentment, whatever its source, into a social interaction seems insightful, a sophisticated piece of folk theorizing. But the aggressor almost never targets a social superior. Like José on that fateful Sunday, he (or, less frequently, she) singles out a João or a Juliana, someone equally powerless.

[5] Sérgio, despite his upper-middle-class origins, seemed just as susceptible as Tito to what we might call an "individualizing" accusation. Like those less materially privileged, Sérgio was living within a general sociocultural environment that sensitizes individuals to feelings of vulnerability and nullification. That the average person must "swallow" symbolic indignities on a regular basis, and therefore experiences the full brunt of the injuries to self-respect dealt out within this environment, does not mean that the materially privileged, who also inhabit it, are not under certain circumstances confronted with similar threats.

[6] The person confronts his adversary with a verbal or nonverbal "Do you know who you're talking to?" (*Você sabe com quem está falando?*). See DaMatta 1978: chap. 4. DaMatta has also argued that urban riots can be seen as the "Do you know who you're talking to?" of "the masses of despoiled individuals who are politically without voice or forum" (1982: 41).

This pattern is not unique to Brazil. It shows up, for example, in Spanish, Peruvian, and Trinidadian festive aggression, discussed in Chapter 1; in the playing of the "dozens" by American slum dwellers (Dollard 1939, Abrahams 1964); in violence among British soccer fans (Dunning, Murphy, and Williams 1986); and in the brutal and indiscriminate beating of young men by older men in a South African segregated township (Mayer 1971 [1961]: 81–89). In Anne Campbell and John J. Gibbs's useful collection of essays on "violent transactions" (1986), Campbell's overview of street violence stresses the link between ghetto brawling and personal slights, and Richard B. Felson, William Baccaglini, and George Gmelch find (with some qualifications) a class component in Irish and American bar fights. In brief, intraclass aggression broadly reminiscent of briga appears to be common.

Although the cross-cultural comparison is suggestive, the inference that such aggression is a narrowly social phenomenon, independent of culture, is unjustified. As Dilthey (1962 [1926]) and Weber (1978 [1922]) argue, it is *meaning* that motivates action. How people construe interpersonal and intrapsychic worlds varies; the degree to which such cultural constructions overlap is at present unclear. I have tried to show how and why brigas occur in São Luís. This has required not just a description of são-luisense social relations, but a discussion of how these social relations translate into experience. Whether this Brazilian case study provides clues for understanding situations elsewhere remains to be seen.

In São Luís, members of the lumpen and working classes experience all manner of indignities in their dealings with superiors, whether persons or institutions, ranging from low wages and disrespect on the job (if indeed they are employed at all) to neglect of basic health, educational, and housing requirements by the government to arbitrary and brutal treatment by the police. Repeatedly in the interviews, people spoke of their need to expel all the burdensome things they had to put up with, among which prominently figured the impositions of the modern hierarchical system in which they live—a hierarchy that concentrates persons (with their privileges, connections, and immunity from the rules) at the top and individuals (at the mercy of those rules and of the caprices of their superiors) at the bottom. By expelling *at* someone else, by relegating another to the scrap heap through an unmistakably self-assertive, dismissive, and counternormative action, one is, in the logic of the system, making a claim to personhood, to a right to be respected, a right to *exist* that, paradoxically from a North American point of view, consists precisely in exemption from purportedly universal laws, regulations, and moral strictures. Given the oppressive realities of that system, the obvious choice of a victim, if one is to have any hope of success at this game, is, ironically, someone who occupies as disgraceful a social position as oneself—a social equal or social inferior.

To be symbolically nullified by such an individual, also a social nullity, is perhaps doubly infuriating. So rank gets negotiated face-to-face in the currency of humiliation, and the status war fought in these trenches of the lower and lower-middle classes frequently degenerates into a literal blood-bath. To "hurl an inhuman cry," Chico Buarque and Gilberto Gil remind us, is, after all, "a way to make [oneself] heard." In Gil's parable, the sacanagem of João and Juliana erases José from both relationships; treated as if he does not exist, he exacts his revenge by physically obliterating the two of them, an irrevocable, if horrifying, existential declaration.

I claim no monopoly on this interpretation, which is, after all, built upon Brazilian understandings. It is hard to say how many são-luisenses observing a briga consciously see it as a "status bloodbath" or could interpret it as such, but some, such as Tito, Joana, and Genival, do and can, and I would submit that in any case most people, upon reflection, associate desabafos, provocations, and arbitrary humiliations imposed by superiors. They sense that a briga has something to do with the indignities they themselves have suffered at work, on the streets, in municipal offices, at the police station— indignities ground out by a sociocultural system that deprives and demeans.

The Psychological Predicament

To say that briga is rooted in socially generated resentment is also to make a psychological argument: that feelings of low social worth, which in São Luís equate more or less to feelings of inefficacy or vulnerability in dealings with others, can motivate one to express hostility in face-to-face social interactions. But briga is more complex psychologically, for there are good reasons not to fight, no matter how much resentment you may feel. Obviously, because brigas are dangerous and unpredictable they induce fear: you could get stabbed or shot, maybe killed. But there is another motive as well to stay out of brigas. Aggression toward others is, generally speaking, regarded as something bad, a sign of disequilibrium or moral rot; moreover, it generates feelings of guilt. As Cravo, the macho pistoleiro, put it, "If you kill, your soul becomes burdened, your spirit becomes burdened. . . . From time to time you dream of that guy you killed, if his name was Manoel, well then, you dream of Manoel, of João."

The point is that fighting is a distressing experience for all but socio-paths. Recall Joana's observation that when the man who goes to the praça to fight tonight wakes up tomorrow, "he's going to remember what he did, [and] he's going to get even more disgusted." The behavioristic as-sumptions underlying virtually all psychological theories would lead us to expect that this should incline people to avoid brigas. But I want to explore here the possibility that the very unpleasantness of brigas can have a paradoxical effect, encouraging continued, perhaps ever more serious, bouts of fighting.

Consider first the onlookers who inevitably gather around a street fight. The intentness with which são-luisenses observe a briga and the intensity with which they verbally replay it suggest that often they vicariously experience the emotions of the fight. Empathy, however, sometimes produces an overlay of agitation compounded of incredulity, excitement, and loathing. I think these two levels of emotion show through clearly in Ezequiel's description of his response to Cosme's initial gunshots:

> I realize that in truth I moved closer in order to understand. When [Cosme] drew the gun and extended his arm, I realized his intention. I thought: He's going to blow Sérgio's brains out. Now that was something that was unbelievable to me, but on the other hand was inevitable. It was as if I was in a nightmare and I couldn't manage to prevent [what Cosme was going to do], I knew that it would happen. The idea of, for example, shouting "Stop!" or "Never that!" never passed through my head, no, my act at the time was an act of understanding, an act of hallucination, an act of madness. I got very sick on account of [all this], I spent several days very terrorized. I somatize all this a lot, all these problems of violence. Since I can't understand it, I somatize a lot.

Ezequiel adopts the point of view of Cosme, recognizing the policeman's intention, playing through a script of Cosme's actions, as if trapped in a nightmare. His "act of madness," I believe, is his identification with Cosme, a concentrated attempt (or compulsion) to understand the sources of the violence. In a sense, Ezequiel himself "kills" Sérgio, in search of an answer he never finds. Yet there is much more here than identification with the killer, for Ezequiel has a profound mental and physical reaction to the scenario, a revulsion produced by his own experiment in empathy.

There is no reason to believe that Ezequiel's complex response is atypical. I have noted previously that brigas seem to transfix onlookers with both terror and fascination. The reader may recall another painful introspection—it borders on a confession—made by Léia, referring to the climactic moments of Sérgio's fatal briga.

> What I would like is really that nothing had happened, not even that the tables and chairs had fallen over, all that interfered brutally in a pleasant moment that we were passing. But I can't, I can't, I can't refuse to admit that [my] paralysis, sud-

denly it seems that an anticipation of something [that might happen] could be touched with a desire that perhaps it would happen, but at that moment I think that this didn't occur to me consciously.

Léia is not a person who enjoys, or enjoys talking about, violence. Like Ezequiel (and almost everyone else who witnessed or heard of the event), she was sickened and outraged by the Praia Grande murder. But what she is revealing here is that, upon reflection, life as she most deeply does not want it may be life as it is imaginatively in one dark corner of the interior world of her own passions.

By this reading, Léia, again like Ezequiel, vicariously participated in this briga, as she had vicariously participated in previous brigas she related to me on other occasions. What is going on here?

It seems at least plausible that briga is a ritualized, disturbing experiment for both participants and spectators that produces characteristic interpersonal and intrapsychic crises. These crises are acute forms of typical dilemmas experienced by those who live within the Brazilian sociocultural environment.

The notion of an iterated, dismaying ritualized experiment calls to mind Freud's discussion of the "compulsion to repeat" unpleasant experiences (1955 [1920]). It seemed to Freud that this compulsion failed to obey the pleasure principle—the principle that mental functioning tends to reduce unpleasurable tension. He thought that the pleasure principle could perhaps explain a child's repetition of a disagreeable experience because such repetition might enhance a sense of mastery over an overpowering and upsetting situation,[7] but other phenomena—transference during psychoanalytic treatment, or the recurrence of traumatic dreams—apparently issued from a deeper, essential compulsion independent of the pleasure principle. Freud identified this source finally (and somewhat reluctantly) as the "death instinct," a fundamentally conservative instinctual tendency to return to an

[7]Children's ritual attention to perceived danger need not, it seems to me, be confined to reenactment of specific real-life situations (e.g., a visit to the doctor), as Freud suggests. F. G. Bailey (personal communication) recalls that in his childhood in Britain boys sometimes lay between railroad tracks: so long as one remained still as the train passed, there was no danger. The situation is contrived, not reconstructed from actual experience. Another example, again involving trains, is "rail surfing" in Rio de Janeiro (White 1990, with remarkable photographs by Miguel Fairbanks). The *surfistas*, youths from Rio's North Zone slums, balance on top of moving commuter trains, dodging the high-voltage cables passing rapidly overhead. This "sport," which seems symbolically counterposed to the wave surfing of the middle-class youths in Rio's South Zone, is incredibly dangerous: in 1988, 144 surfistas died from falls or electrocution. Perhaps it is not forcing an interpretation to suggest that rail surfing is an icon for the fluid psychological equilibrium required to negotiate the dangers of lower-class life in these Brazilian slums, where fighting and police terror are rampant.

"earlier state of things" (p. 63)—ultimately, to a completely quiescent inorganic state. When turned outward, according to this scheme, the death instinct fuels our innate destructiveness.[8]

Freud's argument is (he admits) often "far-fetched speculation" (p. 24), and in the same spirit I will try to adapt it to this discussion. In the case of certain individuals, say, Sérgio or Bocado, we can discern something that looks very like a "compulsion to repeat" the experience of briga. Freud's suggestion that one source of such a compulsion might be a desire for mastery of unpleasant situations seems particularly relevant here. Fighting in a briga simultaneously puts into play one's ability to master others physically and one's ability to master a powerful surge of aggressive emotion, what Tito describes as the "organic necessity to hit, to throw punches, to crush if necessary, to beat someone without stopping, without stopping." Let me suggest that individuals acutely anxious over feelings of humiliation and hostility might engage in brigas, unconsciously seeking a sense of control over these troublesome feelings by re-creating and sharpening them in repeated interpersonal confrontations. In other words, control cannot be convincingly asserted unless the things to be controlled, in this case unacceptable emotions, are given some leeway. This is, I proposed earlier, the rationale behind the dual message of Carnival's "Anything goes!" and its insistence on "playing, not fighting."

The problem is that, aside from their unpredictability, brigas rarely if ever permit the simultaneous mastery of these emotions. Dominating an opponent through violence signifies an inability to control aggressivity and produces guilt; averting violence demonstrates equilibrium but may well entail humiliation. As an emotional experience briga is a recalcitrant enterprise. Any outcome invites schismogenesis: residual frustration can spawn repetitions that create ever more acute versions of the dilemma.

This argument requires no instinctual compulsion to repeat propelled by a death instinct, but at times something like the latter does seem to be

---

[8]Freud's discussion in *Beyond the Pleasure Principle* often seems forced, as if he is struggling mightily to piece together an argument for an instinct whose existence is really proven by his own experience. In *Civilization and Its Discontents*, he is straightforward in this regard: "Men are not gentle creatures who want to be loved, and who at the most can defend themselves if they are attacked; they are, on the contrary, creatures among whose instinctual endowments is to be reckoned a powerful share of aggressiveness. . . . *Homo homini lupus.* Who, in the face of all his experience of life and of history, will have the courage to dispute this assertion? . . . Anyone who calls to mind the atrocities committed during the racial migrations or the invasions of the Huns, or by the people known as Mongols under Jenghiz Khan and Tamerlane, or at the capture of Jerusalem by the pious Crusaders, or even, indeed, the horrors of the recent World War—anyone who calls these things to mind will have to bow humbly before the truth of this view" (1961 [1930]: 58–59). Certainly the events that followed close upon Freud's death in 1939—World War II, the Holocaust, the atomic bombings—would not have led him to a different conclusion.

at work. For might it not be that at some point this increasingly desperate quest for mastery of an impossible situation dovetails with an overwhelming desire for a final reduction in anxiety through self-destruction, through annihilation of another, or, perhaps, through salvation, another regressive solution?

This line of thinking is, of course, prompted by Sérgio's plunge into the briga in the Praia Grande. Sérgio was not able to resolve the emotional crisis he was experiencing; in fact, there is no indication that he had much of an idea about why he felt the way he did. Rather, having reached a point of stalemate, he intensified the very behavior that was causing him pain and frustration in a reckless attempt somehow to discover a way out. Such a do-or-die quality is at the heart of Bateson's notion of schismogenesis, which I pressed into service as an explanation of Sérgio's behavior in the bar. I am now widening the argument to speculate that briga catches up and indeed exacerbates two linked and intransigent psychological problems—one revolving around respect and self-esteem, and another around control of aggression—that are aggravated by certain features of the cultural and social arrangements of urban Brazil. These problems are not, in other words, simply idiosyncratic features of the psychology of this or that individual but instead broadly distributed psychological residues of a sociocultural complex. This is why briga is meaningful as a public phenomenon, as a cultural performance.

Violence, Impasse, and Change

In briga são-luisenses explore certain profound and locally accentuated questions—How can one live without humiliation? How can aggressive feelings be safely managed? Can it really be that the world is ultimately a tragic, dangerous place?—through repetitions and reformulations, firsthand (in the case of disequilibrated persons, usually men, whose anxieties are sufficiently acute) and vicariously (in the case of the vast majority of the population, for whom the event becomes a dramatization of less insistent but nevertheless salient psychological and existential issues).[9] Brigas not only illuminate the deep quandaries and imminent dangers of são-luisenses' socially and culturally constituted world, but also, possibly, represent a feverish groping for a way out of the blind alley, for a "civilized" way of reconciling the antagonistic forces unleashed in the face-to-face encounter.

[9]Most physical violence is initiated by men, but both men and women face these dilemmas. Women as well as men find interpersonal conflict, including violence, a compelling spectacle and topic for conversation, and there is every indication that humiliation is as big an issue for women as for men. But more research is required to identify gender-based differences in the understandings and emotions related to briga and to discover why women are less likely than men to engage in violent brigas.

The evidence belies Freyre's contention that a benign, consistent, and uniquely Brazilian cultural approach to interpersonal conflict already exists, except perhaps as a dream, an exhilarating carnivalesque fantasy, desirable but difficult or impossible to implement, especially under the conditions of widespread degradation, both material and spiritual, that continue to disfigure Brazilian society. But I do not think that things are as hopeless as Cunha intimates. Brazil (like many other nations, including, I would argue, my own) may not as yet have realized a consensus civilization that yields a reasonable degree of social harmony while minimizing the frustrations and anxieties of living within a community. But if a sense that something is gravely wrong must precede significant shifts in cognition and behavior, then Brazilians' contradictory origin myths and their performances of Carnivals and brigas may, ironically, be a crucial civilizing step, for these concrete signs confront them directly with the message that their world is dangerously, deeply fractured.

How Brazilians might find an exit from the many-sided dilemma compressed into briga, or, conversely, how far things might go in the direction of social and psychological disruption, I cannot guess. Probably the violence in Brazilian society has never been more widely and ardently debated, by Brazilians in the street as well as by scholars, clerics, and politicians, than it is at present.[10] This debate, often polemical, tends to focus on crime or on violence by the state. One of my major aims here has been to offer a sociocultural perspective on the problem of Brazilian violence (and, indirectly, on the problem of human violence) by examining briga, a manifestation that, remarkably, has been all but neglected in the public debate although it impinges in one way or another on the personal life of virtually every Brazilian. I would not presume to suggest that my approach or my conclusions are definitive. I have tried, however, to raise issues in the spirit in which Brazilians themselves have wrestled with the problem of violence—to ask yet again, in yet another way: Why?

[10]For a brief but interesting review of Brazilian discourses of violence, see DaMatta (1982). DaMatta's discussion of the "common-sense discourse" of violence touches on issues raised in this book. During the 1980's, empirical studies of urban violence proliferated. Noteworthy are Corrêa's (1983) study of so-called crimes of passion, Fausto's (1984) historical survey of crime in São Paulo, Oliven's (1982) collection of essays on violence and culture, several of the papers in Pinheiro's (1983) edited volume, and Zaluar's (1985) discussion of the meanings of poverty in a notoriously violent neighborhood of Rio de Janeiro. The most telling indictment of state-sponsored violence is the Archdiocese of São Paulo's exposé of torture during the years of military rule (Arquidiocese de São Paulo 1985). These works are the tip of an iceberg: during the last decade, urban violence has been the theme of countless studies, novels, films, political tracts, and press reports.

REFERENCE MATTER

APPENDIX A

BIOGRAPHICAL SKETCHES

I have listed here only those persons interviewed who are cited by name in the text. All names, and in a few cases certain minor biographical details, are fictitious. Biographical information on some persons is incomplete.

BARTOLOMEU   40, born in Rosário (Maranhão). Has lived nineteen years in São Luís. Separated, with children; whereabouts of wife unknown. Bar owner and public employee. Lives alone, in own house in a large, economically diverse conjunto. A practitioner of umbanda. Attended university.

BOCADO   24, born in São Luís. Unmarried, no children. Unskilled casual laborer. Lives with father and numerous siblings in an earthen house in an invasão. Mother died when he was one year old. Father works as unskilled laborer; stepmother is housewife. Finished primary school.

CRAVO   About 50. Stated profession: gambler. Former pistoleiro in interior of state. Lives in Anjo da Guarda, a poor bairro across the Bacanga River from central São Luís.

DENILSON   Early twenties, born in São Luís. Unmarried, no children. Unemployed. Father is unskilled casual laborer; mother, housewife. Lives in Anil, an enormous and diverse outlying bairro of São Luís. Completed primary school.

DIONÍSIO   23, born in São Luís. Unmarried, no children. Unemployed: has heart condition that makes it difficult to engage in strenuous activity. Lives in small house in Center with mother, two sisters, and brother. Father deceased. Mother takes in sewing and works as a monitor of students in a

251

secondary school. One sister attending university. Enjoys pets; breeds cats. Interested in parapsychology. Completed secondary school.

EDUARDO   48, born in São Luís. Married, with three children. Father and mother died in his childhood. Telegraph operator with federal agency; spouse is housewife. At age twelve, was sent to Rio to school, where he learned radio-telegraphy. Has worked many years in both Minas Gerais and Amazônia. Reassigned upon request to São Luís in 1976. Lives with wife and children in own house in predominantly upper-middle-class conjunto. Completed secondary school.

ELENE   Late forties, born in Bacabal (Maranhão). Married, no children. Lawyer in state government agency; husband is middle-level bank employee. Lives with husband in modest but comfortable house in central São Luís. Has worked in various municípios in Maranhão, but has lived for some years in the capital. Became a lawyer against wishes of family. University graduate.

EZEQUIEL   39, born in Campo Grande (Piauí). Married, no children. University professor. Wife is also professional. Lives in apartment in Center. Active in human rights organizations. Postgraduate education.

GABRIEL   22, born in São Luís. Unmarried, no children. Part-time cartoonist and graphic artist. Lives with family in outlying bairro. Family runs small shop in one room of house. Completed secondary school.

GENIVAL   Mid-twenties, born in São Luís. Married, with one daughter. Works as clerk in civilian police department; spouse is housewife. Lives in Center. Completed university course in law.

IVAN   23, born in São Luís. Single, no children. University student. Father is merchant; mother also works. Lives with mother, father, and four siblings in middle-class house in Center. Childhood friend of Sérgio.

JAIR   19, born in Pinheiro (Maranhão). Has lived in São Luís five years. Un-married, no children. Secondary student. Lives with parents and three siblings in Maiobão, a distant conjunto. Father is machine operator; mother, nurse.

JOANA   26, born in São Luís. Married, with a four-year-old son. Unemployed; formerly worked as domestic servant. Lives with husband, child, mother, grandmother, and several others in Desterro, a bairro of the Center. Family income (low) from diverse sources: e.g., peddling, laundry. Husband works as security guard for the city. Father (deceased) was sergeant in military police. Attended (but did not complete) primary school.

LÉIA   35, born in Florianópolis (Santa Catarina). Has lived in São Luís four years; previously lived in various cities of the South and Amazonian regions. Re-cently separated, two children. Artist and teacher. Lives with children in upper-middle-class house in comfortable beach suburb. University gradu-ate.

PATO   22, born in São Luís. Recently married; spouse is pregnant. Unemployed.

Lives in parents' house in Anil with three siblings and wife. Father is un-skilled casual laborer; mother, housewife. Completed secondary school. Known in neighborhood as a benign sort of malandro. Along with Rubem, Waldyr, and Tito, one of a turma that calls itself (with a degree of humorous self-deprecation) the Vagabonds.

PAULISTA   25, born in São Paulo. Recent arrival in São Luís (six weeks before interview). Unmarried, no children. Artist. Only son of an engineer (father) and a lawyer (mother). Attended (but did not complete) university.

REGINA   35, born in São Luís. Single, no children (but is helping to raise sister's son, age seven, whose mother is in the South). Works as a clerk for the state government; also worked many years, until very recently, as a do-mestic servant in a well-to-do suburb. Lives with father, mother, a sister, and nephew in small house in Fabril, a mostly working-class bairro close to the Center. Attends weekly religious services at a Spiritist center. Com-pleted secondary school.

RUBEM   18, born in São Luís. Single, no children. Sometimes primary student, sometimes unskilled casual laborer. Only child, lives in Anil with mother and father in earthen house. Father is truck driver; mother, housewife. One of the Vagabonds.

SANTOS   Mid-thirties. Married, with three children. Works as clerk in police department. Completed secondary school.

TIAGO   Early twenties. No other biographical data.

TITO   22, born in São Luís. Single, no children. Has worked as waiter and clerk in between periods of unemployment. Lives with parents, three siblings, niece, nephew, grandmother, and others in fairly large but unpretentious house in Anil. Father, now retired with heart condition, operated small motor vehicle body shop on premises; mother is housewife. One brother at university; a sister lives in Salvador. Family, like many, has suffered steady erosion in standard of living. Attended, but did not complete, secondary school. One of the Vagabonds.

THE VAGABONDS   Informal self-designation of a group of young men, neigh-bors and longtime friends, who gather in the evenings in a neighborhood of Anil beneath a burned-out street lamp (or, when the lamp is working or the rain is heavy, at a nearby bus stop) to trade often humorous and exciting tales featuring sexual escapades, brigas, and the exploits of notorious malandros and "characters" of the bairro. Included in this rather hazily defined group are Tito, Waldyr, Rubem, and Pato.

WALDYR   25, born in São Luís. Single, no children. Unemployed. Lives with father, mother, and several siblings in modest house in Anil. Father is retired fisherman: now sells fish from house. Mother is housewife. Attended, but did not complete, primary school. One of the Vagabonds.

WILSON   22, born in São Luís. Unmarried, no children. University student. Lives with parents and several siblings in substantial house in Center. Family evidently well off. Father owns business; mother is housewife. Childhood friend of Sérgio.

XAVIER   22, born in São Luís. Unmarried, no children. University student. Lives with parents and siblings in middle-class house in Center. Father is merchant; mother also works outside home. Childhood friend of Sérgio.

APPENDIX B

A NOTE ON METHODS

On São-luisense Realities

Without question my own biography and my own concerns helped shape both my fieldwork and this book; moreover, the shaping has been, I believe, in important respects unconscious, unknowable to me in even my most relentlessly reflexive moments. And yet, if anthropological knowledge is undeniably the contingent product of an encounter, as postmodern anthropological critics (Clifford and Marcus 1986, Marcus and Fischer 1986) have so forcefully demonstrated, I have not the slightest doubt that I encountered something with a life and dynamic of its own, some of which I hope to have captured on these pages.

What is important here is the recognition that those among whom I lived inhabit worlds that are real and vital, largely recalcitrant to my intervention although partially recoverable through it. The são-luisenses I knew were not simply "others," shadowy derivatives of my encounter with them. Indeed, I find the discourse of "otherness" and "alterity" uncongenial, for I believe that, contrary to the intentions of many who employ it, it tends to deny autonomy and what we might call experiential density to the lives of those "others." The challenge, then, is to project what I take to be são-luisense realities through the almost necessarily objectifying prose of an anthropological story. Whether I have succeeded I leave for the reader to judge.

Making Models

Describing events like Carnivals, though not always easy, was usually fairly straight-forward: an exercise in careful, patient, informed observation aided at times by reliable personal or archival sources. Deriving cultural models, however, was a trickier venture. I had to infer the invisible, constructing conjectural representations of what I thought são-luisenses might be thinking and feeling (my models of what I imagined to be their cultural models) and testing those conjectures informally against any evidence I happened to generate or encounter, until I was satisfied that I had identified a construct consistent with what I could see going on around me.

Brigas presented a much more difficult problem in observation than Carnivals, despite the much greater complexity and larger scale of the latter. Unlike Carnivals, brigas are unscheduled. Some situations are propitious for their occurrence—the praça during a festival or a bar on a weekend night—but you can never count on being in the right place at the right time (nor, I might add, would you necessarily wish to be). Furthermore, a briga does not normally attract attention until the people are fighting, and then what you usually see is an exchange of blows followed by the intervention of the Quit-It Gang. The analytical possibilities of dealing with these data are quickly exhausted; the more interesting preliminary exchanges (i.e., provocations and connections) are usually hidden from view.

Thus, few cases can be gathered through direct observation, and what you generally see are certain gross behaviors that, in the end, tend not to be very illuminating. You cannot get "inside" a briga through mere observation. Once in a while I was privileged to witness a briga's origins (or potential origins), as in the story "A Drunk Makes a Desabafo at the Bus Stop." Valuable though such incidents are, the opportunity to observe them is a matter of luck.

There are other avenues to briga-as-event aside from personal observation. Newspaper accounts can be valuable, although unfortunately in São Luís these are often unreliable and I had to use them with care. Sometimes an event can be fixed through consultation with various witnesses or reference to legal testimony, as in the case of Sérgio's murder. Finally, over time I learned whose account to trust and whose not to trust. In this study I chose for the most part to treat accounts as accounts rather than as events, but in many instances I am confident that narratives portray incidents much as they actually occurred.

Of course, as I emphasize throughout my discussion, it makes little sense to talk about "what actually occurred" without knowing how são-luisenses themselves understand what happens in brigas. That is, only by reference to the briga scenario can you give an intelligible rendering of an actual event. To derive this cultural model I relied on accounts of brigas, são-luisenses' explanations and interpretations of the cultural model itself, and what we might call random participant observation offering opportunities to check my own evolving model of their model against the evidence of my own experience.

Accounts of Brigas

Briga stories constitute a very rich data source. In such "episodic scripts" (Abelson 1976: 35)—specific remembered sequences such as "boy did I get spanked the time I sneaked the cookie"—we see how people perceive certain actions as being linked in specific cases. The logic of the briga scenario, which is culturally patterned, emerges from such tales of specific brigas. The stories also provide leads to related cultural models; by following these leads I could discover how the briga model depends on more basic cultural building blocks, in particular, on são-luisense folk psychology.

The art of oral narrative is very much alive in São Luís, and the briga story is a recognizable genre, which, I believe, indicates the great significance of briga as an event. An anthropologist looking for a highly salient and structured region of culture might do well to listen for the *kinds* of stories that people tell, for—if briga is representative—such prominent genres can reveal both shared cognitive structures and shared emotional concerns.

A story is not the same as an actual experience, and a genre's stylistic demands conceivably distort the presentation of cognitive structure. Briga stories are told for dramatic effect; peril is sometimes exaggerated and humorous aspects are often embellished. Nevertheless, a briga story purports to reproduce a piece of actual experience: it is a realistic genre, a bit like journalism or autobiography (or some anthropology). A briga story guides its listeners through the event, striving to create the effect of a meticulous, blow-by-blow replay, encouraging identification with the storyteller as participant or as witness. If, as happens, details are exaggerated, reconstructed, or falsified, the underlying structure and emotionally crucial aspects of the event are nevertheless highlighted and emerge clearly in story after story.

It is hard to say for certain whether in actual brigas people's perceptions follow the model, but I believe that these vicarious replays of brigas provide the best evidence available of what this experience might be like. The evidence becomes all the more convincing when it is corroborated by more general indigenous interpretations and by participant observation.

Most of the briga stories I have reproduced here required surprisingly little editing. In general, each story was told as a coherent narrative, with a definite beginning and end. For the sake of brevity, I usually omitted the interviewer's comments (mine or those of Carlos Ramos). I did not indicate elisions, almost all of which are short digressions or repetitions. I used brackets to summarize repetitious, lengthy, or disjointed segments of transcript. I also glossed references to people, places, or events unfamiliar to the reader or unclear from the cited passage. Finally, I bracketed observations on the speaker's nonlinguistic behavior (e.g., laughter), translations of words or phrases, and occasional clarifications or editorial comments. In no case did I disturb the narrative sequence; I have not reversed the order of a person's statements within a particular story. Pauses, which sometimes betoken heightened emotion or confusion, are indicated by ellipses. The guiding principle has been to preserve the essence of the original narrative without the distractions of a complete, inevitably messy, literal transcription.

Many of the recorded tapes were transcribed in their literal messiness by Cleomar de Jesus Silva, Maria das Graças Pereira, and Carlos Ramos. Because I transcribed a goodly number myself, I am well aware of the unbelievable patience this work required. In all cases I rechecked transcripts for completeness and accuracy, and any remaining errors are my own.

Aside from a general exhortation to give all the details, my research assistant Carlos Ramos and I did not need to do much prompting to get those interviewed to provide full and elaborate stories. Most people seemed to have little trouble thinking of such tales. Indeed, certain informal social occasions (such as the nightly street-corner gatherings of the group I have called the Vagabonds—see the biographical sketches of Appendix A) featured the recounting of briga stories. These gatherings, marked by spontaneity and occasional hilarity, unfortunately did not offer, for a variety of reasons, favorable conditions for tape recording—a necessity if one is to make effective analytical use of the material. Carlos managed, however, by assembling some of the Vagabonds together in a room, to capture some of their stories on tape.

Most of the interviewing was within the capability of my resourceful and sensitive research assistant, despite his lack of training in anthropology or psychology. It is encouraging that both anthropologist and são-luisense were able to collect these stories and that the models underlying them seem consistent. I am grateful to Carlos Ramos for the recordings he made of the stories recounted by Bartolomeu, Bocado, Cravo, Denilson, Genival, Jair, Pato, Paulista, Rubem, Tiago, and Waldyr. All other interviews reported here I did myself. In some instances, I conducted long series of conversations with particularly informative and articulate persons, especially Tito and Léia. Such series, consisting of a dozen or more hour-long sessions, required very close rapport and often touched on delicate matters. Here, I believe my training in psychological interviewing was essential. I likewise handled virtually all interviewing related to the murder of Sérgio.

The approximately sixty hours of taped interviews fell into three main categories. In one type of interview, Carlos or I sought to elicit briga stories and their interpretations. These stories were modifications of the naturalistic narratives that are a readily identifiable genre of popular speech. We encouraged people to relate all the details of a briga and then asked them to make further interpretations. In a second type of interview, I presented several fictional briga stories (derived from actual cases) to two or three people at once, asking them to discuss the stories with one another. In a third type, I explored emotional responses to briga with selected persons. These one-on-one interviews were the most delicate and required the greatest degree of rapport.

These various procedures evoked much more detail, especially with respect to commonsense aspects of briga, than would have been available otherwise. As all investigators of cultural models point out, because such models are intersubjectively shared, people need not specify most aspects of any narrative or description based on them—hearers automatically fill in the blanks from their knowledge of the model. The anthropologist lacks this knowledge. Ethnographic interviewing requiring considerable patience on the part of the interviewee is therefore the greatest aid in discovering cultural models.

The translations presented here are my own, although Jorge and Jordana Soares were helpful in clarifying some last-minute confusions and ambiguities. Where I thought it was illuminating to include the original Portuguese in brackets, I have done so. Often my aim was to demonstrate the rich Brazilian Portuguese vocabulary for certain semantic domains (e.g., the domains of venting and arguing). In some cases, I felt that my English translation could only be approximate and that Brazilians or specialists in Brazil would find the Portuguese word or phrase more precise. I have taken some liberties, especially with translations of profanity, in order to preserve the vitality of the narratives. Ethnographic translations are frustrating, however—one cannot stray too far from literal meanings, or else one risks using or suggesting improper metaphors, a serious danger in this work. I have tried to strike a compromise between ethnographically important literalness and the fluidity that is so much a part of são-luisenses' verbal artistry. It seems to me, however, that there is no really satisfactory resolution of this problem, which is probably even more acute in ethnography than in fiction.

Informants' Interpretations and Explanations '

The general scheme known as the cultural model of briga can be inferred from various accounts of specific brigas, but the model also manifests itself in a more direct manner via people's interpretations and explanations—what Abelson (1976: 35) calls "generic" and "hypothetical" scripts. A generic script—"My doing bad things leads to my getting punished"—is a generalization based on various episodes of the cookie-snitching variety. A hypothetical script is a flexible, conditional assemblage of generic scripts: "My doing a bad thing could lead to my getting punished (unless I could make it look like my brother did it), but if it weren't too serious or they were in a good mood, or if I could sweet-talk my mother and she could get around my father, then maybe I'd just get a mild scolding." Generic and hypothetical scripts are essentially references to the cultural model itself, as in the statement "It's better to not connect with a provocation, because then it becomes very hard to avoid fighting." Not everyone volunteered information at this level of abstraction, but frequently such general statements could be elicited. If they were consistent with my reading of the evidence provided by episodic scripts (stories), confidence in my own conjectured model was reinforced.

The interviewer must be more active when seeking direct commentary on the cultural model. As I have pointed out, few people are able to describe the entire model in detail, but if the model is (as in this instance) rather definite, they can be walked through it. The interviewer uses questions such as "Then what might happen?" or "What would happen if . . . ?" Questions such as "Why would someone do that?" can be used to get at concepts on which the sequence is based.

People do spontaneously offer general explanations, explicit or implicit, during the telling of a specific briga story, but they vary in their ability or inclination to generalize or speak in hypothetical terms. Tito is a good example of someone able and willing to think through the conceptual scheme he is using. Hence with Tito I found it possible to spend sometimes an hour or more talking abstractly about provocations, psychological equilibrium, or other important ideas related to briga, and he was, as in the story "Getting Shoved While Riding the Bus," accomplished at producing hypothetical scripts. With certain persons, however, I could not pursue such topics very far before they circled back to concrete examples, but they often presented a specific case in apparent support of a general point. On two occasions, I assembled groups (once consisting of men, once of women) to discuss briga stories I had written, based on real cases. This stimulated conversation and sometimes dispute, which helped bring to light various underlying aspects of the model. It also pointed up some of the limits of consensus. Not everyone thought the same way in every detail, but in important respects people seemed to be operating with the same basic model.

But can it be said that differentially articulate persons have the same model in their heads? Insofar as something that walks and quacks like a duck is a duck, the answer is yes. Given that this particular duck (the cultural model) is intrinsically unobservable, all we have to judge by is how it walks and quacks. If são-luisenses had a shared cultural model of briga in their heads, I think they would say and do the things they said and did. To the extent that the cultural model gives us clues about those things we call knowledge and motivation, so that we can make sense of observable behavior like Sérgio's unusually determined bar fight, the construct has at the very least explanatory value.

Participant Observation

Briga offers obvious problems for the participant observer, even were he or she inclined, as I am not, to experiment by provoking, connecting, and so on. Nonetheless, a participant observer does have unwelcome opportunities to try out the model. This can happen when from time to time you inadvertently get conscripted (or blunder) into the opening stages of the sequence. This happened to me, for example, on the way home from a championship soccer game, as I was riding in the "kitchen" of a crowded and slow-moving bus with a neighbor, Dudu, a boy aged ten. Several feet away, a young man, very drunk and very displeased at the outcome of the game, was shouting insults at cars through the window. Unfortunately, he then noticed me—not an obvious foreigner, but, white-skinned and wearing eyeglasses, a ringer for the comfortable car owners he had been excoriating. He continued swearing, now with glances in my direction. I avoided connecting to the degree possible— this happened near the end of my fieldwork, when I knew the model well—but did end up feeling somewhat humiliated: the fellow stepped on my foot as he jumped out the back door of the bus, glaring at me as he hit the ground. Dudu and I shared a look of relief, but I also recall my anger at swallowing the attack. In the field perhaps you learn emotions as well as scripts.

So from time to time things happen that put you in a situation to test the cultural model directly in an interaction, but there are other ways that participant observation can be employed. For example, you sometimes participate in a briga as a spectator, and your expectations may or may not accurately predict the course of events. Again, this serves as a check on your own understanding of the model.

Conversations, including the most casual, offer yet another opportunity for verification. You can question, try out explanations, or offer predictably contentious commentary, using your conjectural model as a basis for these conversational techniques. In other words, once you think you have learned the model, you can try to make use of it in various ordinary conversational situations to see if it works. This requires no special observation techniques, simply a readiness to take advantage of unexpected opportunities for informal testing of your guesses and tentative conclusions (D'Andrade 1984: 105–9).

Finally, the anthropologist participates through the appreciation of cultural products—fiction, popular music, movies, and so on. Such products are difficult to work with because they often take a lot for granted that the researcher cannot discover through introspection. You need to have the required cultural keys. But when, with the aid of a discovered cultural model, you suddenly understand what a movie or popular song is about, you have a sense of double triumph—first, because you now have access to the cultural product, and second, because the fact of understanding is yet another confirmation of your conjectures.

It would be disingenuous to claim that I systematically developed hypotheses and then tested them. Like most fieldworkers, I did everything at once—guessing, modifying, refining, and verifying until things fell into place—until, that is, I could derive the construct that made sense of the many phenomena I was examining: the brigas I witnessed, the stories people told, the explanations and interpretations they gave, the cultural products they found meaningful, and my interactions with them.

GLOSSARY

Portuguese words are, with the exception of a few cognates, defined in the text the first time they appear. Below, I give a brief gloss (indicating the contextually most appropriate usage) for those that appear more than once, as well as some other key words and phrases. For fuller definitions (although they may not adequately indicate the relation of the word to the topics discussed in this book), see the standard dictionary of Brazilian Portuguese, the *Novo dicionário da língua portuguesa* (Ferreira 1975).

agüentar   to bear up; to put up with

alterado   literally, altered; in a disequilibrated emotional state

baiana   a woman from Bahia; one of the stock figures of Carnival, a fat woman in a voluminous white dress "typical" of Bahia

bairro   a neighborhood of the city

barraca   a small, temporary stand selling food or drink during festivals or other gatherings

batucada   the rhythm of *samba*; the playing of percussion instruments in this rhythm

besteira   a foolish, objectionable act

bicha   literally, worm, intestinal parasite, female animal; a male who during sexual intercourse is penetrated by another male

bicho   literally, animal, beast, creature; a slang term of address used among young males

Bicho-Papão   a formless, devouring monster of childhood stories

bloco a neighborhood-based group that plays music and dances in the streets during Carnival

botar para fora to expel in a vigorous way one's frustrations and anxieties (noun: *bota-fora*)

botequim a small bar serving drinks and snacks

briga a violent face-to-face confrontation or fight, usually involving two males (verb: *brigar*)

brigão a person who habitually provokes and participates in brigas

brincadeira a playful, joking kind of performance or game

brincar to play; can refer to children's games or to adult activities such as drinking and dancing during a festival

bumba-meu-boi a cultural performance built around the story of a bull stolen by a slave, part of the June festival (*festas juninas*) in São Luís

bunda buttocks

cabacinha literally, little gourd; liquid-filled wax balls hurled during Carnival of the last century (see also *laranjinha, limão de cheiro*)

caboclo a person from the countryside; a person with rustic habits (sometimes used condescendingly)

cachaça a liquor brewed from sugarcane, the most widely consumed distilled beverage in Brazil

cara literally, face; guy; a form of address used predominantly among males

compadre Ego's child's godfather or the father of Ego's godchild; a familiar term used to refer to or address close male friends

conjunto a residential development in an outlying area of the city

corno cuckold

crente the term Catholics most commonly use to refer to a Protestant, with a connotation of uprightness shading into self-righteousness

cruzeiro the currency of Brazil (symbol: Cr$)

delegado the police officer who heads up a department or district of the civilian police force

desabafar to "unsmother" or cast out frustrations, anxieties, resentments, as during Carnival (noun: *desabafo*)

discussão an argument, a discussion

educação childhood training; education; politeness, cultivation, civility

empregada maid, female household servant

engolir to swallow

entrudo the act of throwing an object or a substance (a *cabacinha*, cornstarch, sewer water, etc.) on another during Carnival; another name for Carnival before this century

farinha a starchy, gritty manioc preparation (a staple food)

farinha d'água a coarse variety of farinha

fazenda a large estate

festa   a party, festival, or celebration

festas juninas   the June festival known also as São João, a series of festivities during the latter part of June, celebrated in most of Brazil but with greater vigor in Maranhão

fofão (plural: *fofões*):   a Carnival figure dressed in a baggy, floral-patterned costume and a grotesque mask

folião (plural: *foliões*):   a Carnival reveler

formação   constitution of one's character or mental structures; formal education

fuleiro   a no-account; a worthless, insignificant person (an insult)

gota d'água   that which causes accumulated resentment to overflow; the last straw

grilagem   takeover of land through devious, illegal, or violent means

homem   a man

homem cordial   literally, the cordial man; a characterization of the Brazilian as given to forming intimate relationships with others

igreja   church

invasão   literally, invasion; a settlement formed on vacant land by poor people or those recently arriving from the countryside

invocado   literally, invoked; enraged beyond control

ladrão   a thief

laranjinha   literally, little orange; a liquid-filled wax ball used during *entrudo* (see also *cabacinha, limão de cheiro*)

largo   a large open space in town; a *praça*

ligar   to connect with (i.e., acknowledge in some way) a provocation

limão de cheiro   literally, lemon of scent; a wax ball filled with perfume or some other liquid, used during Carnival (see also *cabacinha, laranjinha*)

loló   an illegal home brew including ether made for and inhaled during Carnival

machão   a very aggressive man, much caught up in *machismo* (can be used to praise, condemn, or ridicule depending on persons and circumstances)

machismo   masculine code of honor, emphasizing courage and quickness to take offense and to exact retribution (a quality viewed positively or negatively depending on persons and circumstances)

maconheiro   a user of marijuana (*maconha*)

malandro   an astute, somewhat devious and conniving individual who lives by his wits (often viewed with ambivalence or amusement)

mamãe   an affectionate term for mother (equivalent to the English "Mom" or "Mommy")

maranhense   a native of Maranhão

marginal (plural: *marginais*):   a thug, criminal, dangerous person, hoodlum

mestiço   a person of racially mixed descent

mocambo   a community in the bush established by runaway slaves (see *quilombo*)

moleque   a black young man or boy; a punk or pretentious young man of no importance (an insult)

movimento   comings and goings in the street or *praça*; "action"

mulata   a woman of mixed European and African parentage (masculine form: *mulato*); a stock figure of Carnival: a young woman scantily dressed, an obvious sexual symbol

município   a local administrative unit, equivalent more or less to a county in the United States

o povo   the people

otário   a sucker, a fool

pa!   an exclamation representing a loud, sudden sound

palhaço   a clown

papai   an affectionate word for father (equivalent to the English "Dad" or "Daddy")

parado   literally, stopped; quiet; in a state of psychological immobility or decay

pardo   a person of European and African descent; *mulato*

passarela   the passageway constructed for the parade of samba schools

patrão   a boss; a patron; a benefactor (female: *patroa*)

pistoleiro   a hired gunman

pivô   a person who instigates or exacerbates a *briga* between others

PM   military police (Polícia Militar) or military policeman

porra   literally, sperm; an obscene exclamation expressing exasperation or anger

poxa   an emphatic exclamation

praça   a public square, a plaza

puxa   variant of *poxa*

quebra-quebra   literally, break-break; the act (by an individual or a crowd) of destroying property in an uncontrolled manner

quilombo   a remote community founded by runaway slaves (see *mocambo*)

quintal   the interior or rear courtyard of a dwelling (equivalent to the American English "yard")

quitanda   a neighborhood shop selling staples and usually beverages and snacks

rapaz   literally, boy; a boy or young man; a term of address, predominantly among males

renunciar   renounce; refuse to fight

revolta   disgust; extreme irritation; anger; resentment; revolt

revoltado   revolted, disgusted; angry, furious; resentful, rebellious

rixa   a feud between two people who see themselves as enemies

sacana   one who engages in *sacanagem*

sacanagem   sexually adventurous activities other than "Mom-and-Dad" type intercourse; devious, conniving, disloyal behavior

safado   wicked; wicked one

samba   a dance and musical form typical of Carnival

samba-enredo   the song and performance devised by a samba school for each year's parade

São   Saint (female: *Santa*)

São João   Saint John; the June festival (see *festas juninas*)

são-luisense   a native of São Luís (synonym: *ludovicense*)

saudade   a melancholy feeling of longing for or missing a person, a place, or a time

senhor   a rich or powerful person; in "*o senhor*," a polite form of address; a title equivalent to "Mr." in English

sertanejo   an inhabitant of the sertão

sertão   the arid interior or backlands

ta!   an exclamation representing a sudden, loud sound

tambor   a drum; refers also to a celebration involving music and dance in a *terreiro* where Afro-Brazilian religion is practiced

tambor de mina   a maranhense Afro-Brazilian religion with many African practices reasonably well preserved

terreiro   an Afro-Brazilian religious center where *tambor de mina* or *umbanda* is practiced

tríduo   the three-day period preceding Ash Wednesday, the period of most intense celebration of Carnival

turma   literally, a gang, more like an age-set; a group of young people of about the same age, from the same *bairro*, who spend much time together and feel a strong sense of mutual loyalty

turma do deixa-disso   the Quit-It Gang, those who intervene in a *briga* to separate the adversaries

umbanda   an Afro-Brazilian religion, typically urban, highly variable in practice, less tied to African forms or preoccupied with authenticity than *tambor de mina*

Vale tudo!   "Anything goes!," the slogan of Carnival

zona   the red-light district

BIBLIOGRAPHY

Statistical Sources

Unless otherwise indicated, statistics cited in the text are for 1980. All figures come from official IBGE (Fundação Instituto Brasileiro de Geografia e Estatística) publications. The following abbreviations of statistical sources are used in the footnotes.

AEB   1984 Anuário estatístico do Brasil. Rio: IBGE.

CDM   1-3-5 1982 Censo demográfico—Maranhão (Dados distritais). Vol. 1, tomo 3, n. 5. Rio: IBGE.

CDM   1-4-7 1982 Censo demográfico—Maranhão (Dados gerais, migração, instrução, fecundidade, mortalidade). Vol. 1, tomo 4, n. 7. Rio: IBGE.

CDM   1-5-7 1982 Censo demográfico—Maranhão (Mão-de-obra). Vol. 1, tomo 5, n. 7. Rio: IBGE.

CDM   1-6-7 1982 Censo demográfico—Maranhão (Famílias e domicílios). Vol. 1, tomo 6, n. 7. Rio: IBGE.

Newspapers

The following newspapers are cited in the text. Abbreviations follow the titles.

In São Luís

A Moderação (AM)	*Estado do Maranhão (EM)*	*Jornal de Hoje (JH)*
Diário do Maranhão (DM)	*Jornal do Dia (JD)*	*Jornal Pequeno (JP)*

O *Conciliador* (OC)   O *Globo* (OG)   *Pacotilha* (PA)
O *Estandarte* (OE)   O *Imparcial* (OI)   *Tribuna* (TR)

Outside São Luís

Jornal do País (Rio)   *Los Angeles Times*

References Cited

Dates in brackets refer to the first edition of the work cited.

Abelson, Robert P.
  1976 Script processing in attitude formation and decision-making. In John S. Carroll and John W. Payne, eds., *Cognition and Social Behavior*. Pp. 33–45. Hillsdale, N.J.: Erlbaum.

Abrahams, Roger D.
  1964 Playing the dozens. *American Journal of Folklore* 75: 209–20.

Akutagawa, Ryunosuke
  1959 [1922] *Rashomon and Other Stories*. Trans. Takashi Kojima. New York: Bantam Books.

Almeida, Alfredo Wagner B. de
  1983 *A ideologia da decadência*. São Luís: Instituto de Pesquisas Econômicas e Sociais.

Almeida, Bernardo
  1978 *O Bequimão*. São Luís: Serviço de Imprensa e Obras Gráficas do Estado.

Amnesty International
  1990 *Brazil: Torture and Extrajudicial Execution in Urban Brazil*. New York: Amnesty International USA.

Arquidiocese de São Paulo
  1985 *Brasil: Nunca mais*. Petrópolis: Vozes.

Asselin, Victor
  1982 *Grilagem: Corrupção e violência em terras do Carajás*. Petrópolis: Vozes/Comissão Pastoral da Terra.

Azevedo Neto, Américo
  1983 *Bumba-meu-boi no Maranhão*. São Luís: Editora Alcântara.

Bailey, F. G.
  1977 *Morality and Expediency*. Oxford: Basil Blackwell.

Bakhtin, Mikhail
  1968 [1965] *Rabelais and His World*. Trans. Helene Iswolsky. Cambridge, Mass.: MIT Press.

Bateson, Gregory
  1958 [1936] *Naven*. Stanford, Calif.: Stanford University Press.

1972a [1949] Bali: The value system of a steady state. In *Steps to an Ecology of Mind*. Pp. 107–27. New York: Ballantine.

1972b [1935] Culture contact and schismogenesis. In *Steps to an Ecology of Mind*. Pp. 61–72. New York: Ballantine.

1972c [1971] The cybernetics of "self": A theory of alcoholism. In *Steps to an Ecology of Mind*. Pp. 309–37. New York: Ballantine.

1972d [1955] A theory of play and fantasy. In *Steps to an Ecology of Mind*. Pp. 177–93. New York: Ballantine.

Berman, Marshall
1982 *All That Is Solid Melts into Air: The Experience of Modernity*. New York: Simon and Schuster.

Brown, Diana DeG.
1986 *Umbanda: Religion and Politics in Urban Brazil*. Ann Arbor: UMI Research Press.

Buarque, Chico, and Paulo Pontes
1975 *Gota d'água*. Rio: Civilização Brasileira.

Buzar, Benedito
1983 *A greve de 51*. São Luís: Editora Alcântara.

Campbell, Anne
1986 The streets and violence. In Anne Campbell and John J. Gibbs, eds., *Violent Transactions: The Limits of Personality*. Pp. 115–32. Oxford: Basil Blackwell.

Campbell, Anne, and John J. Gibbs, eds.
1986 *Violent Transactions: The Limits of Personality*. Oxford: Basil Blackwell.

Chagas, José
1966 Um domingo sério. *Jornal do Dia* (São Luís), Feb. 20, 1966.

Cleary, David
1990 *Anatomy of the Amazon Gold Rush*. London: Macmillan.

Clifford, James, and George E. Marcus, eds.
1986 *Writing Culture: The Poetics and Politics of Ethnography*. Berkeley: University of California Press.

Conceição, Manuel da
1980 *Essa terra é nossa*. Interview and editing by Ana Maria Galeano. Petrópolis: Vozes.

Coqueiro, J. B. Bastos
1966 O Carnaval do passado. *Jornal Pequeno* (São Luís), Jan. 9, 23, 1966.

Corrêa, Mariza
1983 *Morte em família: Representações jurídicas de papéis sexuais*. Rio: Edições Graal.

Coutinho, Milson
1984 *A revolta de Bequimão*. São Luís: Secretaria de Comunicação / Secretaria de Cultura do Estado.

Cunha, Euclides da
1944 [1902] *Rebellion in the Backlands*. (*Os sertões*.) Trans. Samuel Putnam. Chicago: University of Chicago Press.

d'Abbeville, Claude

1975 [1614] *História da missão dos padres capuchinos na ilha do Maranhão e terras circunvizinhas*. Trans. Sérgio Milliet. São Paulo: Editora da Universidade de São Paulo.

DaMatta, Roberto

1973 O Carnaval como um rito de passagem. In *Ensaios de antropologia estrutural*. Pp. 19–66. Petrópolis: Vozes.

1978 *Carnavais, malandros e heróis*. Rio: Zahar.

1982 As raízes da violência no Brasil: Reflexões de um antropólogo social. In Roberto DaMatta, Maria Célia Pinheiro Machado Paoli, Paulo Sérgio Pinheiro, and Maria Victoria Benevides, *Violência brasileira*. Pp. 11–44. São Paulo: Brasiliense.

1983 An interpretation of Carnaval. *SubStance* (Madison, Wisc.) 37–38: 162–70.

1984a Carnival in multiple planes. In John J. MacAloon, ed., *Rite, Drama, Festival Spectacle*. Pp. 208–40. Philadelphia: Institute for the Study of Human Issues.

1984b On Carnival, informality and magic: A point of view from Brazil. In Edward M. Bruner, ed., *Text, Play, and Story: The Construction and Reconstruction of Self and Society*. Pp. 230–46. Prospect Heights, Ill.: Waveland Press.

1985 *A casa e a rua*. São Paulo: Brasiliense.

1986 *Carnaval* as a cultural problem: Towards a theory of formal events and their magic. Working paper 79. Notre Dame, Ind.: Helen Kellogg Institute for International Studies, University of Notre Dame.

D'Andrade, Roy G.

1984 Cultural meaning systems. In Richard A. Shweder and Robert A. LeVine, eds., *Culture Theory: Essays on Mind, Self, and Emotion*. Pp. 88–119. Cambridge: Cambridge University Press.

1987 A folk model of the mind. In Dorothy Holland and Naomi Quinn, eds., *Cultural Models in Language and Thought*. Pp. 112–48. Cambridge: Cambridge University Press.

1990 Some propositions about the relations between culture and human cognition. In James W. Stigler, Richard A. Shweder, and Gilbert Herdt, eds., *Cultural Psychology: Essays on Comparative Human Development*. Pp. 65–129. Cambridge: Cambridge University Press.

Davis, Natalie Zemon

1978 Women on top: Inversion and political disorder in early modern Europe. In Barbara Babcock, ed., *The Reversible World*. Pp. 147–90. Ithaca: Cornell University Press.

Dilthey, Wilhelm

1962 [1926] *Pattern and Meaning in History: Thoughts on History and Society*. Ed. H. P. Rickman. New York: Harper & Row.

Dirks, Robert

1987 *The Black Saturnalia: Conflict and Its Ritual Expression on British West Indian Slave Plantations*. Gainesville: University of Florida Press.

1988 Annual rituals of conflict. *American Anthropologist* 90(4): 856–70.

Dollard, John
1939 The dozens: Dialectic of insult. *American Imago* 1(1): 3–25.

Dorson, Richard M.
1982 Material components in celebration. In Victor Turner, ed., *Celebration: Studies in Festivity and Ritual*. Pp. 33–57. Washington, D.C.: Smithsonian Institution Press.

Dougherty, Janet W. D.
1985 Introduction. In Janet W. D. Dougherty, ed., *Directions in Cognitive Anthropology*. Pp. 3–14. Urbana: University of Illinois Press.

Doughty, Paul L.
1968 *Huaylas: An Andean District in Search of Progress*. Ithaca: Cornell University Press.

Dunning, Eric, Patrick Murphy, and John Williams
1986 "Casuals," "terrace crews" and "fighting firms": Towards a sociological explanation of football hooligan behavior. In David Riches, ed., *The Anthropology of Violence*. Pp. 164–83. Oxford: Basil Blackwell.

Durkheim, Emile
1965 [1912] *The Elementary Forms of the Religious Life*. Trans. Joseph Ward Swain. New York: Free Press.

English, Barbara Ann
1984 *Alcoa na ilha*. São Luís: Cáritas Brasileira (Escritório Regional de São Luís).

Estado do Maranhão
1984 372 anos de São Luís. Special ed. *Diário Oficial* 77(2).

Falassi, Alessandro, ed.
1987 *Time Out of Time: Essays on the Festival*. Albuquerque: University of New Mexico Press.

Fausto, Boris
1984 *Crime e cotidiano: A criminalidade em São Paulo (1880–1924)*. São Paulo: Brasiliense.

Felson, Richard B., William Baccaglini, and George Gmelch
1986 Bar-room brawls: Aggression and violence in Irish and American bars. In Anne Campbell and John J. Gibbs, eds., *Violent Transactions: The Limits of Personality*. Pp. 153–66. Oxford: Basil Blackwell.

Fernandes, Rubem César
1985 Aparecida, our queen, lady and mother, saravá! *Social Science Information* 24(4): 799–819.

Ferreira, Aurélio Buarque de Holanda
1975 *Novo dicionário da língua portuguesa*. Rio: Nova Fronteira.

Ferretti, Sérgio Figueiredo
1985 *Querebentan de Zomadonu*. São Luís: Editora da Universidade Federal do Maranhão.

Foster, George
    1963   The dyadic contract in Tzintzuntzan, II: Patron-client relationship. *American Anthropologist* 65(6): 1280–94.
Frazer, Sir James George
    1959   [1890]   *The New Golden Bough.* Ed. Theodor H. Gaster. New York: Criterion Books.
Freud, Sigmund
    1955   [1920]   Beyond the pleasure principle. Pp. 3–64 in *The Standard Edition of the Complete Psychological Works of Sigmund Freud*, vol. 18. Trans. James Strachey. London: Hogarth.
    1961   [1930]   *Civilization and Its Discontents.* Trans. James Strachey. New York: Norton.
Freyre, Gilberto
    1956   [1933]   *The Masters and the Slaves: A Study in the Development of Brazilian Civilization. (Casa-grande e senzala.)* Trans. Samuel Putnam. New York: Knopf.
    1964   The patriarchal basis of Brazilian society. In Joseph Maier and Richard W. Weatherhead, eds., *Politics of Change in Latin America*. Pp. 155–73. New York: Praeger.
Fry, Peter
    1985   Male homosexuality and spirit possession in Brazil. *Journal of Homosexuality* 11(3–4): 137–53.
Galjart, Benno
    1965   A further note on "followings": Reply to Huizer. *América Latina* 8(3): 145–52.
Geertz, Clifford
    1973a   [1972]   Deep play: Notes on the Balinese cockfight. In *The Interpretation of Cultures*. Pp. 412–53. New York: Basic Books.
    1973b   [1957]   Ethos, world view and the analysis of sacred symbols. In *The Interpretation of Cultures*. Pp. 126–41. New York: Basic Books.
    1973c   [1966]   Person, time and conduct in Bali. In *The Interpretation of Cultures*. Pp. 360–411. New York: Basic Books.
    1983   [1974]   "From the native's point of view": On the nature of anthropological understanding. In *Local Knowledge: Further Essays in Interpretive Anthropology*. Pp. 55–70. New York: Basic Books.
Gibbs, John J.
    1986   Alcohol consumption, cognition and context: Examining tavern violence. In Anne Campbell and John J. Gibbs, eds., *Violent Transactions: The Limits of Personality*. Pp. 133–51. Oxford: Basil Blackwell.
Gilmore, David
    1975   Carnaval in Fuenmayor: Class conflict and social cohesion in an Andalusian town. *Journal of Anthropological Research* 31: 331–49.

Gluckman, Max
  1954 *Rituals of Rebellion in South-East Africa.* Manchester: Manchester University Press.
  1969 [1956] *Custom and Conflict in Africa.* New York: Barnes and Noble.
Goethe, Johann Wolfgang von
  1987 [1789] The Roman Carnival. In Alessandro Falassi, ed., *Time Out of Time: Essays on the Festival.* Pp. 13–34. Albuquerque: University of New Mexico Press.
Goffman, Erving
  1961 *Encounters.* Indianapolis: Bobbs-Merrill.
  1974 *Frame Analysis.* Cambridge, Mass.: Harvard University Press.
Goldwasser, Maria Júlia
  1975 *O palácio do samba.* Rio: Zahar.
Gross, Daniel R.
  1971 Ritual and conformity: A religious pilgrimage to northeastern Brazil. *Ethnology* 10(2): 129–48.
Hallowell, A. Irving
  1988 [1954] The self and its behavioral environment. In *Culture and Experience.* Pp. 75–110. Prospect Heights, Ill.: Waveland Press.
Harris, Marvin, and Conrad Kottak
  1963 The structural significance of Brazilian categories. *Sociologia* (São Paulo) 25: 203–8.
Heath, Dwight B.
  1987 Anthropology and alcohol studies: Current issues. *Annual Review of Anthropology* 16: 99–120.
Hill, Errol
  1972 *The Trinidad Carnival: Mandate for a National Theatre.* Austin: University of Texas Press.
  1976 The Trinidad carnival: Cultural change and synthesis. *Cultures* (UNESCO) 3(1): 54–85.
Holanda, Sérgio Buarque de
  1982 [1936] *Raízes do Brasil.* Rio: Livraria José Olympio.
Holland, Dorothy, and Naomi Quinn, eds.
  1987 *Cultural Models in Language and Thought.* Cambridge: Cambridge University Press.
Hutchinson, Bertram
  1966 The patron-dependant relationship in Brazil: A preliminary examination. *Sociologia Ruralis* 6: 3–30.
Instituto Brasileiro de Geografia e Estatística (IBGE)
  1982 *Censo demográfico—Maranhão.* Vol. 1. Rio: IBGE.
  1984 *Anuário estatístico do Brasil.* Rio: IBGE.

Instituto Histórico e Geográfico Brasileiro

1922 *Diccionário histórico, geográphico e ethnográphico do Brasil.* Vol. 2. Rio: Imprensa Nacional.

Joffily, José

1983 *Morte na Ulen Company.* Rio: Record.

Johnson, Mark

1987 *The Body in the Mind: The Bodily Basis of Reason and Imagination.* Chicago: University of Chicago Press.

Juneja, Renu

1988 The Trinidad carnival: Ritual, performance, spectacle and symbol. *Journal of Popular Culture* 21(4): 87–99.

Kadt, Emanuel de

1967 Religion, the Church and social change in Brazil. In Claudio Veliz, ed., *The Politics of Conformity in Latin America.* Pp. 192–220. London: Oxford University Press.

Ladurie, Emmanuel Le Roy

1979 *Carnival in Romans.* Trans. Mary Feeney. New York: George Braziller.

Lakoff, George

1987 *Women, Fire and Dangerous Things: What Categories Reveal about the Mind.* Chicago: University of Chicago Press.

1988 Cognitive semantics. In Umberto Eco, Marco Santambrogio, and Patrizia Violi, eds., *Meaning and Mental Representations.* Pp. 119–54. Bloomington: Indiana University Press.

Leach, Edmund R.

1977 [1954] *Political Systems of Highland Burma.* London: Athlone Press.

Leal, Ivanhoé A., and Samuel Alves Farias Filho

1982 *Meia passagem ou meia cidade.* São Luís: Esquadrus.

Leal, Vítor Nunes

1948 *Coronelismo, enxada e voto.* Rio: Livraria Forense.

Leeds, Anthony

1964 Brazil and the myth of Francisco Julião. In Joseph Maier and Richard W. Weatherhead, eds., *Politics of Change in Latin America.* Pp. 190–204. New York: Praeger.

Leite, Dante Moreira

1983 [1954] *O caráter nacional brasileiro.* São Paulo: Livraria Pioneira Editora.

Leopoldi, José Sávio

1978 *Escola de samba, ritual e sociedade.* Petrópolis: Vozes.

Levy, Robert I.

1984 Emotion, knowing, and culture. In Richard A. Shweder and Robert A. LeVine, eds., *Culture Theory: Essays on Mind, Self, and Emotion.* Pp. 214–37. Cambridge: Cambridge University Press.

Lewin, Linda
  1979 The oligarchical limitations of social banditry in Brazil: The case of the "good" thief Antonio Silvino. *Past and Present* 82: 116–46.
Lima, Carlos de
  1981 *História do Maranhão.* Brasília: Centro Gráfico do Senado Federal.
Linger, Daniel T.
  1987 Beyond Carnaval: Dangerous Ritual in São Luís. Ph.D. dissertation, University of California, San Diego. Ann Arbor: University Microfilms.
  1990 Essential outlines of crime and madness: Man-fights in São Luís. *Cultural Anthropology* 5(1): 62–77.
  1993 The hegemony of discontent. *American Ethnologist* 20 (1): 3–240.
MacAndrew, Craig, and Robert B. Edgerton
  1969 *Drunken Comportment: A Social Explanation.* Chicago: Aldine.
Malta, Maria Helena
  1990 Tiroteio verbal sem fim. *Veja,* April 11: 72.
Manning, Frank E., ed.
  1983 *The Celebration of Society: Perspectives on Contemporary Cultural Performance.* Bowling Green, Ohio: Bowling Green University Popular Press.
Marcus, George E., and Michael M. J. Fischer
  1986 *Anthropology as Cultural Critique: An Experimental Moment in the Human Sciences.* Chicago: University of Chicago Press.
Marriott, McKim
  1966 The feast of love. In Milton Singer, ed., *Krishna: Myths, Rites and Attitudes.* Pp. 200–212. Westport, Conn.: Greenwood Press.
Mayer, Philip
  1971 [1961] *Townsmen or Tribesmen.* Cape Town: Oxford University Press.
Mead, Margaret, and Rhoda Métraux, eds.
  1953 *The Study of Culture at a Distance.* Chicago: University of Chicago Press.
Meireles, Mário M.
  1972 *História da independência no Maranhão.* Rio: Artenova.
  1980 [1960] *História do Maranhão.* São Luís: Fundação Cultural do Maranhão.
  1982 *França equinocial.* São Luís: Secretaria de Cultura do Maranhão/Rio: Civilização Brasileira.
Meirelles, Sérgio
  1983 *Alcântara na era espacial.* São Luís: Cáritas Brasileira (Escritório Regional de São Luís).
Montello, Josué
  1981 *Largo do Desterro.* Rio: Editora Nova Fronteira.
Norbeck, Edward
  1963 African rituals of conflict. *American Anthropologist* 65(6): 1254–79.
Oliven, Ruben George
  1982 *Violência e cultura no Brasil.* Petrópolis: Vozes.

Ortiz, Renato

1980a Carnaval: Sagrado e profano. In *A consciência fragmentada*. Pp. 13–27. Rio: Paz e Terra.

1980b Carnaval: Sagrado e político. In *A consciência fragmentada*. Pp. 29–44. Rio: Paz e Terra.

Pacheco, Dom Felipe Condurú

1968 *História eclesiástica do Maranhão*. São Luís: Departamento de Cultura do Estado.

Pang, Eul-Soo

1973 Coronelismo in northeast Brazil. In Robert Kern, ed., *The Caciques*. Pp. 65–88. Albuquerque: University of New Mexico Press.

Parker, Richard

1987 Acquired immunodeficiency syndrome in urban Brazil. *Medical Anthropology Quarterly*, n.s. 1(2): 155–75.

1991 *Bodies, Pleasures, and Passions: Sexual Culture in Contemporary Brazil*. Boston: Beacon Press.

Pearse, Andrew

1956 Carnival in nineteenth century Trinidad. *Caribbean Quarterly* 4(3–4): 175–93.

Pereira, Nunes

1979 *A Casa das Minas*. Petrópolis: Vozes.

Perrone, Charles A.

1989 *Masters of Contemporary Brazilian Song: MPB 1965–1985*. Austin: University of Texas Press.

Pinheiro, Paulo Sérgio, ed.

1983 *Crime, violência e poder*. São Paulo: Brasiliense.

Prado, Regina de Paula Santos

1977 Todo ano tem: As festas na estrutura social camponesa. M.A. thesis, Museu Nacional, Universidade Federal do Rio de Janeiro.

Queiroz, Maria Isaura Pereira de

1965 Messiahs in Brazil. *Past and Present* 31: 62–86.

1976 [1965] *O messianismo no Brasil e no mundo*. São Paulo: Alfa-Omega.

Quinn, Naomi, and Dorothy Holland

1987 Culture and cognition. In Dorothy Holland and Naomi Quinn, eds., *Cultural Models in Language and Thought*. Pp. 3–40. Cambridge: Cambridge University Press.

Radcliffe-Brown, A. R.

1964 [1922] *The Andaman Islanders*. New York: Free Press.

Rappaport, Roy A.

1979 The obvious aspects of ritual. In *Ecology, Meaning and Religion*. Pp. 173–221. Richmond, Calif.: North Atlantic Books.

Reis, José Ribamar Sousa dos

1984 *Bumba-meu-boi*. Recife: Massangana.

Rosaldo, Michelle Z.
   1984 Toward an anthropology of self and feeling. In Richard A. Shweder and
         Robert A. LeVine, eds., *Culture Theory: Essays on Mind, Self, and Emotion*.
         Pp. 137–57. Cambridge: Cambridge University Press.

Rumelhart, Donald
   1980 Schemata: The building blocks of cognition. In R. Spiro, B. Bruce, and
         W. Brewer, eds., *Theoretical Issues in Reading Comprehension: Perspectives from
         Cognitive Psychology, Linguistics, Artificial Intelligence and Education*. Pp. 33–58.
         Hillsdale, N.J.: Erlbaum.

Santos, Maria Januária Vilela
   1983 *A Balaiada e a insurreição de escravos no Maranhão*. São Paulo: Ática.

Sartorti, Rosalinde
   N.d. Stalinism and carnival. Manuscript.

Schank, Roger C., and Robert P. Abelson
   1977 *Scripts, Plans, Goals and Understanding: An Enquiry into Human Knowledge
         Structures*. Hillsdale, N.J.: Erlbaum.

Scheper-Hughes, Nancy
   1988 The madness of hunger: Sickness, delirium, and human needs. *Culture,
         Medicine, and Psychiatry* 12(4): 1–30.

Schneider, David M.
   1968 *American Kinship: A Cultural Account*. Chicago: University of Chicago Press.
   1976 Notes toward a theory of culture. In Keith Basso and Henry Selby, eds.,
         Meaning in Anthropology. Pp. 197–220. Albuquerque: University of New
         Mexico Press.

Searle, John R.
   1969 *Speech Acts: An Essay in the Philosophy of Language*. Cambridge: Cambridge
         University Press.

Serra, Astolfo
   1941 *Terra enfeitada e rica*. São Luís, n.p.
   1946 *A Balaiada*. Rio: Badeschi.

Silveira, Simão Estácio da
   1979 [1624] *Relação sumária das cousas do Maranhão*. São Luís: Universidade Federal
         do Maranhão/Serviço de Imprensa e Obras Gráficas do Estado.

Simmel, Georg
   1950 [1902–3] The metropolis and mental life. Trans. H. H. Gerth and C. Wright
         Mills. In Kurt H. Wolff, ed., *The Sociology of Georg Simmel*. Pp. 409–24.
         New York: Free Press.

Stoller, Paul
   1978 Rituals and personal insults in Songrai Sonni. *Anthropology* (Stony Brook)
         2(1): 31–37.

Taylor, J. M.
   1982 The politics of aesthetic debate: The case of Brazilian Carnaval. *Ethnology*
         21(4): 301–11.

Taylor, William B.

  1979 *Drinking, Homicide, and Rebellion in Colonial Mexican Villages.* Stanford, Calif.:
      Stanford University Press.

Tribuzi, Bandeira

  1981 *Formação econômica do Maranhão.* São Luís: Fundação Instituto de Pesquisas
      Econômicas e Sociais.

Turner, Victor W.

  1969 *The Ritual Process: Structure and Anti-Structure.* Ithaca: Cornell University
      Press.

  1982 Ed. *Celebration: Studies in Festivity and Ritual.* Washington, D.C.: Smithsonian
      Institution Press.

  1983 Carnaval in Rio: Dionysian drama in an industrializing society. In Frank E.
      Manning, ed., *The Celebration of Society.* Pp. 103–24. Bowling Green, Ohio:
      Bowling Green University Popular Press.

Velho, Gilberto

  1981 *Individualismo e cultura.* Rio: Zahar.

Verger, Pierre

  1984 [1976] *Procissões e Carnaval no Brasil.* Trans. Emmanuel Ribeiro Guimarães.
      Ensaios/Pesquisas No. 5. Salvador: Centro de Estudos Afro-Orientais,
      Universidade Federal da Bahia.

Wagley, Charles A.

  1971 [1963] *An Introduction to Brazil.* New York: Columbia University Press.

Weber, Max

  1978 [1922] *Economy and Society.* Ed. Guenther Roth and Claus Wittich. Berkeley:
      University of California Press.

Weffort, Francisco C.

  1970 State and mass in Brazil. In Irving Louis Horowitz, ed., *Masses in Latin
      America.* Pp. 385–406. New York: Oxford University Press.

White, Tracie

  1990 Rio's rough riders. Photographs by Miguel Fairbanks. *Santa Cruz Sentinel,*
      March 25.

Wirth, Louis

  1938 Urbanism as a way of life. *American Journal of Sociology* 44: 1–24.

Zaluar, Alba

  1985 *A máquina e a revolta: As organizações populares e o significado da pobreza.* São
      Paulo: Brasiliense.

INDEX

In this index an "f" after a number indicates a separate reference on the next page, and an "ff" indicates separate references on the next two pages. A continuous discussion over two or more pages is indicated by a span of page numbers, e.g., "pp. 57–58." *Passim* is used for a cluster of references in close but not continuous sequence.

Library of Congress Cataloging-in-Publication Data
Linger, Daniel Touro.
    Dangerous encounters : meanings of violence in a Brazilian city /
Daniel Touro Linger.
    p. cm.
Includes bibliographical references and index.
ISBN 0-8047-1926-8 (cl.) : ISBN 0-8047-2589-6 (pbk.)
1. Violence—Brazil—São Luís do Maranhão. 2. Carnival—Brazil—São Luís do
Maranhão. I. Title.
HN290.S32L56 1992
303.6'0981'21—dc20   91-28599